the Th____ on the CROSS

"The Trial Of Sundown"

The Story of one of the longest active members of the West
Coast's bloody prison gang and criminal organization
known as La Nuestra Familia "Our Family"

BY RICK L. RILEY
AKA "Sundown"

PAGE PUBLISHING, INC.
New York, NY

First originally published by Page Publishing, Inc. 2015

ISBN 978-1-68139-551-7 (pbk)
ISBN 978-1-68139-552-4 (digital)

Printed in the United States of America

Dedication

This book is dedicated first of all to the Lord God and Jesus Christ who formed me in my mother's womb and kept me, saved me and redeemed me and my family. Also to my wife Lori, who completes me. To all the prisoners still locked up and to all those caught up in the gang life. To my parole officer Mr. Houston, out of Stockton, who graced me and encouraged me to write my story. Lastly to you the reader who I hope come away with a different understanding and compassion for prisoners.

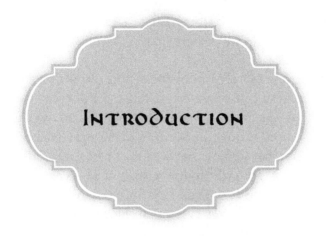

Introduction

When telling any story, the beginning is always the best place to start.

—From the Trial of Sundown

I am Sundown. This is *my* story. Let me tell it. When you tell it, you can be the hero. You can even say that you look like me—tall, dark, and handsome, Hollywood's dream of the ideal gangster leading man. When you tell it, you can even say that you too danced upon the volcano's edge, laughing at the pain, shouting at the madness, and singing into the darkness like the madmen that we were, and still are, once upon a time here in America, the land of the free and the home of the brave and of bloody opportunities they never taught us about in school and of bloody men like me who were baptized in blood and fed from the tables of bloody men, taught in the knowledge and ways of tried and proven warriors who had been to hell and back again.

Home of murderers and thieves who dared to believe that we could become something and somebody not just inside California prison walls but even reaching out into the very streets and society from which we had been sentenced to be forgotten by the rest of the world. But we were men who refused to be forgotten, and with the blood of our enemies, we would carve our names on the pages of criminal history. We would create and establish our own family, La Nuestra Familia, which in English means "Our Family"—a family made up of Carnales, brothers, men of common chains, enemies, and cause. Bloody desperados with nothing left to lose but our lives, lives that, without something to still believe in, held little or no value or sense of self-worth to us.

We believed that even from the depths of the darkest corners of our prison hell, we could have everything to gain if only we were willing to spill enough blood toward achieving it. First, we had to take control of the prisons from the Mexican Mafia and Aryan Brotherhood or anybody else that stood in our way then take control of the streets. We would recruit prisoners and men such as we were, and so like the ancient Aztec warriors of our common ancestry, we sacrificed the blood of our enemies, and if necessary, even the blood of our brothers, to that ancient left-handed god of war, Huitzilopochtli. And with a warrior sense of courage and pride, we embraced our bloody heritage. We were, all of us, Pancho Villas and Joaquin Murrietas with a dash of Michael Corleone of the movie, *The Godfather's*: poet warriors, and butcherous men, knights in slightly tarnished armor. At least we believed we were, and we butchered as if we were.

While this story is about me, it must also be about this bloody prison gang and criminal organization known as La Nuestra Familia, or NF for short. It has to be, because inside this thing called me, I will always be La Nuestra Familia. I cannot bring back the dead or undo all the things that have happened inside me because of La Nuestra Familia, which have forever helped to shape and form me into this man that I now am still today—the man who but for the grace of God would forever be a monster and a madman because of all the bloody costs that I have paid and all the ghosts that still haunt my knife-wounded and bullet-riddled heart, soul, and spirit. With the regret for all the innocents who got caught up and killed or destroyed in this forever war of love and rage, which we agreed to fight for and defend.

It has been said that the road to hell is paved with good intentions. Speaking for myself and for most of the men, "Brothers," "Carnales," who all stood together in this bloody quest with me for our goals, we were sincere in our dedications and commitments. We were searching for some kind of redemption, respect and honor, and even life. For in the beginning we understood and accepted that some of us would not make it to that age of honorable retirement written in our Constitution and that many of us would never be free from prison and might die behind the cold cement walls from which we were born. But we believed that at least in providing for this family, Our Family, La Nuestra Familia, we could still have worth as men and as warriors of honor in the defending and spilling of blood for it and in the having had to sometimes kill our closest friend or brother because of an allegiance we had vowed to our Constitution of laws and demands.

And because when telling any story the beginning is always the best place to start, then, in the beginning of the La Nuestra Familia, remember that we were heroes to anyone and everyone inside the California prison system who were afraid of, or tired of, being ordered around and taken from by the Mexican Mafia and Aryan Brotherhood and various other prison cliques. We were heroes, like knights in shining armor, riding to enemy territory and killing any and every enemy, oppressor, and persecutor of the prison masses. We took no shit for anybody, inmate, staff, or civilian. A death-on-sight rule of engagement policy was what we employed when it came to any of our enemies whose names appeared on our hit lists. Even those of our own brothers who had broken their vows to the Constitution and Our Family, seriously enough to warrant the death-on-sight status that we had employed against our main enemies, the Mexican Mafia, or EME for short, or the Aryan Brotherhood, or AB for short.

In the beginning, whenever any member of La Nuestra Familia drove up to any prison yard where there were any active Mexican Mafia or Aryan Brotherhood members, the prisoners would come to us and would point them out to us. They would give us weapons or weapon stock, from which any Familiano had been taught how to fashion the tools of death and destruction. Then they would just be sure to stay out of the way, because a Familiano of the La Nuestra Familia was on the yard now. He would be taking care of some business real soon and removing the hated and feared Mexican Mafia or Aryan Brotherhood member or shot caller, at first sight, even underneath the gun towers if need be. There was going to be some shooting going on today from the gun towers. So you better bring your popcorn and get a good seat. The real *Gladiator* show was on as brought to you by the good folks of the Department of Corrections, who ignorantly and deliberately put known enemies on each other's yards to ensure that the continuance of any real unity between prisoners, especially of the Mexican American prisoners, would be impossible because of all the lives and blood that had been lost and shed by and on all sides.

But remember, in the beginning we were heroes. We pressured no one; we took from no one. We were merely fighting for and defending our own rights under the United States Constitution, which guarantees to all its citizens, whether imprisoned or free, the right to pursue our rights to life, liberty, and the pursuit of happiness.

Sometimes we were even concrete Robin Hoods, taking from the richer and giving to the poorer, and sometimes we had no idea what the hell we were doing. This newfound power was all new to us, but we learned, and we grew both inside California prison walls and in the streets of the cities throughout the state of California. And courtesy of the federal racketeering laws, we have spread across the United States the same way in which we began, drawing recruits from fellow prisoners, to family members and criminal elements on the streets of California and America to the point that there now exists two separate factions of the one original La Nuestra Familia, as will be revealed in this story.

But I am getting way ahead of myself in this story, because the real beginning of my story begins with me. And so because of any potential future criminal prosecutions that could occur against myself because of there being no statute of limitations for some crimes such as murder, kidnapping, etc., and because of federal racketeering laws, i.e., RICO, and also to protect the innocent as well as the guilty including myself, I must now change some names except for some names that are already a matter of public record or names that I wish to give honor to for their sincerity and loyalty. And now I write this book as if it were just a story, a fiction that was reality. Also, if questioned by any law agencies or prosecutors with respect to anything revealed in this book, let it be known that I will swear in court that none of this is true and there is no such thing as La Nuestra Familia, and I will stand upon my Fifth Amendment rights as guaranteed by the Constitution of the United States of America. Those who know the truth and those who matter and who were there, they will know the truth of my story.

This story had to be told, and I was the one chosen by those who matter to write it just as we once had a song written, recorded, and released throughout California, called in English the ballad of La

Nuestra Familia, so too has this book been encouraged and approved by those who matter to me. "Que mi importa mi muerte, si no hay importance en mi vida, pero si con mi muerte o mi vida yo desfendo las esperanzas y fe de mi gente, es todo que mi importa. Y con eso digo todo." (Of what importance is my death if there is no importance in my life, but if in my death or my life I defend the hopes and faith of my people, this is all that matters to me, and with this I say it all.)

Love and rage,
Sundown

Operation Knockout: Gang raid targets Nuestra Familia in Salinas

By JULIA REYNOLDS Herald Salinas Bureau Monterey County Herald
Posted:

MontereyHerald.com

An ambitious multi-agency operation aimed at dismantling the Central Coast leadership structure of the Nuestra Familia gang resulted in more than three dozen arrests during sweeps early Thursday.

At least 37 alleged gang members and associates were in custody after hours of coordinated raids across Monterey County, ending months of investigation that culminated in what some call the largest law enforcement operation ever to target the Nuestra Familia, one of the West's most violent crime organizations.

The operation, which will continue to play out in state and federal courts, aims to disband the Salinas-area regiment of a gang that for three decades has dominated criminal activity in farm towns across Northern California.

For months, gang investigators from the California Department of Justice, the federal Bureau of Alcohol, Tobacco, Firearms and Explosives, the Salinas Police Department, the Monterey County Gang Task Force and the FBI worked to prepare arrest warrants for more than 40 high-ranking members of the gang in Salinas and nearby counties.

U.S. Attorney Joseph Russoniello said the mass arrests sent a direct message to the gang's followers: "Stop the violence. You can't win this fight."

The Nuestra Familia gang, which operates in and out of prisons, influences much of the criminal activity of thousands of Norteño gang members in Monterey and other California counties by ordering "hits" and demanding payments from drug sales, robberies and other gang crimes.

Norteño gang members, who police say number about 6,000 in Monterey County, act as street-level soldiers for prison-based Nuestra Familia, which operates as the "parent company" of the Norteños.

State gang experts credit the Nuestra Familia with about 1,000 killings since it began in the late 1960s, with Norteño gang members claiming hundreds more lives.

State and federal law enforcement officials chose Salinas for the raids because for years the city has been known as a hub of Nuestra Familia's activity.

Largest bust

THE THIEF ON THE CROSS

Section I. The primary purpose and goal of this organization is for the betterment of its members and the building up of this organization on the outside into a strong and self supporting familia.

Section II. All Members will work solely for this objective and will put all personal goals and feelings aside until said fulfillment is accomplished.

Section III. A familiano will not be released from his obligation towards the organization because he is released from prison, but will work twice as hard to see that a familia is established and will work in the hand with the organization that's already established behind the walls (pinta).

Section IV. A familiano will remain a member until death or otherwise discharged from the organization. And he will always be subject to put the best interest of the organization first and always above everything else, in or out of prison.

Section V. An automatic death sentence will be put on a familiano that turns coward, traitor or deserter. Under no other circumstances will a bother familiano be responsible for the spilling the blood of a fellow familiano. To do so will be considered as an act of treason.

Section VI. In order for (ART. II, Sec. V) to be invoked, the regiment governing body will hold a vote amongst themselves and pass sentence. Majority rules. In the case of a tie vote, the decision will lie with the captain, and his decision shall be final.

Bakersfield Californian (Bakersfield, California), Edition – Page 3
Printed on May 7,

Prison gangs tied to drugs, rackets

SACRAMENTO (AP) — Inmate gangs have turned California's prison system into a battleground for control of prison drug traffic and rackets, a secret witness has told a Senate subcommittee.

The testimony, taken in closed session March 15, was released Monday without the names of witnesses by the Senate Subcommittee on Civil Disorders.

A witness identified only as a prisoner recently incarcerated in the state prison system said prison violence had become "outrageous."

"One can no longer serve his own time without having to answer to some violent member of an organization," the witness said. "Nowadays an inmate must think and act violent in order to survive the forces and pressure that he is confronted with in a violent prison environment."

The inmate said he believes half the system's inmate population is connected with one of the gangs. He identified the groups as the Nuestra Familia, the Mexican Mafia, the Black Guerrilla Family, Black Liberation Army, Black Guard Family and Aryan Brotherhood. He said their influence extended throughout the system.

"Members of the Nuestra Familia organization and the Mexican Mafia who are locked in some of the most maximum security adjustments centers in the prison system can still send orders to any prison in California or out to society to have people executed," he said.

12

THE THIEF ON THE CROSS

Nuestra Familia: The Real History
By Gabe Morales
Published: 02/18/2008

Editor's Note: This story is being shared with us by Gangs Across America. http://www.gangsacrossamerica.com/ an online source providing strategies to combat gangs across the nation. From time to time, Corrections.com will publish articles from the Gangs Across America website.

By late 1965-1967, the California Mexican Mafia or EME controlled many prison yards in the California Department of Corrections (CDC) and had already started to victimize Northern California inmates and inmates from Southern California who would not join their gang.

Some EME members were against Mexicans victimizing Mexicans, especially some members from Maravilla, which was a large area of East Los Angeles. The first Nuestra Familia Mejicana Constitution was written between the lines of legal work. The draft was covertly smuggled out to others who voiced concerns about La EME's tactics.

Voted to the first Mesa or Board of the Organization was "Lipu/Lil John/Juan" from San Gabriel Valley's Big Bassett gang, "Chalo" from Bakersfield (and EME Leader "Cby" Cadena's cousin), "Huero" from the West L.A.'s Clantone gang, "Freddy/Ferny/Wolf" Gonzalez from Los Angeles' Temple St. and San Diego, "Diara" from Paicoma in the San Fernando Valley, and "Black Jess" from Oxnard-Chiques. Note: All of these initial NFM leaders were from Southern California cities!

The objectives of the NFM group according to their constitution were social, political, economical, and cultural. The NFM did have an alliance with the Black Family, which later was named the Black Guerilla Family, against the Mexican Mafia-Aryan Brotherhood Alliance.

By 1967, many NFM members were being sent to San Quentin. This is about the time period of growing dissatisfaction with the EME and growing numbers of NFM. "Black Bob" Vasquez, who was later an NFM General, states he was introduced to the group and "Babo" Sosa was later elected as the sole "Nuestro General", but neither started the NFM.

There has been some historical misunderstandings about La Familia Cinco which was a separate group from the NFM ran by an inmate named David Corona. This NFM "Blooming Flower" was spreading forth in CDC at a time when the Mexican Mafia was dominant in controlling the Mexican-American inmate population and soon led up to confrontations around September 16, 1968, which is Mexican Independence and on December 17, 1972, which resulted in the death of Rodolfo "Cheyenne" Cadena at Chino Prison (CIM) Palm Hall.

This killing was depicted in the movie "American Me" with actor James Edward Olmos playing "Cby" as the character "Santana". White convict Joe Morgan's (J.D. in the movie) power grew within the Mexican Mafia, *but he and other* EME did not have Cadena killed, it was done by the Nuestra Familia. In the mid-1970s the NF started to use younger Norteno 14s to do their bidding and by the late 1970s to early 1980s the Sureno 13s were doing a lot of work for La EME as more and more prison gang members were locked down in Segregation Units.

By the 1980s, the Nuestra Familia recruited almost exclusively from Northern California. These historical events and *we created the Norteno structure in West Nell Tract. All Northern Mexicans were used to do our bidding* bloodshed during this gang civil war between North and South are some of the main reasons that many young Mexican/Chicano kids fight today, they fight each other on the street and in prison, and sadly many really don't even know why. *WE utilized and manipulated and spread this to insure our control (*

Gabriel Morales has worked in the area of gang prevention, intervention, and suppression, both in the adult and juvenile system, for over 25 years. His experience includes working with at-risk kids in Seattle and the suburbs, rural areas, and L.A. youth gang diversion programs, many years as a Correctional Peace Officer at Folsom State Prison in California, as well as classifying and dealing with violent offenders in the jail setting of a large city.

He also teaches about Black gangs, Asian gangs, White Supremacists, and other Security Threat Groups. Gabe will be an instructor in Las Vegas for the Homefront Protect Conference on prison gangs. He has a book coming out on "Prison Gangs in the United States" that will be released Fall 2008.

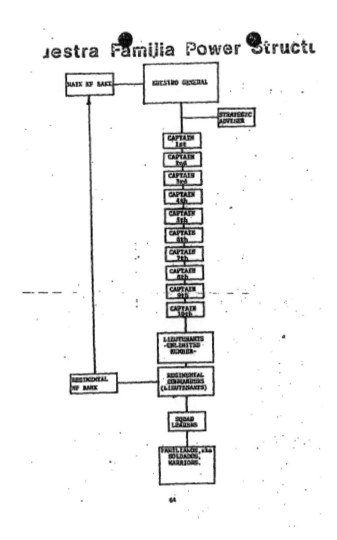

Nuestra Familia Power Structure

Chapter 1

I was a miracle baby. I was born in answer to my grieving parents' prayers for their recently lost firstborn child, Ricky Lee, whom they lost to SIDS, or crib death. They were so devastated that when they returned that day from the hospital, they could not even enter their trailer home ever again. They simply walked away, leaving everything behind them that reminded them of that once happy life they had begun so young. The only thing my mother had kept to remind them of Ricky Lee was a small photograph of him taken on his first and last birthday, which she had kept in her wallet.

One year later, I was born Ricky Lamon Riley, of Irish, Mexican, and Native American heritage. In the Bible, King David writes in one of his Psalms that he was cast upon the Lord from his mother's womb. And because of some stupid and cruel insensitive stuff, a Catholic priest had ignorantly said to my parents that their deceased son, Ricky Lee, was in hell because they had not been faithful to the Catholic Church and had not attended mass regularly; and because they did not have their son baptized by the Catholic Church, their son was in hell now and could not be buried by the Catholic priest.

So to be safe, she had with her second son, me, Ricky Lamon, cast me upon the Lord from her womb too, by dedicating me to God with constant prayer and when I was born she had me circumcised. On my first birthday, because I had been born looking exactly like Ricky Lee,

17

she had a photograph of me taken in the exact same type of outfit as Ricky Lee had worn in the picture she carried in her wallet. To this day, if both pictures sat side by side, no one could tell which one was Ricky Lee and which one was me. Even our smiles were exactly the same. You would have thought they were the same picture and the same child, but only she knew which one was which.

I would be saved at the age sixteen at a revival I had arrogantly attended in Santa Maria, California, in my own personal Damascus road conversion. But as Jesus was driven from the baptismal waters into the wilderness for forty days and nights, I was driven straight from the waters of my baptism into the wilderness of sin for forty years. I would go on to become a vicious animal, a killer hit man in organized crime—from born again to a *soldado* (soldier), a *guerrero* (warrior), a criminal, a master criminal. Not only would I be this, but also I would teach this, and I would lead this and a lot of the gang violence going on in the streets of California, still today is because I shared in its creation and growth. I taught it, I led it, I ordered a lot of it, and I willed it too. I was part of it, and it will always be a part of me.

But before all this, I was a child. My father had come back from the Korean War, and he had his ghosts and nightmares and scars that he had to deal with. Alcohol and fighting were often the ways he tried to deal with it. He had to fight his way back from behind enemy lines. He won medals for valor, only to be demoted in rank for chasing his own superior down the Korean beach shore, shooting at his feet and telling him he had no right to try to stop him and his men from celebrating and getting drunk after they fought their way back across enemy lines in time to pull out of that godforsaken war-torn country before being left behind. This superior had never even seen battle action, nor had he killed as many Chinese and Korean soldiers as they had to in their squad's fight to make it back alive from deep behind enemy lines.

My mother was only sixteen years old and a virgin when my father married her, and after having lost her firstborn the way she had, when I was born looking exactly like him, even though she would go on to have five more children after me, she cherished me and doted on me. I would always be her favorite. She believed I was special, an answer from God to all her grieving prayers.

People don't believe me when I tell them how far back I can remember, becoming cognizant and aware. I don't care if they believe me or not; I know the truth, and I can even remember when I learned how to crawl. I can remember in my mind figuring it out and understanding the concept of crawling from one side of the yard to the other side I wanted to get to. I remember the whole process of moving my body and straining to crawl. I remember sitting in a high chair watching Popeye and being excited to eat my spinach so I could become strong like Popeye. My mother told me that I stopped sitting in a high chair at eighteen months old.

I began drinking milk from a glass at one year old. But I still clung to being breastfed until I was three, and I was so jealous of my little sister Penny being breastfed that when Penny was two, I pushed her down and she hit her face and went to the hospital and was in a coma for two days. Somehow, I blocked that out of my memories and had to be told about it years later by my mother. I still can't remember it or Penny until she was about three or four years old, though I remember all my other brothers and sisters every moment and age. I believe I felt so bad and guilty that I completely blocked Penny out of my memory until she was about three or four years old in my family.

My mother always loved and cherished me, and it seemed I could do no wrong in her eyes. She began sitting me on the kitchen counter while she cooked or washed dishes and taught me to recite my alphabet, spell, do math, and read. By the time I was five years old, I could already read and knew my multiplication and spelling to the point where my mother would be so proud that she would have me compete with my older cousins and her friends' older kids. I would outspell them and outmultiply them, and because this always made her so happy and proud of me, I would excel in it. My mother throughout my life would always stress to me the importance of education. I would even teach myself and read everything I could—newspapers, books, everything I could lay my hands on.

It is important that I tell this because it all goes to the makeup and character of the man that I would grow up to be and why I would become such a gifted criminal and excel in the criminal lifestyle, this organized crime life I would choose to live.

Until about the age of five or six, I remember that we had lived in a big white house in Hayward, California. Everything was great. The people who had owned the house we lived in owned a big ranch that this house was a part of, and they lived in the back part of this big ranch-like property. The grandmother lived in a two-story-high tower type of condo right next to our house. Her family lived in the bigger ranch-style house behind ours; there was a big barn between our rental house and their living quarters. When you are a child, everything seems so much bigger than it actually is, but it was all beautiful to me, and I was happy.

They had a fourteen-year-old daughter named Annie. She was very pretty to me and had a body like a full-grown woman's, with large breasts for her age. She had long very light brown hair and hazel eyes. She was my babysitter, and she was always nice to me. I was madly in love with her of course. They had a son named Joey; he was thirteen and big for his age, but he was really slow mentally for his age. Playing with him was like playing with a nine-year-old. He would build these little go-carts and let me drive them while he pushed me around in them all day, so that made him my pal. The youngest sister, who was ten years old, had reddish-colored hair and brown eyes, and she was covered with freckles. She hated me in the beginning; her name was Cecilia.

I had an older cousin. He wasn't actually a cousin, but because we grew up living together a lot of the time, we considered his whole family cousins. He was a juvenile delinquent if ever there was one. His sister Racheal, according to Mexican tradition, had been promised to me to be my wife when we were grown up, as I had also been promised to her by our mothers. Her two brothers, Anthony and Ronnie, would be close to me too, all my life. They were living with us in this big white house when he had come to live with us from a juvenile facility he'd been released from when he was only ten years old and already a little terror. I would protect them from their own brother.

He was much bigger than I was, and he was a little bully. But my father had already taught me how to stand up to bullies when I was just in first grade. There had been this third grader; he was your typical big fat kid for his age. He would terrorize all us smaller kids every day at the school bus stop, which was close to where I lived. It was during the year when Kennedy and Nixon were running for president. The school sent home notices to the parents that we, children of this school, would be given presidential election candidate banners to wear to show our patriotism and support. Our parents would write on the notice we'd been sent home with which presidential candidate they favored, and that candidates banner would be given to each of us schoolkids to wear every day for a week leading up to Election Day.

Now I was already having problems with this bully and his two little sidekick third graders every day at the bus stop. My mother decided she likes Nixon for president and was so proud of me when she put the Nixon banner over me to wear to school during election week. The only problem was that in the whole school, I was the only child wearing the Nixon banner. This bully and his buddies threatened me one day on the bus to school and on the bus back from school about how they are gonna beat me up and take my Nixon banner away from me and make me eat it if I ever wore the banner to school again. I told them, "No, sir, not my banner. My mama put it on me, and only she has the right to tell me not to wear it anymore." Well, this pissed them off, and they chased me from the bus stop all the way to my house about a block away.

I'll never forget it because I'd come tearing up our driveway into our yard just ahead of them chasing me and calling me names and shouting threats to me about how I was dead if I wore that banner to school tomorrow. My father happened to be in the front yard when he saw me come tearing into the yard and crying, scared, so my father asked me what was going on and why I was crying like a little baby. I told him all about the bully and his two little buddies, how they terrorized all of us smaller kids every day at the bus stop before and after school, about what he threatened to do to me if I wore my Nixon banner to school the next day, and how I did not want to hurt my mother's feelings by telling her I didn't want to wear the Nixon banner to school anymore because of how proud she was when I wore it for her. I was hoping my father would be sympathetic to my plight and talk my mother into not making me wear the Nixon banner to school the next day so I wouldn't get my ass kicked at the bus stop by the bully and his little sidekicks. Instead, I'll never forget that look of disgust and shame in my father's eyes, for the first time in my young life. I remember, he told me instead, "You don't ever cry or run from anybody, especially a bully." I said, "But, Dad, he's bigger than me and older, and he's got two other third graders with him." And then my father said something to me that stayed with me for the rest of my life and affected the way I would come to face any threat against me ever again. When my father told me, he said, "Son, I want you to pick a stick the next time this bully tries to do anything to you, and I want you to swing that stick with all of your might, and I want you to hit that bully right between his eyes."

I asked my father, "Won't I get in trouble for doing that?" My father looked at me with a little pride in his eyes instead of that look of disgusted shame that I had seen earlier. My father said, "Don't you worry about getting into trouble. As long as you stand up for yourself, I'll be proud of you." To this day, this is my father's favorite story to tell about me. I thought about it all the whole rest of that day and all night until I fell asleep. The next morning, I got up extra early and went outside, and I found a good-size stick. I hurried down the street to the bus stop, and I hid that stick in the tall grass that grew around the bus stop area, then I hurried back home and got ready for school. My father had mentioned it to my mother that the Nixon banner she was so defiant about my wearing had been the source of some bullying and that maybe she ought not to make me wear it to school anymore. My mother asked me about it as I was getting dressed, and I remember that for a moment, I felt elation and relief that maybe I wouldn't have to wear that damn banner anymore and thereby avoid conflict with the bully and his little sidekicks. Then I saw something in her eyes, like she felt guilty for having imposed her political stance upon me. My mother was proud to be among the minority who stood for Nixon in a Kennedy-dominated town and neighborhood. I knew in that moment that between her eyes and the look the day before in my father's eyes, I was wearing that damn Nixon banner and that I would rather die and get beaten up than ever see shame or disgust again in my father's eyes or sadness in my mother's eyes.

So I insisted to my mother that I wanted to wear my Nixon banner and the heck with all the other people who were for Kennedy. With a mother's concern and pride, she walked with me to the bus stop that morning and waited with me for the bus to make sure no one bothered or threatened me. I was grateful to her, but once I got on the school bus and away from the safety of her maternal love and protection, that bully started in on me. He started calling me a little sissy baby who had to have my mamma walk with me to the bus stop to protect me, and his two little buddies of course were chiming right in with him. That bully threatened me, saying my mamma wasn't gonna be there at the bus stop after school and he was gonna tear my banner off me and beat me up. When we got off the bus, I ran over to where I had laid that stick earlier. As he and his little buddies came at me, I did exactly as my father had told me to do: I swung that stick with all my little first-grader might, and I hit that bully right between the eyes, breaking his nose in the process. There was blood everywhere. This kid took off running down the street past my house, as my father loves to tell the story, screaming and holding his nose, crying all the way home.

I remember, for better or worse, feeling the power as I looked around me at the stunned and shocked faces of all the other kids at the bus stop. How powerful I felt when I turned to that bully's two shocked sidekicks, waving that stick and asking them if they still wanted to try to take my Nixon banner off me too. Both of them took off running and crying after their bully friend down the street. I received cheers from all the other kindergarteners and first and second graders at what I had done to the bully and his two friends, who had been making their lives miserable too. I was a hero to them that day, and I saw the pride in my father's eyes when he asked what happened and why that bully kid had run by screaming bloody murder and holding his bloody face.

The reason why I bring this up is because I had learned that to win my father's affection, to win his approval, I had to be this violent kid and I had to be tough. That was a good thing in that it served me well and prepared me for the drastic changes in my young life that were soon to come. The other thing I learned, more importantly, was the importance of having an equalizer, a weapon. As long as I had some kind of weapon, I wasn't afraid of anybody. That would turn out to be important, because throughout my life, as you know, I turn out to be a gang member and a leader, specializing in weapons and guerilla warfare. But I think it all started right there that day, when I hit that kid as hard as I could with that stick and I saw the results. Also, just to throw it in there, the next day, that kid's father had the nerve to come to our house, complaining to my father about what I had done. My father just told him, "Hey, your son has been bullying everybody," and said he had told me to do what I did and that if that kid's father didn't get off his property and go home, that he would be going home in an ambulance, because my father was going to beat him up. Well, the kid's father just left, and we never heard from him again.

So now, here was this ten-year-old sort of cousin being released from juvenile hall to come live with us, and he was a bully too. He would say nasty things and used cursing language about my babysitter Annie. He would say how he was gonna fuck her and suck her big titties and how he just knew Annie had a big hairy pussy and stuff like that. I was so innocent I didn't even know what any of that really meant. I just knew that they were dirty by the evil way he said them. I would tell him to stop talking like that about Annie, and we'd get into a fight. One day both of our mothers heard us fighting over Annie. This time, Annie happened to be there. I told my mother all the things David had been saying about Annie. David called me a liar and tried to rush me. We were rolling around together on the living room floor, fighting, when our parents said they'd had enough of our fighting. My mother grabbed me and David's mother grabbed him, and they told us that since we couldn't get along, we were gonna have to go outside in front of everybody and have it out once and for all.

Now remember, I was six; he was ten and much bigger than me, so my mother must have had confidence in me. This time there would be no stick in my hand to help me, and this time my mother had a big belt, as did David's mother. They were whipping us to make us fight each other, and worst of all, all the other kids were watching us fight, including Annie. To lose and get my butt kicked in front of Annie would be too embarrassing to me.

I did not understand why my mother was whipping me. I was her pride and joy. I looked at her, and I said, "Mamma, why are you hitting me? Why are you making me do this?" I'll never forget what she told me. She said, "You don't ever quit a fight. Once you start it, you finish it." Well, right then I realized that the only way I was gonna get my mamma to stop hitting me was to knock this kid out. I don't know how I did it; I just knew I had to take him out. I charged him, swinging as hard as I could. I knocked him out, and I knocked him smooth out, unconscious. Everybody that was there was cheering for me because nobody liked David, even the ten-year-old girl Cecilia and Annie too. Everybody knew that fight was over Annie and that I was defending her honor. After the fight, Annie came and she hugged me and kissed me, crushing my head against her young big breasts. I was in heaven. I didn't know what all this stuff meant; all I knew was that being crushed against Annie's big breasts and having her kissing me and praising me felt so good. She was talking about how I was her knight in shining armor defending her honor and all that. But I saw how Cecilia looked at me; she had a new look in her eyes toward me, and I didn't even understand what it was. One Saturday morning, I was waiting for Joey. I was sitting on my front step, waiting for him to come. He's going to take me on a new go-cart he built, and we were going to go driving all over the place in it. Instead, around the corner came Cecilia. She started talking to me, and right away, I was suspicious. This girl's never liked me; she's always been mean to me. So I asked where Joey was. She answered, "Oh, Joey can't come today. Joey's gotta do something. He had to go somewhere." He wasn't going to be able to come play with me. I was like, "Oh man, no go-carts. I was really looking forward to it." She told me, "You want to play with me?" And I was like, "Why would I want to play with you? You don't even like me, and you're a girl." She said, "No, I'll give you a puppet show, come with me." So she promised me a puppet show. She took me into this big barn and made sure it's all locked up. She sat me on a bale of hay. I was sitting there; I was waiting for a puppet show, and she told me to close my eyes. Next thing I know, she started taking off her clothes. She took all her clothes off, and she was standing there naked right in front of me. I had a lot of girl cousins, and I had seen them naked because we would always bathe together. It never impressed me one way or the other. I did notice the difference with Cecilia, because she had already started growing pubic hair, and she had begun to have little breasts. That was different; still I was waiting for the puppets. I asked her, "Where's the puppets?" She told me, "There are no puppets. I brought you in here to show you a dance. I'm gonna dance for you." I was heartbroken. All I could keep saying was, "No puppets! Man, where's the puppets? No puppets!" She was like, "No, I brought you in here so you can look at me," and I looked at her because she said, "Look at me!" So I was looking at her, and like I said, I noticed the differences. I still was not really impressed, but then she started to do this little kind of a dance. She turned her back to me, she bent over, and she started moving her butt in my face, literally inches from my face. For the first time in my life, I felt something in my groin. I felt something in my blood I'd never felt before. Next thing I know, I had this erection. I was like, "Wow!" This feeling I'm feeling for the first time is intoxicating to me. She took me, and she got me undressed. She had me lie on top of her. She showed me all those things that she wanted me to do to her, and I liked it. I was like, "Wow, this is fun," and she gave me a quarter to keep quiet. She kept telling me, "This is our secret, don't tell nobody." So my innocence was taken that day. I lost my innocence that day in that barn. Every chance we could get, Cecilia would take me into that barn and use me to satisfy her desires, and every time she would give me a dime or a quarter after we had finished. After that, every girl I saw, I was trying to get her panties off. I was just a little pervert now, but it's interesting. I always think back and wonder when was it that I lost my innocence, and it was then, that day.

Funny thing about this family, you gotta realize, okay, here I was, I think I was six. I had fought to defend Annie's honor, and I had won from somebody much bigger and older than me. The brother had taken me in a go-cart to a liquor store, and there were newspapers out in front, Sunday papers. I remember they had comics out there. I asked Joey, "Why are those papers out here like that all the time? Are they for free?" And he told me, "Yes, they are for free, take one." Something told me not to listen to him, but he was older, so he must know. I took one of the newspapers. The storeowner came running out; he called the police and everything. I was taken home by the police. So here, I had my first crime. So I had defended the honor of the older sister, I had committed my first crime with the brother, and now my first sexual experience was with the younger sister. You would think that's the weird thing and it stops there, but it doesn't. These people were kinda gypsies, and their father was killing a goat one day. They had it hanging upside down. He was cutting its throat. He was drinking its blood straight from the cut, and he asked me, "You want some blood? Drink it, try it, it will make a man out of you." So I went in and drank the blood. There is a prohibition against drinking blood in the Bible, by the way, but I did not know this. I remember when I drank the blood I got kinda drunk, like, you know, I was kinda woozy and lightheaded. I remember going out and kinda stumbling out into the field and passing out, lying down and then waking up, you know, wondering what happened. The grandmother, she used to let me spend the night in her house. Unfortunately, she was into witchcraft, so was my mother, to a little degree, not realizing what she was really messing with, and all she knew was this kind old lady who actually owned all the property, including our house, adored me, and I adored her. It all seemed harmless enough. So anytime she asked my mother to let me spend the weekend with her and offered to babysit me, my mother would ask me, and of course, I would be begging her to let me stay the night with this grandmother. I loved staying with her because she would bake cookies, cupcakes, muffins, and pies for me. She taught me how to play rummy, and we would play cards all night, eat treats, and listen to her records. She treated me like a king, and I loved being spoiled by her. She always gave me money and little gifts. She would bathe me and tell me how handsome I was going to grow up to be. She would warn me about girls who might try to do nasty things with me because I was so handsome and mature for my age. She even warned me against her own granddaughter Cecilia, to be careful with her. I remember thinking maybe she knew about Cecilia and me and about the games we played in the barn. *But how could she know?* I would tell myself. Cecilia and I were always very careful and secretive. Then after bathing me and drying me off with a towel and putting me in my PJs, she would begin adding more water to my bathwater left in the tub, saying she was just saving water by bathing in the same bathwater. She would take off her robe and get naked in front of me before getting into the tub and would tell me to go wait for her in the living room and watch TV while she bathed.

I remember that before Cecilia seduced me in the barn, I never paid any attention to the grandmother when she took off her robe and was naked. But after my experience in the barn with her granddaughter, now I wanted to see her naked body. She noticed too, because she would ask me things like if I was frightened by her nudity and if I liked what I was seeing. Then she would tell me I must never tell anyone ever that I had seen her naked. When she saw how fascinated I was by how thick and hairy her pubic hairs were and how big her breasts and especially her nipples were, she would ask me if I wanted to touch her so I could see that there was nothing to be afraid of. I had to promise not to tell my mother, or I would never be able to stay there with her anymore. She let me suck her nipples, asking me if I remembered sucking my mother's breasts when I was a baby. She said it would be like the same thing, so I said okay and promised never to tell anyone. She told me that after her bath, she would let me suck her nipples and she would hold me like my mother used to and it would be like I was her baby too. That night, before I went to sleep, she laid on the couch with me, holding me and letting me suck her nipple while she hugged me and told me how special I was to her and how this would be our own private secret. I fell asleep with her nipple in my mouth. The warm chocolate milk she had me drink before bed had made me very sleepy. Looking back, I realize now that I always got sleepy after the chocolate milk I drank before bedtime. I think she was drugging me. One night, I woke up in the middle of the night. I was very groggy, but I remember looking down at my waist. She was kneeling beside me, and my pajamas were down around my knees. Her face was where my penis was, and it was in her mouth. She told me to go back to sleep and that I was just dreaming. And because it was her, and I trusted her. I fell back to sleep. As I drifted off to sleep, I remember wondering why she had my penis in her mouth. Looking back it's obvious now she was performing fellatio on me. It was not until many years later that I would even recall these events and all the things she used to do to me when I stayed overnight with her.

This woman was into witchcraft and tarot cards, herbs, and spells. My mother unwittingly admired this woman because witchcraft was one of the ways of Mexican people, and this woman treated my mother really good and was always nice. She gave her gifts and things, so my mother trusted her with me. And because of the loss of her first son, when this woman would predict great things over me from her tarot cards, my naive mother would just be grateful for her, not realizing the doors that were unwittingly being opened over me and my future.

I bring this up because this family really did a lot of things to shake my innocence. Shortly after my sixth birthday, my mother and father were divorced. We went to live in a ghetto in Santa Maria, California, you know, a labor camp. I remember that my mother told me, "You are the man of the house now, so I need you to help me with your brothers and sisters." I took that very seriously.

So here I am now. It's different, besides the fact that we were living poor. The kids there were a lot tougher and rougher than I was used to. I found that out. On the other side of the fence to the labor camp was the county park. The other side of the park was a country club with a golf course. One of the things that the ghetto kids would do would be to shag golf balls; they would sell golf balls that they found back to the golfers. Well, I found a golf ball. These two older boys, around twelve, saw me when I was showing off my golf ball. They told me to give them my golf ball. The ball was worth twenty-five cents. When they told me that, I said, "No, I'm not giving you my golf ball." So here they are now, beating me up to get that golf ball, choking me out on the ground. I was about to pass out, but I was not about to give up that golf ball. My cousin Jimmy Ray, who was older, happened to come by at that time, and he ran those kids off. He was about the same age as they were, so thank God he was there. When I got up and told him what happened, that they wanted the golf ball, he explained to me why they wanted it. You know, apparently twenty-five cents was a lot of money back then. Fifty cents was a lot more. Sometimes you could get that for one ball. So I gave it to Jimmy. I said, "Here, you take the golf ball." All I wanted was a nickel. You know what I mean? So I can get something off the doughnut truck for cookies or something. Also, it kept him in my good graces so that if I ever needed backup again, and from the look of this labor camp and the toughness of these poorer kids, I was gonna need it. I wasn't dumb. I tried to keep my cousin Jimmy Ray on my side, and Jimmy always did look out for me whenever he could. He was always good to me. He was my favorite cousin and always stood up for me and sometimes let me tag along with him. He also would take me to the Junior Park Rangers meetings; he taught me how to say the Lord's Prayer during the meetings. As Junior Park Rangers, we would help by picking up trash around the park and promise to help protect the animals in the park and report any abuse by other park visitors if we saw it. The funny thing about this is that because we were so poor, the park became my hunting grounds to put food on the table. I would poach ducks, squirrels, and fish and take them home to my mother to cook to feed all us kids.

Chapter 2

So here I am at around seven years old. I have had all these things go on in my life. I had my first encounter with the police for the theft of a newspaper, my first defense of a girl's honor, my first sexual experience, and my first two beat-downs of bullies prior to moving to the labor camp. So now, here I am in the ghetto labor camp. It's much harsher and tougher, so I learned a lot of things growing up every day when I went to school. There were mostly Mexican kids in the labor camp, also a couple of black families, one or two Indian or Asian families, and one or two poor white families. For the most part, there were mainly Mexican families living here. Because I was half white and half Mexican, I would fight every day at the bus stop before school because I was a gringo and patty; these were racial slurs from the Mexican kids. I would fight on the bus on the way to school because I was a patty. I would fight in school with the white kids because I was a spick, a taco bender, a greaser and a beaner, which were racial slurs by the whites against Mexicans. After school, at the bus stop, I was fighting Mexicans again because I was a patty and a gringo.

Here I am; I grew up fighting the very things that I was Mexican and white. It got to be so that at the words *patty*, *gringo*, *spick*, *greaser*, or *taco bender*, I would charge and fight with no more conversation. I remember thinking and wishing that these people would make up their minds, which one I was, so I didn't always have to fight both sides. I fought blacks, Indians, and Asians too, I fought everybody. The blacks seemed to embrace me more as did the Indians and the Asians. I guess it was because we had the same enemies. I had a little bit of an allegiance going there. This stuff's important. The reason why I'm saying this is because it was forming the man who would one day grow up to be an executioner, a hit man, a leader, a teacher of criminal organization and alliances, and eventually becoming one of the last original La Nuestra Familia generals. That is what I became; it finally fell to me, because for us, the original La Nuestra Familia, there had always only been Babo Sosa as our Nuestro General. Then after the split and the civil war began, those of us who remained loyal to the original La Nuestra Familia voted, and Babo had to step down as our Nuestro General. We voted Fig as our Nuestro General, with Casper as our new first captain, and me as the second captain. After ten years of civil war, Fig stepped down according to our Constitution and Bylaws; he was allowed to retire with honors.

Our Nuestro General was required to be in prison in order to ensure the power of the La Nuestra Familia always remained behind prison walls. This was done so that no matter how big the outside division of our criminal organization grew to be, the prison body and soldiers would never be forgotten or not provided for. The real power and leadership had to always remain behind prison walls, where we had been born and formed. It wasn't until I, as the second captain, returned to prison in 1993 that in 1994 a vote could confirm me as the Nuestro General, and once I returned, I blew the doors wide-open for new recruiting and reentry criteria. Now we recruited from all races, except the blacks (we left them to our allies), the Black Guerrilla family, the Bloods, and the Crips. Now Indians, Samoans, Asians, and others were welcome to join, but everything had to be *Omerta*, which means silent. We were to deny even the existence of any original La Nuestra Familia 1, as we were designated by the Department of Corrections and its security units. We were also to deny any knowledge or affiliation with any active prison gangs. We were to say we were nonaffiliated so we could be allowed to be released to prison main lines rather than sit among the famous in the holes, allowing us to make the money and protect and support each other while letting the others dance in the spotlight of the daily gangster news. Let the famous for a few days take the long bus rides and airplane trips to the federal prisons and lockdown units across the state and country, courtesy of RICO federal racketeering and all the new gang taskforces. I also made peace with the ruling body of the new La Nuestra Familia 2, as they were designated by the Department of Corrections and law enforcement agencies. After ten years of civil war, we would leave each other alone for now and hopefully pursue a possible reunification of the old original with the new structured La Nuestra Familia. Then all hell began to break loose, with special task forces and federal racketeering cases, and we had no more time for killing each other. We are all too busy trying to survive the onslaught and storms of the new task force prosecutors. We needed to concentrate on making arrangements for all the possible outcomes and challenges we had long ago foreseen coming, now thrust upon all La Nuestra Familia, such as convictions and transfers across the state and United States. The Aryan Brotherhood and the Mexican Mafia were also going through all the same changes and challenges brought on by all the same law enforcement agencies. I of course continued to follow our number 1 rule of Omerta; I denied being a member, active or drop out of any prison gangs. I denied any affiliations or even any concerns for or about any criminal gangs, be they prison, street, or whatever.

Like the song by the Animals said, "I'm just a soul whose intentions are good, oh Lord, please don't let me be misunderstood." I walked almost every active prison yard. Mostly all enemy held for the next eighteen years straight. I paroled from an active general population yard, although I didn't simply parole. I actually had to post bail to get out on a parole because I had caught a new case after serving my eighteen years straight. I was facing another new life sentence before I was even able to make parole.

In this rabbit trail I've taken, I've said more than I maybe should have, but as I said in the beginning of this book, if questioned or charged by any law agency with any type of crime or crimes committed by myself in behalf of any ongoing criminal organization, I plead the fifth amendment and deny all charges. I deny even knowing anything about anything called La Nuestra Familia, 1 or 2. Thank you very much, sir. Now I will move on back with my story of the thief on the cross.

So anyway, where did it all start for me? It all started back there in the labor camp. Throughout all this, my mother kept telling me,

"Get your education, get your education, get your education." So I excelled in my education. I even won a contest when I was in the third grade. I had the highest IQ of all the kids in Santa Barbara County from the sixth grade down. As a reward for winning this contest, I got a two-week stay at this resort camp and exclusive club for rich kids for the summer, with crafts, boating, and all that stuff. My mother was so proud of me she bought or borrowed every item I would need to make this trip—from sleeping bags, flashlights, clothes, and shoes, everything I would need to be able to at least look like I belonged there with all those little rich kids. I had an awesome time, and on the last day of one of the best experiences of my young life, while all the little rich kids were busy having a last-day family celebration and BBQ before leaving, since I had no family able to be there, I was free to go through all the rich kids' luggage. I came home with an extra suitcase filled with stolen gifts for my family, as well as over $150 in cash, which I had stolen from the various rich kids' luggage and the little camp store where they sold us treats. I was not dumb, I was smart, and I worked hard too. When my mother told me I was the man of the house now and she needed my help, I took her seriously. One of the things that there were a lot of in that ghetto labor camp were single moms with cloth-diaper-wearing babies, so the first job I ever had was washing diapers. Pee diapers were two cents, but diapers with poop in them were a nickel. I made good money washing diapers. It seemed like every women there had a baby. I had to fight to protect my money; everybody made fun of me, even my own cousins. In Spanish, we call shit *caca*, and because my family nickname was Kiki, sometimes they would say, "Hey, there is Kiki Caca," or "Caca Kiki," because of the diapers I washed. I would have the last laugh though, because every time that bread truck ran through the neighborhood, I'd be there getting a bag of doughnuts or cookies with my money. I would give the rest of my money to my mother. I made a couple of dollars a week washing diapers. Then I started doing other stuff for money by the time I was nine years old. Where we lived in the camp, the nearest store was like two miles away. It was a little bit of a walk. One day, this lady told me, "Hey, Kiki, you going to the store? Can you get me this? I'll give you a dime." Before you knew it, I had everybody wanting me to go to the store for them and paying me to do it. They would all give me a dime or a nickel; I did pretty well. One day, I only had one customer, and I remember thinking I needed more money than that. I wanted to get myself something too. Everything she wanted was just a dollar fifty. I was only going to make a dime. I thought, well, that's not gonna cut it. I was at the store. I was watching, and I observed that they had the store brand on every bag, not just the paper bags, but also on the produce bags. I noticed nobody took their receipts; everybody just threw them on the ground. I picked them up, looked at them, and said, "Wow, this is going to be important. I don't know why, but it is." So I took a few receipts with me and put them away, then I thought, "These are the items she is asking for. I could hide them under my clothing. I could put them in my pants and my shirt, walk out with it and not pay, and then I could have the whole dollar fifty plus my dime." So I did it; I became a thief. No one paid attention to a child just walking around the store unless they were in the candy aisle. As long as I stayed away from the candy aisle, I went unnoticed, so I just stuck this stuff down my pants, front and back, and had on a big jacket because it was cold out. I remember my heart pounding with excitement and fear as I walked calmly out of the store past all the cashiers and bag boys, fearing at any moment I would hear a voice yelling, "Stop, thief!" As those automated doors opened and I walked out unnoticed and once I got around to the side of the parking lot safe, I realized I was rich. I couldn't believe it—a whole dollar and sixty cents to buy all the candy I wanted. I stashed the items I had stolen and walked back in the store with confidence. I went straight to the candy aisle, and sure enough, it seemed all eyes were on me as I shopped like I was rich, and I only spent sixty cents on the candy. Back in those days, sixty cents would buy you an entire bag of candy and treats.

I hurried home; I gave the woman who sent me her stuff and her forty cents change from the two dollars she had given me. She even gave me an extra dime tip. Now I had a full bag of candy, a dollar to give me to my mother, and a dime for ice cream later when the truck came by. I remember telling my mother that I found the dollar on the floor outside of the store as I was coming out. I even told her that I looked around to see if anyone had just dropped it on their way out before me but that there was no one around, so I picked it up and kept it to give it to her. She was so proud of me for not spending it on candy and giving it to her that she gave me a dime to get myself a treat from the ice cream truck or the bakery truck, whichever I decided, but not to eat it in front of my brothers and sisters.

I knew exactly what I was gonna do with my two dimes and my hidden bag of candy. I was gonna use it all to get me some pussy from the neighborhood little girls who, in exchange for some ice cream or candy, would go someplace hidden with me and let me play doctor. I would give some of the candy to my little followers who looked up to me as their leader even way back then. At nine years of age, I had learned the politics of being poor and how to use the other kids to my advantage. All that Cecilia had taught me all those times in that barn had affected me like I said. I was a little pervert set loose in a ghetto where all the girls around grew up very fast. I could preach here about how it was all wrong and sad that this was the culture of ghetto labor camp and poverty, but at that time, it was what it was, violence and perversion. I used to wonder even way back then when I was with a lot of these girls, where and how some of them learned to play these nasty sexual games we would play. Sadly looking back at my conquests, I was sometimes the first one and as guilty of the sin as any and everyone else who might have abused or took advantage of all these girls, though we younger boys were growing up just trying to emulate all the older teenage kids who were doing it for real all around us. We would brag to each other about our so-called stud sexual experiences, but as much as possible I wouldn't brag. I would instead try to keep my perverted conquests as secret as I could. I didn't want to get caught and in trouble, and more importantly, I didn't want anyone else to know about which girls I was with because I didn't want the competition. They were mine. I wasn't sharing any of them with any of my friends, relatives, and followers. I wasn't like all the other boys bragging and telling anything. These girls trusted me and were easier to convince into sneaking off with me somewhere hidden and secret if I didn't tell.

I knew what I was doing with these girls was wrong. I remember a few times being convicted inside of myself that what we were doing was shameful and wrong. Unfortunately, just like stealing, the forbidden fruit aspect of it all just made it more exciting and irresistible to my young and twisted wicked soul. Like drugs, I was addicted, and soon girls my own age were not enough for me. I wanted real sex with a real woman. By the time I was nine years old, this was my desire. I remember that after Cecilia had seduced me and taught me those perverted pleasures of the flesh, I would fantasize that I had this gigantic penis. Every girl I liked I would stick them on my dick like a shish kabob, all different girls and even a few women I had crushes on. Whoever was my favorite at the time would be the last one on the head of my penis.

Looking back over it all, I believe that between Cecilia's actual physical sexual seduction using my innocent young body and Cecilia's grandmother's witchcraft and fellatio of my young penis, they introduced a sexual demon in my loins. At the age of nine, I would actually have intercourse with a fully mature fifteen-year-old horny girl. It seemed my penis had a perverted mind of its own, but I'm getting ahead of myself again.

I started boosting, shoplifting. As all the women started giving me their orders to pick up from the store for them, I would boost what I could. Then I figured out something. I said to myself, "You know what? If I take this store receipts and I figure out what's on there, I'll get these items and I'll put them in one of the produce bags with the store name and then walk out. As long as I have the receipts, if I get stopped, I'll show them the receipt." This gave me confidence in what I was doing.

Before long, I had all the kids in my circle working for me. I was teaching them how to boost, and we were keeping the money the housewives were giving us. They would boost a dollar's worth of stuff, and I would give each kid a quarter. I'd keep the rest. None of the women knew what we were doing; my mom either. All my mother knew was that when I did a grocery run, I would come back and give her a couple of dollars, every day, which added up to about ten dollars a week. We were poor, and that was a lot of money to us. So this began my life of organized crime. I had organized the neighborhood kids and taught them how to boost. I taught my cousins, my brothers, and my sisters. I kept it in the family as much as possible. So here I was, running an organized boosting ring of kids. There were many other things I did too. I started hustling and stuff like that. I would sell newspapers. You could go down to the newspaper business, and they would give you twenty papers at a time. They wanted a nickel a piece for those twenty papers. They had about twenty boys every day picking up batches of twenty papers at a time. Everything you made over the nickel a paper was yours to keep. So we would go out and try to sell each paper for at least a dime. If you were smart and hustled, I learned that at bars and certain other places, you could get a quarter, and that was our hustle. I learned that shining shoes was also a good hustle. So here I was, selling papers and shining shoes with my little circle of followers, who were hustling with me too. Still washing the diapers, I never gave that up until I was about ten. I think that is when Pampers started hitting the scene, and I think it was Pampers that put me out of diaper-washing business. I had also learned to babysit and to clean restrooms and gas stations and fast-food places and movie houses. I would get paid for stuff like that. So by the time I was about eleven, I had about five jobs that I would do before and after school, as well as the hustling. For a kid, I think I figured it out; I was bringing home a minimum of twenty-five dollars and sometimes thirty-five dollars a week and giving it all to my mother. My mother would give me five dollars a week allowance from that money, which was a lot for an eleven-year-old back then. Back then, the average man's paycheck was about thirty-five dollars a week, maybe forty. Here I was, a little kid bringing in as much as a man was bringing in even though it was hustle, stealing, and working. I always had my hands in something to make money.

Throughout this time, the one thing that ruled my world was girls. That little girl in that barn had turned me out, even though there were other experiences with other girls, which I don't know if I'll ever tell about. There was a certain older relative who was about fifteen at the time when I was nine. She had come to stay with us for a while because she had been caught being sexually active with some of my older relatives; she was sent to live with us. One night, she was babysitting us, and I got up to go to the kitchen; I wanted water. She was in the living room, on the couch; she was playing with herself. I remember she had big tits with big nipples, and there she was, masturbating and sucking on her own breasts. I had never seen a woman suck her own breasts before; it fascinated me. As I watched her, instead of her stopping what she was doing or running me off, she just kept playing with herself. She started talking to me; she asked me if I knew what sex was. I said, "Yes, I know what it is. I've had sex," trying to sound more mature than I was. I remember she told me mockingly that I was lying and "You can't even get a boner," so I said defiantly and proudly, "Yes I can!"

She said nah in disbelief. "Let me see." So I pulled down my pajamas and showed her that I had a boner. As soon as she saw that I indeed had an erection, her eyes lit up, and she was like, "Come here, come here." Even though I was only nine years old, here I had at least about a four-inch hard dick. She asked me if I wanted to suck her nipples; of course I did. So I did. She had tried to get me to kiss and lick her pussy too. I balked, just as I had the first time Cecilia had tried to talk me into that. I said, "No, that's where pee comes from." Then she took my penis in her mouth to show me how good it felt, and it did feel good, so I said okay. I tried to use my mouth on her as she was instructing me to, but she smelled unpleasant, and I didn't want to continue. She locked her thighs around my head and started pulling my head against her so tight I couldn't breathe. Finally, she let me go and settled with my just sticking my penis inside her while following her instructions of how to thrust my hips. We would go at it, seemingly for hours, until one night, my mother came home early from work and almost caught us red-handed. There I was, a nine-year-old actually having sex, with my penis in a red-hot pussy. Even though I couldn't ejaculate, I really enjoyed it. Throughout my whole young life, it was now always about girls, girls, girls, like the Elvis Presley song and movie *Girls! Girls! Girls!* Sex just seemed to rule my world, especially the white girls, the little rich white girls that lived on the other side of town. For poor boys like us from the poor side of town, they were like the forbidden fruit. For me, it was like, if I could just get them and I could get them naked and could do things to them, then I felt powerful. Even though I was this poor kid, I had rich white girls submitting to me. I was a pervert, yes, I was a pervert. A lot of the things I did to get money were so that I could go wherever those girls were. I would grow up to be a handsome man. I mean, I'm not gonna lie. I was handsome, and I have always known it. I remember reading a book that came out when I was about thirteen, called the *Sensuous Woman*; it described everything that woman like sexually. I was just a kid, but I did everything it said to do, and the girls loved me. I'm telling you: the girls loved me—junior high school, high school. I was not like the typical kid just trying to get his dick wet. I learned through that book that hey, do this to a girl, and you will get what you want, so I guess I was mature, you know. Is all this good? Is all this bad? I don't know, I just know that pussy ruled my world for a long time, until I finally grew up and realized that I made pussy my idol. The altar where I worshipped, the sex I sought, was like a religious experience to me. I'm running through this stuff and leaving out so much. I think it's important, though, that you know what kind of a man grows up and becomes a killer for organized crime. This is the kid I was. I never really grew up. This is why I became what I became, or what influenced what I became, I guess. I grew up learning you had to fight any man who stood in your way, and I used sex to dominate and conquer women.

I grew up. At first, everything was so good. I mean, I lived a good life until I was six. It was so beautiful, so innocent, so nice—no problems, nothing. Then I started learning about all this other stuff. I moved to a labor camp, the ghetto. I learned that you had to be a good fighter; you had to fight. So I learned to fight, and I was a good fighter. I could fight. I would fight at the drop of a hat, and I would protect everybody around me, and so everybody liked me. Kids around me liked me; they would come to me. I guess I was kinda charismatic; I don't know. I would protect them, and I would defend them. I hated bullies, so I always beat them up. There are so many stories about bullies I beat up in my life. I learned that you had to work hard; you had to hustle if you wanted things. I learned about sex. For me, I think the combination of violence and sex in my life is what kinda formed me. I mean, can you imagine I started taking judo when I was eleven— karate, judo, boxing? Anything I could learn to do to fight better. Girls, I already told you, I loved them, older girls too. You know, as soon as I was old enough to start having sex with older girls, I was having sex with older girls. When I was fifteen, I was having sex with women. The oldest woman I ever had sex with was sixty-three. She would pay me to come by once a week. This is the kind of guy I was, and I always had guys flocking to me. People were always around me, and I always taught them. I organized them, and I always had a group with me. I had followers. I taught them how to do crimes, taught them to fight, so, you know, that is what I was as I was growing up. I grew up in an era of Michael Corleone, the Godfather, and gangster movies. I did my best to act as they would, treating it like research. Martial arts, guns, and knives became my gods. I would sometimes have three or four of my guys surround me and attack me all at once, and I would defeat them all. I practiced with handguns so that I could shoot birds out of the air. With knives, I would tie them to my hands and practice stabbing and slashing the shit out of the targets I would set up. I called a sawed-off pool stick my wife and would beat many older and much bigger opponents into submission with it. By the time I was sixteen, I already knew what I wanted to grow up to be. I wanted to be the best hit man in the world. Can you imagine that? A kid grows up and he is sixteen years old and he wants to be the best killer in the world. He hones himself to that, and he trains himself to that.

Me, my mother, and my brothers and sisters

Chapter 3

It was the time of hippies and free love, drugs, sex, rock and roll, and the Vietnam War. My father had been a war hero, and while I may have participated in the protest against the war and the establishment, I did it more for the free sex from all the young hippie and runaway girls and what I called the twenty-five-cent fuck. A single marijuana joint cost twenty-five cents, and whenever you would ask a girl to smoke a joint with you, the two of you would go off somewhere private to smoke the joint. It would almost always end up with you having sex, so I always referred to that as the twenty-five-cent fuck. Everyone would attend protest rallies and concerts and party with drugs and alcohol. We would have love-ins and sex orgies after the events. Growing your hair long and protesting against the establishment and the war was popular, so I grew my hair and attended all protests, concerts, and rallies in search of new, strange, and different pussy.

I had always been a sports jock too. I excelled in football and basketball, and I was good at baseball. But like I said, I excelled in football and basketball; I even set a record in high school for scoring five touchdowns in a single game. The record was not that I had scored five touchdowns, but that I scored five touchdowns in every way that a touchdown could be scored in a single game. I scored a touchdown by receiving a pass. I scored another touchdown by intercepting a pass on defense and returning it for the score. I scored a touchdown by return-

41

ing a kickoff all the way for the score. I scored a touchdown by returning a punt all the way for the score. The last touchdown I scored was by
taking a handoff from the quarterback. I was very proud of all that. For
the first time in my life, my name was in the newspapers for something
I could be proud of. I had always planned to go to college, hopefully
on a sports scholarship. Back then, I was considered too small for a
professional career in either football or basketball. While I could still
go to college on scholarship for football at that time, I could not see
it turning into an NFL career because I was not over six feet tall and
two hundred pounds. The air force could afford me my best chance for
a career in the world of professional sports. I had it all planned out. I
would win a gold medal in the Olympics for boxing, because I believed
I was that good. I would continue with the money from the air force
into college as well as pursue my education in the air force. After discharge from the air force, I would join either the CIA or FBI or even
become a police detective. Being in the air force intelligence pretty
much guaranteed these types of careers, and the idea of having a license
to kill was very attractive to me then. This was still the era of the draft,
and at age eighteen, you had to register for it. Burning draft cards and
fleeing to Canada was popular, but I knew that because of my father, I
could never be a draft dodger. While I did not necessarily want to go to
Vietnam, still I knew that when the time came, I would not avoid the
draft. Instead of waiting to be drafted, upon my eighteenth birthday, I
would enlist in the air force.

I was sixteen years old when I began committing armed robberies
and dealing drugs. By the time I was seventeen, I had a woman who
was thirty-one years old and an exotic dancer. She was called the Satin
Doll. Then, exotic dancing was just really taking off. She had some
humongous tits. They were silicon though. I did not like silicon-en-
hanced breasts, and I have never liked false tits. I like the real thing, no
matter what the size. Everybody was in love with this broad; she had
dope houses where she sold her drugs. Like I said, she was thirty-one,
and I was seventeen. She saw in me something, and she decided she
was going to get me, and she was going to turn me out using sex. She
was going to put a pistol in my hands, and she was going to control me
with that pussy, like she had always controlled all the men. One thing
led to another. One night, she came to scout a friend of mine's house
as a potential dope house because a lot of traffic went through there, so

she figured she could sell dope there too. She was beautiful, like a cross between the movie stars Jane Russell and Jayne Mansfield. I watched her shoot down many men who were older than me, men who had things and who were supposed to be somebody. I mean, they were drug dealers. They were supposed to be gangsters and pimps, and she was just shooting them down, treating them like they were just clowns. So I just observed her, and we talked. I knew to be careful with this woman. Whatever you do, be very careful; she was unlike any woman or girl I had ever known. She was impressed by the fact that even though I was the youngest person there, I was treated with respect by everyone and was known by everyone. Anyway, one night, she came to this friend's house, banging on the door at two o'clock in the morning, all excited, saying that she wanted Riley. "I want Riley; get me Riley." That was my last name and what everybody called me at the time. So my friend told me, "Hey, Satin came by looking for you. She wants to see you. She say it's really important." So I was thinking, "Wow, all right, because this is one fine bitch and she wants me." So the night the meeting is set up for, that afternoon, I went to go to see the movie *The Godfather* again before I met with her. The first thing she asked me was if I have ever killed anybody. I asked her, "Why do you want to know." She said she had a contract killing she needed to have done. Now I was looking at this sexy-ass bitch and thinking to myself, "What answer is gonna keep me still in the game of trying to get in her pants and not come off sounding like one of the lames I'd seen her shoot down the night I met her?" So I told her, "No, I've never killed anyone, but I would if the price was right."

She told me, "The price of the contract is five thousand dollars." Trying to sound more professional, mature, and experienced than I was, I told her, "That doesn't sound like a whole lot of money to me." She said this was an easy contract at five thousand and that it was fair for such an easy job. I countered with, "I'll determine how easy it is." Then I told her, trying to sound serious and experienced, that we were now having a conversation that could put both of us in jail. She began to explain how easy this contract would be to me. There was this guy who wanted his older aunt killed so that he could inherit everything since he was her only heir. Still trying to sound like an experienced gangster, I said to her, "If I do this, it's double, and I gotta have five thousand up front and another five thousand after it's done." I even told her, "I should even double that because I'm going to have to probably kill him too." I never intended on really killing anyone even though I wanted to be a hit man. I didn't want my first hit to be some old lady. I wanted to keep stringing her along, sounding like the gangsters in the movie *The Godfather.* I never figured this guy would agree to my doubling the price, and I wouldn't lose face in front of her. So this guy agreed to my price. This surprised me. He owned a dress shop, and he wanted to meet me. We were not to talk about the contract; he just wanted to observe me. He had a bodyguard-driver-type guy who drove him around, a big fat guy. So I went into his shop to meet him. While I was there, I observed his bodyguard leave the shop. I thought that was unusual. Satin and I left after the meeting. I told her, "Just wait here in the parking lot, I want to see something." Sure enough, I see the fat bodyguard driver getting into his car. I told Satin, "He is sending his driver to try to follow us." We let him follow us for a while to make sure that was what he was in fact doing. Then we lost him on the free-way. Later Satin and I had a conversation. I told her, "Look, we should double the price because of what he is doing. He is trying to follow us to find out where I live, and that ain't cool. The only reason he would want to know where I live is because he has plans to try to do some-thing to me after I fulfill the contract. Like not pay me and to have me killed so he won't have any witnesses." Satin said, "Well, he won't pay that much. Why are you asking for that much?" I said, "Because of this shit you've now got me in. After I kill her, I'm gonna have to kill him, and I may even have to kill you too." I told her, "This guy has no intention of paying me the second half; he wanted you to bring me there so that his goon can get a good look at me so they could take me out. How the fuck do I know that you're not a part of this too?" My accusing her of possibly being involved in the whole plan of using me to do the dirty work then having me killed stunned her. I pulled my gun, and I told her, "Bitch, you better not be fucking playing me." She swore she didn't know anything about what he's doing, but she agreed it did look like that could be a possibility, but she didn't think this guy was that smart. She said, besides that, what about her? He would have to kill her too. I laughed, and I said, "Maybe he is planning on killing you too anyway." She asked me, "What do you want to do?" I told her, "Let's get the money." This seemed to intrigue her. She smiled, and she said, "What do you mean let's get the money?" "Let's go ahead with the contract, get the first half, get the instructions, tell him it's a go. I don't want him to think that we are aware of his plans. Bitch, you better not be playing with me because I don't care how hot your fine ass is, I will kill you." She laughed and said, "I knew when I met you, you were going to be trouble, Riley."

So the guy told me through Satin this was the setup and how he wanted it done: His aunt was eighty years old, she lived in a big condo, and she had a bad heart. He was going to have her go to the bank and withdraw a large amount of money on the day of the hit. So she was known to have withdrawn money that day and that a possible motive for her killing would be that someone saw her withdraw the money, followed her home from the bank, robbed, and killed her. He gave me a key to her place, and what he wanted me to do was go in there and take the money she withdrew from the bank. Also she had a big ring with a big ruby that was an heirloom. I was to take that ring; that would be proof that I had been there and I had done the deed. When I gave him the ring and she was dead, I would get the rest of my money. I could keep the money she withdrew from the bank. It would be a few thousand dollars. So I said, "Okay, set it up. I'll do it. I'll kill the old lady." Let me say something right here. I never intended on really killing this woman. I wasn't going to kill her. I was not going to kill any old lady. What I was going to do was take the money she had from the bank. I was going to take her ring, and then I was going to warn her that I had been hired by an unknown source to kill her. Then I was going to go back and say, "Dude, hey, you got to get me the rest of the money or I'm going to tell your aunt that you're the one who hired me, then you will be cut out of her will." So I was going to blackmail this punk, and the old lady would have put security around herself. I thought he was a punk for wanting to kill this eighty-year-old lady. Why couldn't he just wait for her to die naturally? So that was my plan. My intention was never to kill this old lady, and I still couldn't trust Satin enough to let her in on my plan.

I was still trying to impress her with how mature and advanced a killer I was for my young age, and I was afraid that if I told her the truth, she would bail on the contract with me and hire someone else. Going along with taking this contract would keep me close to her, which I wanted to be, but on my terms, and possibly save this woman's life too. Until I could get Satin's pussy and get the money from this contract too. She was more than eager to give me her pussy, but I was actually intimidated by her sheer physical beauty and obvious gangster bitch quality. The last thing I wanted to do was stick my dick inside her and come in the first few seconds. This is how hot and sexy a woman she was. I was a young seventeen-year-old wannabe gangster, and here was this sexy, seasoned, experienced thirty-one-year-old exotic dancer. I had just seen the movie *The Godfather* the second time when our paths met, and I tried to imitate Michael Corleone to the best of my young ability. I knew this woman was dangerous, and I wanted to get me some of everything she had to offer a young stud like I was. Not even for all my young wild sexual fantasies being fulfilled with her was I ever gonna kill some old lady. No pussy in the world was worth doing such a cowardly act as this to me. Burning this piece of shit nephew, now that was very attractive to me. By the time it would finally all go down, I would have gotten close enough to Satin that she would agree with me to just burn this dude, and she would still respect me even though I refused to kill an old lady. Either way, it would give me time to work my charms on Satin and give me a chance to have sex with this beautiful, dangerous bitch. The funny thing is that she had her own agenda for her plans to seduce me and get me into bed with her from the first time she had me come to her house and met me in a completely see-through baby-doll lingerie. She walked around me the whole time I was there practically naked, tempting me, observing me and my reaction, even showing me the dance routine she did in the clubs. She would ask me what I thought of how she looked for her age of thirty-one. I knew then she was trying to seduce me, but I told her that I was a professional and believed in business before pleasure. I said this with a false confidence and the best imitation of the Hollywood classic gangsters I had grown up idolizing. The truth was, I had never had a woman as sexual and beautiful and experienced as she was in my life. I was scared that I wouldn't be able to satisfy her, so I tried to play it cool and wait until I felt confident enough. This only made her want me more.

The night I was going to do this robbery, I was dressed all in black except for a white turtleneck under my black shirt and black sport coat. Back then, turtlenecks were fashionable, and I always dressed sharp. Still to this day, people say I dress sharp. Anyway, when I entered the condo—remember, I had a key—I made no noise. I looked around the house and headed for the master bedroom. I wanted to catch the woman off guard and control her immediately so that she was quiet and not screaming and alerting her neighbors. I couldn't find her in her bedroom. I could see her clothes on the bed and her purse on her dresser, and then I heard a crashing sound, a thud, and water splashing coming from her bathroom.

I figured this was where she must be, but what was all the splashing sounds? So I eased the bathroom door open, and what I saw shocked me at first. This woman was naked, trying to pull herself up out of the tub and slipping and splashing water everywhere. I instinctively knew she was in trouble by the look on her face. I don't know why I did it at the time, except that I didn't want to frighten her any more than she looked already. I pulled my ski mask completely off my face and rushed to help her. That's when she noticed me for the first time. Like I said, she was naked, and I just instinctively understood that a man in a ski mask suddenly in her bathroom was not going to help the situation. More than this, I sensed that this woman was in serious trouble and that she might be having a heart attack. One of the things her nephew stressed was that she had a bad heart and that killing her would be easier because of that and because she was so old. I rushed to her side, kneeling beside the tub, telling her not to be afraid and that I was there to help her. I kept repeating those words to her, "Don't be afraid, I'm here to help you." She grabbed on to me, almost pulling me down into the tub with her. She said she was having a heart attack and wanted me to get her out of the tub. She threw her arms around me, and I tried to lift her out of the tub. There was soap and water everywhere, and in pulling her out of the tub, we slipped and fell. Now there we were, both on her bathroom floor. She was naked, half on top of me and clinging to me for dear life so tightly I could not get her to release me so I could get up and call for help. I slipped my gloves off as we lay there together. They were wet, and I didn't want her to notice them and maybe become suspicious or even more frightened.

As we lay there on the soaking-wet bathroom floor, I kept trying to reassure her that everything was gonna be all right but she had to let go of me so I could get up and help her, call an ambulance, and for her not to worry because I was there to help her. Now this woman couldn't have been but five foot two and weigh no more than a hundred and twenty pounds soaking wet. She would not let me go, and she didn't want me to let go of her either. She kept calling me "Father." Her nephew's orders were that I was to let myself in with his key that he had provided and catch her asleep in bed, and I was to make it look like I had broken in and had tried to rape her then rob and kill her. There had been a few burglary rapes in the news, and the suspect was black. This was why I had dressed completely in black except for my white turtleneck. When he first gave me his instructions to Satin to pass on to me, he'd actually suggested that I did in fact rape her, rip off her clothes, and penetrate her before strangling her. That way it would look like it might have been this black guy in the news. I told Satin I wouldn't penetrate her, but after I killed her, I would tear off her clothes to make it look like someone tried to rape her. Because even though I wanted to be a hit man, I wasn't gonna rape an eighty-year-old woman for no amount of money, and besides that, how was I even supposed to get an erection with an eighty-year-old lady? This nephew was so sick he suggested that if I couldn't actually have sex with her, I should shove some kind of object up her vagina so it would point toward a rape burglary gone wrong.

Like I said, I never even intended on harming a hair on this old lady's head when I agreed to the contract. I was just gonna take her ring and the money he'd had her withdraw from the bank for him earlier that day, then blackmail the nephew for the rest of the contract money. But now, here I was lying on this poor woman's bathroom floor, all wet and holding her naked body in my arms. Because she was a devout Catholic and Italian and because of the way I was dressed, she thought I was a Catholic priest coming to help her in answer to her prayers to the Virgin Mary earlier in the evening. She told me that when she first started having her chest pains, she knew she was going to die but wanted to bathe her body and get dressed so that when she died, she would be clean. She had been praying for the Virgin Mary to send her a priest to hear her last confession, and here I was, in answer to her prayers.

Then it hit me that to her, with the way I was dressed, she mistook me for a priest. As soon as she saw me, she did not want me to call for an ambulance. She only wanted me to hear her confession before she died. I had come into this only wanting to do two things: one, burn this piece of shit nephew of hers, and two, I figured that by taking the contract and burning him, at least he would not have hired another hit man to do it and so I would actually be saving this lady's life. I would warn her after I robbed her that I had been hired to kill her, and she'd put security around herself, and her nephew would be too afraid to try it again. He would just have to wait for her to die of natural causes to collect the inheritance.

Now all I knew was that I wanted this woman to live with every fiber of my being, that if I went along with her thinking that I was a priest sent to her in answer to her prayers, and if I listened to her confession, that maybe she would then let go of me and let me get up to call an ambulance. I wanted to call that ambulance for her to save her because I didn't know anything about how to perform CPR or how to save her myself.

So I patted her head that was on my shoulder, and I played along. I had grown up going to Catholic masses a few times and even knew about confession. I told her, okay, that it was all right. I would hear her confession.

There we were, I was not even eighteen years old yet, but Satin had taught me about disguises and makeup. So I did have gray hairspray in a can, streaks in my hair, moustache, and sideburns. Maybe that helped her to think I was old enough to have been a priest. Maybe it was just her condition at the time, and when I had asked her if maybe we should get up off the floor and let her put some clothes on first, then I could hear her confession better. She just squeezed on to me tighter and said, "No, there's not enough time for that." As I looked at her naked body in my arms, I thought of what her nephew had said to Satin at first, about wanting me to actually rape her before killing her. He had said for me to do it to give her one last thrill before she died. For the first time, I actually looked at her full naked body. I was shocked to realize how sexually aroused her naked body was beginning to make me. I could actually see how beautiful a woman this lady had been at one time and still was at eighty years old. She looked like Barbara Stanwyck, the movie star, with her wet silver hair and her big naked breasts and thick Italian bush and big buttocks. I felt so ashamed for looking at her like I was and thinking what I was thinking in those moments. I held her closer to me and tighter, and I told her as I kissed her forehead, "Go ahead, my child, give me your confession."

She seemed to relax and took a break and said to me, "Forgive me, Father, for I have sinned. It has been two weeks since my last confession. But I have never confessed my real sins before, Father." Then she shocked me with her next words. "I murdered my husband so that I could inherit all his wealth. I poisoned his food and his drinks slowly, until one night while he was angry with me and beat me before he had sex with me. He had a heart attack and died."

I was stunned, but I was also curious, so I let her go on with her confession. She said that when she married him, he was old like she is now and she was young and very pretty and poor. She married her husband because he was old, rich, and had a bad heart like she did then. She thought that she would have so much sex with him that it would eventually kill him, and she would have all his money. But after they were married, he changed. He began to beat her and make her have sex with him. Sometimes he would make her have sex with other men and even women while he watched. Then he would have what she called perverted sex with her. She seemed embarrassed as she looked into my eyes and admitted that at first, she hated it, but later she began to enjoy it. She began to be afraid that someday he would grow tired of her and replace her with a younger, prettier, poorer girl who would be happy to marry him like she had for his money. So she had begun to poison him, but he only seemed to get stronger and more perverted in his requests. The night that he died, he was beating her because she refused to have sex with this young prostitute he had picked up off the streets. She thought she looked like a dirty drug addict, and while he was beating her, he had his heart attack and died. I asked her if this was all the sins she had wanted to confess, and she said, "No, Father, there's more." So I said, "Okay, go ahead and finish your confession." She told me that it was really embarrassing what she still had to confess. I squeezed her and told her, "Go ahead, my child, get it off your chest." She said that after her husband died and she inherited all his wealth, she still practiced some of the perverted sex acts her husband had used to beat her to perform with other men, even with married men, and that she has even committed incest with her nephew. I asked her what she meant by this because now I was really curious about the piece of shit nephew, the one who hired me to kill her. She said that now that she's an old lady, it's harder for her to find men who want to have sex with her. So she paid her nephew sometimes to have sex with her, and sometimes her nephew would find her younger men that she would pay to have the perverted sex with her, which she still liked to have sometimes. She said she was trying to make up for it by leaving her nephew half of her estate when she died and had instructed him to change her will so the other half would go to the Catholic Church.

I can't describe the things I was feeling then or why I told her that she was still a very attractive woman who shouldn't have to pay anyone to have sex with her. Crazy thing to say to a dying woman who's lying there naked in the arms of the supposed hit man who was hired by her only living relative to rob, rape, and kill her. I asked her if that was all her sins she wanted to confess to me, and she said yes. Now I knew from my childhood what the priest says next to the confessee. But instead, I told her, "I absolve you of all your sins. You did not kill your husband. He killed himself with his anger and his bad heart, and he is the one to blame for all your sins," not her because of the things he did to her that made her do the sins she committed. She was relieved to hear me say that I absolved her of all her sins. I don't know what inspired me to say what I said next, but I told her that I was there like I was because God heard her prayers and knew she was sincere. Or what inspired me to ask her what I had remembered being asked myself by a Baptist preacher who had baptized me only two short years earlier. Except that I gave her a more Catholic version, I said, "Do you believe in Jesus Christ, that He is the Son of God, born of the Virgin Mary, crucified under Pontius Pilate for all your sins, and resurrected on Easter morning for your justification?" She answered me, like, for a moment, she was an innocent little girl, "Oh yes, oh yes, I do, I believe in Jesus." I remembered then what the Baptist preacher had told me just before he dunked me under the water, what in that moment seemed a million years ago. "Do you love the Lord with all your heart, and will you serve Him now for the rest of your days here on earth and in heaven, forever?" She clutched me as tight as she could, and she said, "Yes, yes, yes. I will serve Him. I love Him so much. Thank you, Father, thank you for absolving me of all my sins." And then I said to her, "Okay, can I get up now and call the operator for an ambulance for you?" She got really excited and told me, "No, Father, it's too late for an ambulance. My Jesus is here. He's here. Do you see Him, Father? He's here to take me away with Him. Look, do you see Him?"

I got a chill across my entire body, and I was afraid and started looking around the bathroom everywhere, looking to see if He really was there, because she was so sure and so excited. And that's when she hugged me and died. I started tearing myself loose from her, trying to get up off that wet, slippery floor covered with bathwater and bubble bath. I was yelling at her no and calling her name, telling her not to die, to please live, but it was no use. She was gone, and all that remained there was one stupid fool who thought he was so wise and who was gonna be the greatest hit man that ever lived, and the naked corpse of a once beautiful woman who, even in death, still looked like a beautiful dead movie star.

They say that when a person dies they evacuate their bowels, but this was not true for her. I know; I looked as I managed to put her bathrobe on her dead body. I did that so when they found her, they would not find her naked and exposed on her bathroom floor. I carried her to her bed and laid her on top of it. Then all I could think about was how her nephew had used me and set me up. He knew how bad her heart was, and I vowed vengeance right then and there as I slipped the big red ruby ring from her dead finger. I took the money from her purse. I left; I had not made it look like a burglary by trashing the house. I had not made it look like I raped her by leaving her clothes torn off her or penetrating her with some foreign object. Instead, I had put her bathrobe on her and had laid her gently across her bed. I had Satin go to a phone booth and make an anonymous phone call to the local police, to say that she heard a woman screaming at this address, yelling for help, and that she saw some black guys around her door and windows, then hang up before they could trace the call.

I left there filled with so much guilt, shame, and anger—guilt because I had played my part in her dying and had been set up by her nephew. I was gonna make him pay in the worst way possible if I had to. Shame because I couldn't save her—I didn't know CPR—I had seen her naked, and she died naked in my arms and because I had felt arousal at her naked body. Satin had timed me. I had only been there nineteen minutes, yet it seemed like forever, and it will live in me forever.

I realized, after she had said in her confession that she had instructed her nephew to change her will to divide her estate in half between her nephew and the church, that this must be the reason the nephew was in such a hurry for her to die, to have her killed before the new will could be discovered and put in to effect. He was her only living relative and the executor of her estate. He had no intention of allowing half of her estate to go to the church, so he hired me. Now it was time to make him pay. I had her ring and the few thousand from her purse with the bank slips and the truth about his incest with which I could blackmail him. I had a rage to avenge not only myself but also this woman, who had died in my arms. Maybe I hadn't killed her, but I didn't save her either.

Chapter
4

So now, I told Satin everything that happened, and I gave her the big ruby ring with instructions to go get the remaining five thousand dollars I was still owed from the nephew. I told her to tell him that I knew everything about the incest and about the change in her will to give the church half of her estate. I said she needed to tell him that unless I got my money, I will use that information against him and that she was not to give the ring until I was fully paid.

This asshole nephew turned around and told Satin that because his aunt died of natural causes and because I didn't rape her or make it look like a robbery, he wasn't gonna pay me the rest of the money. As far as he knew, all I did was find her already dead and just took the ring off her finger, that I was trying to collect for a job I didn't even finish. He did want the ring though and offered her a thousand dollars for it.

Satin already had instructions not to give him the ring until he gave her the remaining five grand. When Satin refused to give him the ring and warned him against not paying me, the nephew threatened her and me. He basically told her to tell me, "Shut up, punk, kick rocks. You ain't getting shit," and just like he had hired me, he could hire "a real hit man" to kill her and me and Satin's two sons if we didn't shut up and get lost.

When Satin told me all of this, she expected me to get angry and go into his store and start shooting and killing him and his bodyguard driver. She was surprised I was so calm and I said, "Okay, I figured as much. Let's just wait here in the parking lot for him to close up and then follow him."

We waited; she asked me what I was going to do. I told her, "I'm gonna do what I told you in the beginning, when you first approached me with this contract, that I'd probably have to do, I'm gonna kill him and leave no witnesses." She looked at me with a new respect and a little fear as she asked me, "What about me? Are you going to kill me too?" I played the part of this experienced killer hit man I had been playing from the beginning with her, and I answered her, "I should, but won't, not yet anyway, not as long as I can trust you. Can I trust you?" "Of course you can. How could you even ask me that after all of this? I'm getting burned in all this too by him," she said. "How are you getting burned too?" I asked her. That's when she confessed to me for the first time that she had jacked the original price of the contract to fifteen thousand instead of the ten grand I had agreed to. When he gave her the first half, he actually gave her seventy-five hundred, of which she had kept twenty-five hundred. "A girl's got to make something off this deal too. I have to take care of my two sons, don't I?" she said.

I laughed and told her I figured she got more for setting it all up than that. "You knew?" she asked. "It's what I would have done in your place," I answered, acting more mature and professional about it than I actually was. She leaned over in the car seat, kissed me, and told me, "I'm with you, let's make this son of a bitch pay." We waited, and we followed him to an apartment complex and watched as he left his bodyguard driver in the car waiting for him. He went into an upstairs apartment, and a young woman met him at the door. She kissed him and let him in the apartment. Satin said, "He always did like them young and dumb and with big tits and a lot of ass." This pretty much described the girl who greeted him at the door.

He stayed in the apartment for a little over an hour, then left. We followed him to his home; he lived in a secure complex. We followed him for two more weeks, getting his routine down; we observed that he visited this girl twice a week, and each time he never stayed over an hour. His bodyguard always waited down the street in the car for him. I decided that this was where I was gonna get him.

One night, when he went to see his girlfriend, I found my spot beneath an open stairwell that he walked up and down on his visits to see her. It was dark beneath the stairwell, so I was able to hide there unseen. My original plan was to just shoot him in his back through the stairs as he walked down to the pavement below. I had Satin parked directly across the street from where I was where I could see her and she could watch the apartment door. She was supposed to signal me when she saw him coming out of the apartment; she will do this by lighting her cigarette lighter in the dark car. Once she lights her lighter, I'll see it from my hiding place under the stairwell. If he isn't alone when he leaves or if the bodyguard shows up or if anyone else is around, she would hit the car horn one quick time to warn me and to call off the whole thing; but if she lights the lighter twice, it's a go.

I remember that it was cold out that night and there was a bright full moon in the night sky. A light drizzle of soft rain had begun to softly sprinkle. I thought of how this woman had died in my arms, of all the sick shit this bastard had wanted me to do to her before killing her. I thought of how he had told me to kick rocks and that how he would hire a real hit man and not some punk kid to kill me if I didn't just shut up and go away. The more I thought of these things, the more I thought that shooting him in the back wasn't what I wanted, although shooting him in the back as he came down the stairs would have ensured a quick getaway. I didn't care about that anymore as I stood there in the damp darkness beneath the stairwell.

It was personal now, so I wanted him to see my face and to know that it was me killing him. Satin had warned me that he always carried a .32 revolver in the back of his waist like I wore mine, and to be careful. I waited for Satin to give the signal, and then I saw it—the lighter flicked, once and then two flicks. It was now or never as he came down the stairs. As he stepped down onto the cement pavement, I met him with my gun drawn. He was startled, and as soon as he recognized that it was me, he started offering the money. He was telling me that he was sorry he had burned me and how he was rich now and he could give me more money than I ever had before in my life. I told him to shut up. I didn't want any noise. I took a quick look around to make sure no one was watching, and then I told him, "You should have waited for her to just die. You knew how bad her heart was. You set me up and used me, then you have the nerve to threaten and disrespect me." That's when he told me he had to do that because she had told him she wanted him to change her will to give half to the church. He had no choice but to kill her before she could finalize the new will. He would now make it all up to me; he always intended to pay me the rest of the money he owed me. He said, "Here, kid, I got money, let me pay you off." And he started to reach for his back pocket like he was going for his wallet. I remembered Satin's last words to me about being careful because he always carried a gun in the back of his waistband underneath his coat. I fired my first shot, hitting him in the chest. He fell over backward. I stood over him as he cried, "You shot me! You shot me! I was only gonna pay you! I was getting my wallet out to pay you, and you shot me! I have money in my wallet!" He tried to reach underneath himself again, as if he was going for his wallet, but I stepped on his arm and pointed the gun toward his heart. I told him, "You keep your money, take it with you to hell!" and I squeezed off two more shots, killing him dead.

I looked around again to see if the gunshots had alarmed any of the neighbors or his bodyguard driver. But it was strangely quiet. I thought to make it look like a robbery gone bad, so I emptied his pockets, which were full of cash, and I took his jewelry. He had gold chains and a watch, and I saw that .32 revolver fall out of his waistband, and I realized this bastard had no intention of paying me. He was in fact reaching for his gun when I shot him both times. I took his wallet and his gun, then I reached in my pocket and took out that big ruby ring I had taken from his aunt. I shoved it in his dead hand, and I told his dead corpse, "Contract fulfilled."

I thought about his bodyguard driver then. I walked down the street to where he was parked in the car, waiting as usual. At first I thought I would have to kill him too. So I went down. He was sitting there, listening to music and smoking a joint, rocking out like everything's all good, you know, with the windows down too. So I just leaned in with the gun, put it to his temple, and told him, "If I ever see you again, if I even smell you or think of you, I'm gonna kill you." I didn't kill him; I should have. But there had been enough death already; I didn't need another ghost to haunt my soul. He never turned around; he never saw my face. He sat there frozen, afraid to move. I left, and he disappeared. He never said anything to the police, nothing; he just disappeared. He didn't even come back; he was gone. He just got ghost because that's what I told him to do. So now, I felt better. I felt like I had got revenge, you know, for the old lady and for me. I don't know if that makes any sense to anybody, but I just felt better after I killed him.

That's a bad thing to say. I would come to learn later on that killing people was not as much fun as I thought it would be. Maybe that's why I didn't kill the bodyguard driver; I wasn't a hit man after all. I was just an idiot who grew up believing the Hollywood version of what a hit man was supposed to be, until the reality of it all actually hit me later on. I wanted to grow up to be the best hit man there was. Sadly, my first kill was not anything, and it was an accident. He wasn't though, so I had my first kill after all. I had the money. He ended up having nine thousand on him, and his jewelry was worth a lot too.

While we drove back to Satin's house, she had a lot of questions about what happened, how it went, and where I went when I left the apartment complex. She said she lost sight of me. I explained to her about going after the bodyguard driver and what I did. How he never saw my face, or me, how he was driving away as I'd told him to do as I was walking back to where she was waiting. She wanted to know why I didn't just kill him too. I told her, "Nobody paid me to kill him, I don't kill for free," still trying to sound like some actor in a movie playing it cool with her. When we got back to her house, we went into the bedroom, and I took everything out of my pockets that I had taken from the nephew. I took it all and threw it on the bed, even the .32 revolver. She looked at me, and she asked me again, "What about me? Are you going to kill me someday because I was a witness?" I sat her down on the bed, and I told her, "I don't know, maybe someday I might have to kill you if you ever do me wrong, but no, it won't be because of any of this. This is the life I've chosen, and if it's with you by my side, for however long it lasts, I don't know this either, only time will tell, but from now on, you don't ever withhold anything from me like you did by jacking the contract fee. You don't ever lie to me, and you give me wings to do whatever I feel like I have to do. If you're loyal to me—and I don't mean with sex, you can fuck whomever you want—I mean loyalty in all our business affairs. I know you saw me. You know the potential in me, and you thought you would put that pussy of yours on me. You thought you would put a pistol in my hands and you'd control me. This is why I never had sex with you until the other day. I never had sex with you because I knew how you worked and how you use that body and your beauty to manipulate and control men. Believe me, it's been really hard to resist you, when you're always naked around me in that see-through baby doll. I wanted you to know that with me, that wouldn't work."

She laughed at that and admitted that since she'd met me she'd done everything possible to try to seduce me, like I had just said, that the other day, when we finally did have sex, she had to trick me into it. That while the sex was great, she knew it was only because we were both like professional prizefighters trying to use our bodies and the sex to outfuck each other. This was not what she wanted either. I said, "Good. Now we have an honest understanding of each other, and here, there's nine thousand dollars here in cash. Here's the other twenty-five hundred this guy owed you for your share of the original contract."

The jewelry she can keep or dump. I didn't like having a dead man's jewelry on me. I was superstitious about it. She asked me if she could keep the revolver because it was originally hers before she sold it to him a couple of years before. I told her to keep it.

We sat there quiet for a moment, I asked her to make me a drink, a strong one, and to roll me a joint. She seemed to sense what I needed, I was gonna try to get drunk and smoke away all the emotions I was still reeling with from just committing my first murder.

She began to clear the bed of everything and told me, "I know what you need, just trust me," as she reached under the bed and pulled out her stash tray; she usually kept her rolling papers and weed on it. This time there was also powdered cocaine and powdered heroin. She said she knew I would be a little on edge after the night's events, so she got some for us to do together to help me take away what I was feeling. I told her, "No, just a drink and a joint should do it." But she told me to trust her and that she would still fix my drink and roll my joint. I needed to do this, what she called a speedball. It would relax my nerves and help me. Besides, she didn't want me to get all drunk and useless and pass out on her. She had plans for tonight, for us to celebrate our first kill together. And for this, she wanted me wide awake and functioning. I said, "Sex? Really? I don't think I can even perform after tonight, I'm sorry." She just told me to relax and to put myself in her care; she knew what I needed. As she handed me my drink and lit my joint for me, a couple of tokes later and a few sips on the vodka and orange juice, I began to relax a little more. She locked the bedroom door and began to undress me. I was still telling her I didn't think I'd be able to perform tonight, when she made me snort a small mixture of powdered cocaine and heroin, saying the whole time, "Just trust me, Daddy." This was the first time she had ever called me Daddy. As the warmth and rush of the speedball mixed with the vodka and weed, it began to rush through my body and my senses. She had me undressed in just my boxers on her bed. Then she did a striptease in front of me like she had performed so many times in the strip joints. Her name was on the marquee outside the club that night, "The Satin Doll" live. But this was not like any public performances she had ever done before. She seemed to know exactly what I liked and how to reach and awaken in me strange new erotic feelings. As she did things no other girl or woman had ever done before, I began to relax, to enjoy her private personal performance just for me. As she danced so slowly, naked before me, she said, "I know you don't like silicone breasts like most men do, but I do know you like them big, and I do know that you love my big thick nipples. I want you to enjoy them and play with them like this. She pinched them really hard until they were swollen and stood out like an inch thick. "I want you to lick and suck them like this," she said as she took them in her mouth, licking them all around and sucking them deep and hard. She said, "And I know you love my big hairy pussy, with these big meaty lips, because I can see it in your eyes when you look at me. Watch these big meaty pussy lips bloom into a rose," and as she stroked and parted them, they grew like big rose petals. Then she said, "I know you really like how big and swollen my clitoris gets when it gets aroused just from you looking at me. Look at it, Daddy, see how big it is, and it's all yours, baby. Look how big she gets. She's as big as your thumb, and she wants you, Daddy. Have you ever seen a clit this big?" It was almost as big as the top half of my thumb. I almost told her that I had seen one other woman whose clit was even bigger, it seemed, when Annie's grandmother let me touch hers the night I awoke to find her with my six-year-old penis in her mouth. But I didn't. She stopped to give me another snort of cocaine and heroin before turning back to me as she began moving her body and buttocks, slowly, inches from my face as Cecilia had first done that day so long ago, when my innocence had been shattered. She parted her buttocks, revealing her asshole. She said, "You like that, don't you, Daddy? You want it, don't you?" It was like she had transported me away from all the haunting images of the death that stained me. She turned and laid me back on the bed as she could see the effect her actions had produced in me. As she took my erection in her hands, she told me, "Let me worship you, I want to worship you.'

I felt electricity in my loins as she knelt there on the floor between my parted naked legs and stroked my penis with her hands. She licked me all over with her tongue, everywhere her tongue could cover. When I felt the hotness of her breath and her mouth engulfing the head of my penis, I surrendered to her adoration of my young strong body. She rode me to her first orgasm, facing me, playing with her clit, and sucking her own breasts, putting on a show for me to see. Then she gave me another snort of a speedball and rode me with her back toward me, reaching back and spreading her big creamy-white ass cheeks to let me see everything she knew that I wanted to see. With each circular thrust, up and down, and just when I thought I wouldn't be able to hold back anymore, she announced that she wanted me to fuck her in the ass. I had fucked her in her pussy and between her massive double D thirty-eight-inch tits, even in her armpits and mouth. But now she said she wanted me to cum in her ass. I thought she had been wild and nasty before, but then she lay on her stomach, reached back, and guided me into her anus. She asked me to rub her clit for her while I was pumping in and out of her ass, but when I couldn't do it sufficiently as I gave it to her as deep and as hard in her ass as I could, she moved my hand away and said, "Here, let me do this." She began to masturbate her own pussy and clit, begging me not to stop giving it to her in her ass. She went wild, moaning and crying how she had never known a man like me and how she never let just anyone fuck her in the ass. She never wanted to give herself in this way to any man but me. I knew she was probably lying to me, but all her nasty talking had made me feel more excited and stimulated.

After we had finished and she had come back with warm soapy water and towels, she cleaned my penis. We lay there together, and she told me, "Damn, Riley, I think I'm falling in fucking love with you. I know you don't want to hear this and I don't want to say it, but I think it's true. I'm falling in love with you, and it scares the hell out of me. I swore when I was fifteen years old and on my own that I would never fall in love with any man ever. I know you have a girlfriend, and I ain't never gonna be jealous of any woman or girl you may be involved with. I know were not gonna ever play house or have no white picket fence, but I'm yours and I'll never betray you. I would kill for you if you ever asked me to. There is something about you. I've known a lot of men in my life, most of them tricks or fools. I've known real gangsters too, and none of them holds a candle to you. What's so scary is that you're still so young and are only just beginning. I just want to be part of it. I'll always have your back, and I'll never lie to you or be disloyal. You'll never have a more gangster bitch than me in your corner."

I told her, "Okay, as long as you don't get jealous of the other women and are honest and loyal to me and you have faith in me and do what I tell you when I tell you, then we can continue on this road of danger and adventure together that we seem to be on." She said, "Hell, if you want to just fuck some other bitch, you tell me, and I'll get her for you as long as you don't go falling in love with some dumb bitch who isn't even worthy of you. I'll even do threesomes with you if that's what you want, but I'll have to agree to who it is, because I like girls sometimes too. Especially younger, innocent-type girls, not tramps or bitches with diseases." So now, I had a crime partner, a gangster bitch who could still teach me so much that I still needed to learn. I told her no more contract killings unless it's for a lot more money than what we made off this train wreck, and no women or children. She could see I was still shaken about the old lady, and she told me that she knew I never intended to go through with hurting her and that I didn't really kill her, that maybe God or whoever is out there in control of the universe used me to help this old lady out when she was already gonna die anyway. From everything I told her about what happened, that's the way it looked to her, and besides, we both knew that if I hadn't said yes to the contract, her nephew would have just hired someone else who might have actually done all the sick shit he wanted done to her. That as far as the nephew went, he deserved what he got and that she knew that when he told her to tell me to kick rocks, he was going to hire a real hit man to kill us all, instead of a young punk-ass kid like me. She knew I was gonna make him eat his words, and she knew that when he threatened her sons, I wasn't gonna ever let her boys be in danger like that because of how much her boys looked up to me. She knew how much I cared about them too, so she was glad he was dead because now her sons would be safe. The irony of it all is that while this was true, not only would she be involved in the murder of my mother years later but so would one of her sons. Again, I'm getting ahead of myself in this story.

So I had all this money, and I was trying to drink, trying to smoke, trying to do everything I can to deal with the fact that I just killed a man, and an old lady, if you want to count her. I didn't kill her, and I never intended to, so I didn't count her. I had just killed a man, and by the same token, this bitch, now all of a sudden, I was a god in her life. She thought she was going to turn me out; I ended up turning her out. So we organized our own little gang. We started doing robberies, major armed robberies, and we were good. I had my crime partners, Tony and Dorian; she had hers. Her main crime partner, Jimmy, he was a stone-cold killer. He came from the war in Vietnam, he had come back from Vietnam, and he ended up getting out of Leavenworth. He had to go to Leavenworth because when he was in Vietnam, he was smuggling dope back with corpses, and they caught him. This guy was like twenty-nine, but he was a killer. Somehow, Satin had hooked up with him, and he was her pistol guy. If she had something that needed to be done, she would throw it to him. So we got hooked up together, and his crime partner was this big fat faggot that he butt fucked. He also had an old lady; she was cool. Jimmy was bad. He had a nice old lady, loyal bitch, and he had his punk too. So then I had my partners too. One night we were sitting around, Jimmy was about money; that's all he was about. So she was pairing Jimmy and me together. She wanted us to do this particular job to see how well we work out together. Satin had a job planned for us to do. I told Jimmy, "No, let's do a different job." I explained to him, "This one will be easier, and we'll get more money." So he looked at her and said, "You know what, I'm gonna go with his plan." And I could see right then and there she was like, "What?" She didn't like that she had just lost control. We went, and we did the robbery and everything went according to how I had said it would. We made a lot of money. Then there was another incident where we had a major job she had planned. We were supposed to take this guy out; he was supposed to have hundreds of thousands of dollars. This guy used to be one of Satin's boyfriends. Now he was a major pimp. He had massage parlors and all that, but he was also an illegal alien. So anyway, the plan kept falling through; we had cased this guy for weeks. We had his program down, but he was in a secure building, so we didn't know how to get him. We had to get him there, so the long and short of it is that I came up with the plan. I said, "Look, we're gonna do this," and Jimmy said, "Again, I'm going with him, he makes the money, so I'm gonna do what he says." We went in, and we took this dude. We got him. Now how do we get the money?

The money's not in the house, except for what he had in his pockets, which I think was less than a thousand dollars. He had jewelry, which was worth a lot, but where's all this money Satin said he had. We got his bankbooks, and he's got most of it in the bank. But it still didn't add up to everything she said. There's money somewhere. All this money this guy's got, how are we gonna get it? So I told Jimmy to just play along with me. Jimmy's like, all right, because we had already done a few robberies together, and we worked really good together in the other jobs and had developed camaraderie and could communicate and improvise together well as good crime partner do. So we took this guy out, and I was talking to him in Spanish. I told him that he must have crossed somebody and that we were there to take him out and kill him. But we were only supposed to kill him if he doesn't come along with us to see our "Big Boss." We made up who hired us to bring him to him. He wasn't paying the protection money he should be paying for his massage parlors and drug dealings and stuff. So we took him out to the country. We pretended we're going to this other place, and we told him we're taking him to go see the guy who hired us. I have him on the floorboard of the backseat of his Cadillac; I was in the backseat with him. He was at my feet, and I got him covered with a floor mat. All the time we were driving, I was talking to him. "What did you do? Who did you piss off?" So we got into the country, this place I knew where we used to go to and party. He could not see anything, and we pretended we're at a security gate. We even pretended to have a conversation with people to let us in. I said, "Jimmy, you go on in and find out what he wants us to do with this guy." So Jimmy went in to see what he wanted us to do, but what Jimmy really did was walk over to the field and take a leak, smokes a cigarette, and come back.

I was watching him right, but this guy couldn't see anything. He's on the floorboard covered, with my feet over him. Jimmy came back in and said, "He wants us to take him out and kill him." And man, I could just feel that guy under my feet. All the air just went out of him, like he knew it was over. I said, "Well, okay, let's go." So Jimmy's still like, "What are we doing?" And I was like giving hand signals in the rear-view mirror. Jimmy's reading my lips for instructions, "Just keep following me." We went out to this other place in the country where we used to get high. We used to take girls out there and have sex with them and get high and throw parties. So it's real secluded, and it's like, right now, it's about three o'clock in the morning now, four o'clock in the morning. So all the while I'd been talking to him, so I took him out, and he's offering to pay us off not to kill him. "I'll give you money, don't kill me." And we're like, "We can't do that." And so we started playing good cop and bad cop. And I was like, "Well, how much money?" and Jimmy's like, "Hey, we can't do that, man, if we let him live, they'll kill us. We have to do the contract." I was like, "Wait a minute, he's offering us more money." So Jimmy said, "No, no." This fictitious guy we made up, Big Al, or whatever name we gave him, would kill us if we didn't take this guy out. So I told Jimmy, "Just give me a little bit of time with him." So I took him, and I walked him into the country right. I walked him up this hill with trees; the hill was secluded. The moon was shining right through there, so it's lit. I threw down my big bowie knife right at the ground, and I said, "Start digging." I had him digging his own grave. All the time, he's talking to me, and I was telling him, "How can I trust you?" He said, "I'll give you the money." I said, "Where's the money?" He said, "Well, I got to go to the bank." So I said, "Oh, hell no, you'll go in there and tell on us and shit, then we'd get killed anyway if I let you go." So the long and short of it, I knew things about this guy. He's a child molester, I knew that. I knew a bunch of stuff that I found out through Satin about him, because she used to be his old lady. And she had helped him get established, set up with the massage parlors, and all that, then he kicked her to the curb. That's why she wanted us to take him; she was trying to use us to get revenge. So I got him up there, and I told him, "Look, we're gonna play a game here, and it's called a game of trust, you know, because if I agree to take your money, I could be killed, and if I take your money, you have to promise me that you will disappear, because if you don't disappear, then they'll just send somebody else to get you." He said, "I swear to God, I'll leave. I'll go back to Mexico." He's telling me all this, so I said, "Okay, let's play this game of trust." So I got him standing there blindfolded, and I told him, "Okay, I'm gonna ask some questions, and if you lie to me, then how could I trust you?" So I started telling him, "You like little boys, don't you?" "Oh no, no." *Bam!* I hit him with the pistol and knock him down. I picked him back up, and I told him, "You just lied to me. Every time I get a lie from you, I'm gonna hit you, and if I can't trust you, then we can't trust each other and I'm gonna go ahead and just kill you and be satisfied with the money from the contract on you and not worry about getting killed for letting you live." I only had to hit him two more times for giving me the wrong answers to my accusations of his acts of child molestation. In the end, I had him confessing that he was a child molester, that he liked little boys, describing all things that he liked to do sexually with little boys. I became angry because this brought back old memories of an unresolved issue in my life from when I was a young boy and had an older male relative try to molest me. I remembered hiding all that night behind a large box in the bathroom with dirty clothes, afraid to return to the bedroom, and waiting in the dark all night for daylight to come so I would be safe again.

So I hit him one last time with my pistol, which made him roll down the little hill. I picked my bowie knife up from the ground near the hole he had been digging. I took a few steps down the little hill. I stood him up, I walked him back up the hill, and I removed his blindfold while telling him, "I think I can trust you now." A few hours later, after returning to his car, where Jimmy was, I gave Jimmy the signal to continue following my lead by agreeing with me in front of him that we would risk our lives and trust him to buy off his contract. Once the banks opened and Jimmy had managed to notify Satin and the rest of the gang by phone of our new plan, while I sat in the car with the guy. The original plan was to have him withdraw fifty thousand dollars from his account through the outside window teller where we had told him we would be watching him and have a gun on him at all times. In case he tried anything funny, we would just kill him. But we had failed to do our research properly and didn't know that because the amount of money he would withdraw was too large a sum to withdraw from the outside teller, he had to go inside the bank, and he did. We lost sight of him at that point. I began to panic a little. I thought that was it, we lost him. He would be in there screaming for the police. Why else had he deviated from my instructions and entered the bank? I was the one who walked him to the intersection across the street from the bank, talking to him the whole time, convincing him that he was doing the right thing by buying us off and saving his life. He would pay us the money and disappear into the sunsets of Mexico. Now that he had gone into the bank, I was to wait where I was five minutes and then be picked up by Satin and Tony and swooped out of there. Three minutes came and went, and I bailed. I knew the taxi station was only a few blocks away. I took off my jacket and threw it away, as well as my shirt, leaving them in the alley along with my gun, stashed. I made it to the cab station in just my T-shirt as it began to sprinkle rain. I got lucky, caught a cabbie ready to take me right then. As we were driving up to the same intersection, we caught a red light. From inside that cab, I looked out and saw him walking like a robot, going to the phone booth we had instructed him to leave the envelop full of money at. We had someone watching to pick up the money once he made the drop. He was to continue walking up the long street; we told him where his Cadillac would be. Throughout the ordeal, he seemed to be more interested in his Caddie and getting his car back than he was with paying us the fifty thousand dollars. I remember watching as he walked away after the drop and seeing Satin's car swoop in the parking lot and Tony getting out the car and grabbing the money from the phone booth. I could even see the big white envelop in Tony's hand as he jumped back in Satin's car and they sped away. Just then, the light turned green, and as we were pulling away, I remember feeling so excited and surprised that he actually went through with it and we pulled it off. I was so proud because it was all my idea, all my work; I had saved the mess that Satin had sent us into.

I headed straight for Satin's house, which was not that far away. I knew everyone would be heading there after they drove around looking for me first, because I had left from my pickup spot. About fifteen minutes later, they all showed up. Sure enough, they had been looking all over for me. Finally, they figured I'd probably head there. Then they came and threw me the envelop full of money on the bed where I was lying. They were all excited and happy that we pulled it off, especially Satin's Jimmy, my partner in crime. He picked me up, hugged me, and told me I was the baddest young motherfucker he had ever seen. He couldn't believe that it worked. I finally spoke and said flatly to Satin, "You were late picking me up. I had to bail." I knew this stung her as she proceeded to blame it on Tony mixing up direction. She said they went to the wrong alley. She drove around looking all over for me, as I could see by how long it took them to get back to the house. I said, "Don't ever let it happen again." Then I yelled excitedly and playfully, "We did it, now let's divide up the money." I was now the undisputed boss and leader of our gang of seven. We split the money, with me and Jimmy each getting ten grand a piece while the rest got six thousand each. Everyone was to kick in a thousand dollars of their share to save for lawyers and the bail fund that we had. Satin objected to the split, but everyone else agreed, so she was outvoted. In that moment, she knew she had lost leadership and control of everyone. This is funny to me; I always remember it smiling, because nowadays, at the end of every Super Bowl, they ask the winning quarterback what he's going to do now that he has won the Super Bowl. Nowadays, they are paid to say, as a commercial, "I'm going to Disneyland." This was the early seventies when we committed this crime, so they had not started saying this yet. All of us were asking each other what we were going to be doing with our share of the money. Back then, this was a lot of money. Jimmy said, "I'm going to Vegas." Tony and Dorian said, "We're going to Reno." When they asked me what I was going to do, I shouted, "I'm going to Disneyland," just like those winning quarterbacks now say at the end of the Super Bowl. I ended up falling in love with Disneyland. I had a room up on the tenth floor of the original Disneyland hotel for the whole summer. But that's another story. Anyway, now I was taking over the gang. That day, I took control, and Satin knew that I was now in absolute control of the gang. We did a lot of major robberies and kidnappings and other things after that job. Satin could see that I was now becoming the person that she had wanted to create and control. She had thought to put a pistol in my hand, teach me things, and control me. The irony is this woman loved me. She worshiped me; she really did. She fell so madly in love with me that it was crazy. She was obsessed with me, and yet years later she would be involved with the murder of my mother.

That night, we were all sitting around, feeling good about our success. Everybody else was drinking cocktails, rum and Coke, vodka and orange juice, stuff like that, except for me. I was sitting there, dipping cookies in milk. I laughed at the thought that here I was, the leader of this gang of older, more experienced and seasoned felons, and here I was dipping cookies in milk.

Our bank was Satin's idea so that we could have bail money, lawyer money, and bribe money, plus money to pay for our supplies and rental cars that we would use in all our future crimes. I knew Satin was not an enemy to make, and while it became clear that day that I now was the leader, it made her feel better about it that I put her in charge of our bank. Years later, when I would join the La Nuestra Familia, I would be in charge of establishing regiments on the streets with regimental banks. This experience would give me the advantage over other soldiers and their trying to establish regimental banks and securing bail bondsmen, lawyers and judges, and police we could bribe. Remember at this time, I was not even eighteen years old yet. All these early experiences were preparing me for a few short years later when I would join not just another prison gang but an organized crime family, La Nuestra Familia.

After everyone had gone and Satin and I were alone, I told her that I knew the truth: That she had seen in me the potential and that her plan had been to put that pussy of hers on me and put a pistol in my hand, teach me things, use me, and control me to be her personal gunfighter and gangster. That even with this job we had just finished, that she picked this guy because he had used her to help him get organized and then he kicked her to the curb. She knew we wouldn't find all that money she said he had and that either I or Jimmy would get so pissed off that we would just kill him. But I spoiled her plans by coming up with my own plan once her plan had failed. That I felt she owed me an apology and proof of loyalty to me like she had pledged to me after the contract killing fiasco the night we fucked each other's brains out.

She was too quick to apologize and reaffirm her loyalty and her word to me. She asked me what I wanted as proof of her loyalty and acceptance of me as the new undisputed leader of the gang. Did I want her to kill someone to prove her loyalty? I said, "No. I'm gonna want something you promised me. You said you would never be jealous of any other woman that I wanted to fuck and that you would even get the woman for me if I told you to." Satin always had a few girls that hung around her, worshipping her and admiring her. Eventually, she would turn them out to work for her or to just have sex with them. There was this English girl; she had been grooming for her own seduction. She was actually just a plain square hippie folk singer, but I found her accent sexy, so I told Satin I want her to bring Jenny with us to Disneyland as a nanny for the boys. I wanted to fuck her while we were there, and I didn't want no jealousy shit. I didn't want a threesome; I just wanted her to myself.

I saw in her eyes I had hit a nerve; she was jealous. I wasn't sure if she was jealous because I wanted to fuck the shit out of this square-looking broad or jealous because she had wanted to eat this girl up first before I had her or jealous because I had refused her compromise of a threesome. Satin was a professional, and she knew I would just fuck the shit out of this little broad and forget all about the broad once I had satisfied my own lusts with her, and there would be other times to still try to regain control over me. So she agreed, and we had a great time going to Disneyland and staying there for few nights.

Like I said, Satin was beautiful, like a cross between Jane Russell and Jane Mansfield, five foot six, 130 pounds, jet-black hair, dark eyes that were almost black, and white creamy skin. Thirty-eight double-D breasts, twenty-eight-inch waist, and a thirty-eight ass. Since she was fifteen years old, she had been an exotic dancer and in the gangster lifestyle. While she definitely knew how to be a whore in the bedroom, she could never be a lady in the living room, and this is why she could never be my woman alone or ever be my wife.

My mother had told me that she understood that her son was a whore, as she would jokingly introduce me to some of her girlfriends as "My son, the whore."

I was even fucking the shit out of a lot of her girlfriends; my dick did most of my thinking when it came to women. She told me that my father had told her that the secret to happiness was to marry a woman who knows not just how to be a whore in the bedroom but who could also be a lady in the living room. I guess these were words I lived by in my relationships with all women for the rest of my life. Satin would never be a lady in any living room. Heck, she seldom wore any clothes in the living room even when around her own sons, who were seven and nine years old when I came into their lives.

I know that everybody sees his mother naked at one time or another growing up, even me. I'd seen my mother naked once when I was six years old. I had walked into her bedroom early one morning to ask her for money for the bakery truck that was in the neighborhood, and my father had surprised us with his first visit since the divorce. I was used to walking into her room in the mornings to get money. I was shocked and stunned to walk in and discover a naked man on top of her naked body, doing what I thought at first was hurting her. After a few seconds of shocked undiscovered silence, I realized this man was not hurting her as these were not sounds of pain coming from my mother but of something I was too young then to understand was pleasure. This naked man seemingly pounding her into the mattress was my father. Quietly I backed out of the bedroom, and they never even realized I had come in. I ran to tell my brothers and sisters, "Daddy's here, Daddy's here." The next time I saw my mother naked, I was thirteen years old and had come running into the bathroom from diarrhea, not aware she had been in there showering and had just thrown open the shower curtains to reach for a towel to dry off, when I burst in trying to reach the toilet before I shit all over myself. She yelled at me to get out as I tried to explain I had diarrhea, bad, and while she was wrapping herself in a towel to cover up, I ended up shitting all over myself before I could get my pants down and sit on the toilet. She realized I had just shit all over myself. Her anger turned to warm, loving compassion and laughter at my embarrassment.

Satin, however, was constantly naked in front of her boys. I'd tell her that it can't be good for them in the long run. She would just say they were her sons, and she didn't hide anything about her life from them and it didn't bother them. I could see that sometimes it embarrassed them, especially when men were around and they would ask her to put some clothes on and stop embarrassing them. She would make jokes about it and tease them a little, but she would put some clothes on for them.

So like I said, Satin could never be my woman, although I did care for her, and in my own way, I even loved her. In spite of what she thought, it was never the age difference. I loved older woman. No, it was that she was the best whore in the bedroom I'd known yet in this early age of my life. But she was not and never could be a lady in the living room.

Chapter
5

For almost a year, our gang robbed everything and everyone who had money or large quantities of drugs that we would sell for money. My eighteenth birthday was drawing near; I had my plan to enlist and not wait to be drafted and to leave my criminal lifestyle behind me as well as the gang.

I would go straight. I would marry my childhood sweetheart, Patty Ely, who loved me very much and who was tall, blond, and beautiful, the girl all the guys envied me having and at the time, I thought I was in love with her too. I had never let her know about my double life of crime activity. She knew I sold weed on the side, but she never knew about the robberies or Satin or that part of my life until I took her on a prehoneymoon to Disneyland and my two friends were arrested.

I remember her parents did not want her to see me. She was crying about it one day, about how her father had told her to stop seeing me or else she would have to move out of their home. I got pissed off. They had sent her older brother to come get her and to try to warn me off from her. I met him in the street outside my parents' home. I told him to back the fuck up. I told him I loved his sister, she was mine, and I was going to marry her, and I'd hate to have to kill him because he was her brother, but I would if he didn't stay the fuck out of our business and our relationship. He looked in my eyes and knew I meant every word I said. He ended up extending a hand of friendship to me.

Then I told Patty, "Let's go, we are going to your parents' house right now. We are going to deal with this now. I ain't having you crying over what your father's saying." So we went to her parents' house. I walked in with her, and I told her father straight up my feelings and my intentions to marry his daughter, that there was nothing in this world that he could do to stop it, and that if he didn't like it, Patty could pack her stuff right then and come live with me right now and they would never see her or any grandchildren we might have ever again. When they saw I meant it and that though their daughter didn't want to hurt them she would leave with me right then and there, they had a change of heart and embraced us and gave us their blessing but asked Patty not to move out until we got married when I finished basic training in the air force. We agreed, but I told him I was taking Patty with me to Disneyland for a few days because they had stressed her out so bad I felt she needed to get away for a few days. I told Patty not to pack anything, not even underwear. I was gonna buy her everything she needed brand-new. So we left for Disneyland, caught a plane, had limousine service to the hotel, and checked in. I took her shopping there at the Disney hotel; they had everything there in the shopping area, stores, shops, restaurants, and nightclubs. For the next few days and nights, it was like a honeymoon for us that would end up we would never get to ever have. We had so much fun.

All the time we had been there, everything we purchased we had charged to our room key. On our last night there, I had her call down to the desk to find out how much our bill was. I'll never forget how she looked that night, sitting on that big bed in just a pair of turquoise panties, her tanned skin, and long blond hair. As they told her what our bill was, she was shocked. She couldn't believe we owed so much money. She looked at me while still on the phone wide eyed. I laughed and told her it was okay. "Tell them thank you. We will be checking out in the morning, and we will be requesting a limousine to take us to the airport."

As she hung up the phone and sat there in shock at the large amount of money we owed, I told her to reach over into the drawer and get my money roll and to count out the amount we owed. This shocked her even more when she pulled out the roll of money and counted out the amount for the hotel bill. I knew she wanted to ask me where I had gotten so much money, so I teased her and told her she could ask me whatever she wanted. Before, I used to tell her, acting as Michael Corleone did from *The Godfather*, not to ever ask me about my business, and so I answered her question with a question. "Where do you think I got it?" She said, "I don't know, from the weed you sell?" She looked so beautiful there in that moment, that image of her stunning sheer physical beauty in those turquoise-blue panties so innocent. I laughed and told her the money I made from selling weed barely paid our daily cost of living back home and that I gave away more weed than I actually sold. Then I told her about the robberies, all the things I had been doing, except for the contract I had taken. I promised her that I was done with that whole life. I promised her a future with me in the air force. When we went back home, I had planned to go into the air force, and once I finished basic training, we would get married, and she would come live with me on the base wherever I was stationed.

We came back home, and the devil was waiting when my little sister Cindy told me that Tony and Dorian had been arrested and had called asking for me to help them get out of jail. I saw the fear in Patty's eyes when she heard Cindy tell me about my friends. I reassured her, "Don't worry, I'm gonna talk to Jimmy and Satin and make sure they are taking care of this."

I went to Jimmy and Satin to find out what went down and what they were doing about it. They told me what happened, that Dorian was strung out on heroin, talked Tony into robbing a drugstore with him, and everyone agreed, but they were busted. And now, since I had left, Jimmy had brought in a new guy named Ben, and they were working on some plan to do some robberies to get them out. I told them, "Well, let me see what you've got going on." They broke it all down for me, and Jimmy told me, "I'm not gonna lie, Rick, we fucked up and fucked off all the money you left us with, with trips to Vegas and Reno and partying. We haven't done a job since you left. The job Dorian and Tony were doing was our first one since then. Without your help, I've gotta try to use this new guy and my punk to come up with the money. This new guy has never done anything before." I told him, "I told you guys I was done, I left you guys set up good." Jimmy said, "Yeah, you did your part and you don't owe us anything, but it sure would be easier with your help." I told him I had to think about it, and in the meantime, I was gonna talk to this lawyer who owed me for taking the rap for his nephew when I was fifteen years old. He was an Italian mafia lawyer and a friend, and I would get back to them after I talked with him. At least I could find out for them what they were going to need.

I called Dominic Sposeto. He was associated with the Bonanno crime family, and one of his nephews had been a good friend of mine growing up. His name was Phil Harris. Phil's mother and Dominic's sister was a blind and a beautiful woman. She was like a second mother to all us kids who hung out at their house. Dominic was blind also, but he was powerful, and when I was fifteen, Phil had done a burglary and left his handprint on the outside of the window of the house he had burglarized. He stashed all the stolen property there in his bedroom, so when the police came, they found everything, and because of his record, he was done this time. Even his uncle couldn't save him, and there I was, listening to his uncle tell him with his mother crying that this time Phil was gonna go to YA (youth authority) because they caught him good.

I don't know why I did it, but I couldn't stand Isabel, Phil's mom, crying and brokenhearted. Phil was my friend, so I told Dominic, "What if I say I did it and I stashed all my stuff in Phil's bedroom, and the reason Phil's handprint was on the window was because he had been with me there the day before, casing the house, and he leaned against it? But he got scared and refused to do the job with me, and he left. I came back the next day and did the job by myself, and Phil knew nothing about the stuff I hid in his room."

Dominic asked me why I was willing to do this. I told him because I loved Isabel and Phil, Frank and Mary, Isabel's other kids, and I knew who Dominic was and the family's connection to the Bonanno family. Maybe one day I might need a favor. Dominic said that if I did this for his family, he would never forget it and that if I ever needed a favor someday as I said, all I had to do was to call him.

So I went to juvenile hall and did a few months at a young boy's juvenile ranch in exchange for saving his nephew from going to YA, which is a prison for juveniles. Phil would have done eighteen months with hardened tough guys where he never would have made it. The time I did in juvenile camp shaped me. I learned more about committing crimes while I was in there from all the other juvenile delinquents than I could have ever had learned otherwise. I learned how to be even tougher and harder and more of a leader because of my time served as a juvenile delinquent. Now here it was, three years later, and I was going to see Dominic. He agreed to see me on behalf of my friends, and by the time I saw him, he had all the police reports and information he needed to know about my two friends. Dominic advised me to walk away from it and to just go into the air force. I told him I would get back to him either way in a few days.

In the meantime, Tony and Dorian were calling my parents' house every chance they got, begging me to help them because their parents were refusing to help them out in any way. I put cash on their jail accounts so they would have money for the store in there. I went and I did something I hadn't done in a couple of years since the day I had been baptized at sixteen in Santa Maria: I talked to God.

My mistake was that I didn't talk with God; I talked at Him. I just told Him what I felt I had to do and ask Him to bless it and to let me do this one last thing and I would go straight. Go into the air force, marry Patty, and try to do right. I reminded God of all my Robin Hood acts of kindness, even though I had been a bad boy. But God could not interfere with whatever free choice even though it was wrong. I was choosing for myself, no matter how noble my intentions were. Now I had to go talk to Patty. I had given a promise of forever, and now I was thinking of risking that forever I had promised her. Only she had the right to tell me no, not to do anything and to stick to the promise I had made to her. I told her all I felt. I told her to tell me no; it was her right. I have to give this respect to Patty Ely. She loved me, and she had proven that to me when I told her everything and what I was feeling I had to do. I told her, "Patty, I promised you forever and a life with me. I'm about to risk it all. You and only you have the right to tell me right here and now, don't do it, and I won't, and we will just go on with our plans with the air force and our marriage and our life together. I'll tell them, 'I'm sorry, guys, I can't save you this time.' I had left them with money in their pockets and had told them that I was done and owed them nothing anymore. Whatever road they chose to go down was their free choice and not mine." She thought for a moment and then she told me, "I love you, I've always loved you, and I want to marry you and be with you forever, but I know you, Rick, and if I tell you not to do what you feel you have to do to try to help Tony and Dorian, your two best friends, you will regret it, and you will hold it against me if I stop you. I don't want to lose you, and I'm telling you right now that if you go to prison, I won't be able to stand that. It will destroy me, so I hope you're as good at what you say you've been doing all this time, as your promising me you are. Because I won't tell you not to do what I know you believe you have to do. I'm giving you your freedom to make your own choice. You decide what you think you have to do. Please don't get caught. I mean it, Rick. I couldn't take it if you went to prison."

I was so proud of her because I knew what she was risking not to stop me from doing what I felt compelled to do to try to save my friends. I had brought them into the crime lifestyle with me and had left them addicted to it. I grabbed her and kissed her and promised her I wouldn't get busted. I would be very careful. I'll just do this one and never commit another crime. I'll get away with it; I always do. We'll be married, and we will leave all this behind us, and we will live happily ever after. We made love, and for the first time, I was certain and sure I really did love her. I went to Jimmy and Satin and told them everything the lawyer told me and told them that if I help them, we do it my way, and the one condition was that no matter how much money we get, everyone has to agree ten thousand goes to Tony and Dorian's cause, even if that's all we get. Everyone agreed, and I told them, "First, flush that shit you guys are planning. It won't bring in enough money, and it's too risky. Second, wait for me, I'll be right back. I'm gonna case a couple of spots that I think we can rob the easiest for the most money." Everyone agreed.

After they left and I was alone with Satin, I asked her what happened to the bank we had set up before I left. Why didn't Philipeli, our bail bondsman, get them out? We had him on retainer of five grand. She got nervous and told me she had taken the retainer back from him. The gang had agreed because everyone had needed money, and she got the retainers back from both the lawyer and the bail bondsman. Something told me she was lying to me about everyone agreeing and how the split went down. Then she did something that should have set off alarms in me. She started getting jealous about Patty and how I was bailing on her to marry someone who didn't deserve a man like me. She started talking shit about Patty and about how I was weak and had become pussy whipped by an air-head blonde with big tits. I don't know why, but when she challenged my manhood and telling me I was pussy whipped, I bit. I grabbed her by her throat and told her, "Ain't no bitch or pussy ever gonna pussy whip me, bitch, and you of all people should know this, as hard as you tried to control me with your sex." I had never been violent with her before like this. Instead of scaring her, it seemed to turn her on. She reached down, grabbed my crotch, and said, "Prove it to me." This threw me off. What the fuck did she mean, prove it to her? I said, "What do you mean prove it to you, how am I supposed to prove it to you?" I was standing there with my hand around her throat. She had my dick and balls in the grip of her hand, and she challenged me with her eyes and with her next words out of her mouth. She began to massage my penis and balls through my slacks and said, "Fuck me, right now." I thought this broad's crazy, but there was that look in her eyes, the same look she had the first time we ever met and she told me, "I've heard about you." I asked her how my fucking her right now was gonna prove to her that I wasn't weak or pussy whipped. She had this evil smile as she continued massaging my crotch and said, "If you can't fuck me right now, then it's because she has you whipped and you're not the same Rick Riley you used to be."

I squeezed her throat and put my face inches from hers, and I told her, "Ain't no bitch ever gonna control me or change me, and if you ever speak Patty's name again, it had better be with respect. I'm gonna marry her. If I ever think you're even thinking of doing anything against her, I'm gonna kill you. You stay away from her, you evil sick bitch. Do you hear me?" She nodded yes, and I shoved her against the wall and ripped the top off her house gown down to her hips. Her big silicone tits popped out naked. I crushed my lips against hers, even biting her lips as I tore the rest of her gown off her. I threw her now-naked body down on her bed, as she lay there naked on her bed. I spread her legs apart as I began to unbuckle my pants, getting undressed. I looked down at her, and she was excited. This was what she wanted. I told her, "I'm gonna teach you once and for all, bitch, just who the fuck I am." She was pinching her swollen nipples, sucking on them and rubbing her pussy, sticking her own fingers inside herself, looking up at me like a bitch in heat. As I stood there beside her bed, now naked, hard, and erect, I was stroking my own penis just as she was fingering and rubbing herself, saying, "Show me, baby, fuck the shit out of me. Prove to me that young dumb blonde hasn't pussy whipped you." What followed was too X-rated to even describe. I was like an animal intent on complete and absolute sexual domination of this dangerous sexy evil bitch. I now felt fear and worry for the first time over what she could and might do behind my back to my poor innocent fiancée, Patty, once I was gone to basic training. I needed to tame this unbroken wild evil woman right here and right now in this bed or die trying.

At the same time, she was trying to use all her nasty sexual prowess and experience to convince me that she was the only woman who was woman enough to handle and satisfy the real me, the real tiger that I really was in this jungle world in which we were the predators of.

It was wild, and it was crazy. It seemed that the harder and rougher I was with her, the more excited and pleased she got. I dominated her with all my body, fire, passion, and rage. She worshipped my body as if I were her angel fallen from heaven just to satisfy and complete her. Time stood still. It was hours, not minutes, and it was multiple orgasms, not just for her, but for me too. In the end, she was like a little kitten, satisfied and full, purring beside me.

She had gotten up to go make me something to eat and to drink, and as I rolled over to get up and get dressed, I remember feeling guilt and shame thinking of my poor loyal Patty waiting for me at home. But I had to make sure she would be safe from this dangerous evil woman. I had made a pact with Satin for better or for worse that began with the spilling of blood and would end one day with the blood of my murdered mother. After I had showered and dressed and ate the food she had prepared and drank the drink she had poured, I told her once again before I left, "You treat Patty with respect and you leave her alone, do you understand me?" She assured me that she wasn't jealous and that I could have my little square girl wife as long as every now and then I remembered to satisfy her.

What she did not know was that I no longer trusted or believed in her. All I was doing was trying to keep the peace to get the job done, get the money to help my friends, go into the air force in a few weeks, and take Patty with me as soon as I finished basic training and hopefully never see Satin again.

Little did I know that this psychotic bitch did not intend to ever let me just ride away into the sunset with some other girl.

Chapter

6

There was a supermarket in my hometown where mostly the wealthier people of our community shopped. I happened to be casing it, not really sure I wanted to do a job in my own backyard, so to speak, but I needed to come up with a job that would have enough cash to help Tony and Dorian. I was standing in line at the cash register, and all the wealthy housewives were going through and having their asses kissed by the cashier, when this little blond hippie woman was in line behind me. I told her to go ahead in front of me, and then I watched the same cashier who, seconds before was kissing a wealthier customer's ass with courtesy and praise for shopping there, actually had scorn and contempt for the little blonde because she was paying with food stamps. I said to myself, "Yeah, this is the place we are going to rob." That shitty attitude for the poor sealed it for me.

I was Robin Hood after all, taking from the rich and giving to my friends, to the poor. I even gave to religious causes. I went and told Jimmy and Satin, "This is the place, let's case it and plan it out." Sometimes we would find out who the manager was of the particular target we were going to hit. If it was a big score, like a major supermarket chain, we would try to hit the manager at his home before he left to open, and one of us would stay with his family while I would go with him to the store and have him unlock the safe, then be picked up by someone as I left the store with all the money. We were good at this and never had to hurt any manager's family members. I would simply explain, "We only want the money. It's insured. It's not worth losing your life or your family's over it." They would go along with my instructions to the letter. But this job, I made a mistake. I knew the owner's name was Jim, and he was also the manager. I did not know that there was another manager named Jim there also. He had his nametag, "Jim, Manager," so we cased him and decided he lived too far to take him at his house. This would have to be a takedown as he arrived to unlock the store. He was the first one there at six a.m. every morning. We figured this was our guy.

We had never worked with this new guy Ben before; he was the husband of one of Satin's latest young girl followers. Satin was working on her to seduce and turn her out; her name was Stacy. I didn't like him. I was uneasy with his bravado and big wannabe gangster talk. But we were stuck with him for this plan, because when we did these types of robberies, we used three cars, one to take us there, one to leave in, and the third one to transfer into after our getaway. The way this supermarket was set up and where this manager, Jim, parked his car, we would have to have Ben on the pay phone. Ben was supposed to be pretending to be arguing with his girlfriend on the phone as the manager walked past him. Once he walked past Ben and crossed the street entering the store's parking lot, Ben would hang up and follow slowly behind him.

Jimmy would come from the manager's left, and I would come from his right. We would surround him as he neared the store door so he couldn't escape. Once we get him to unlock the door and turn off the alarm system, Ben would go to change to the second car and be ready to pick us up as we exited with the money.

I was all in; this was my last job. I had not come here and risked so much to fail. The spot I had hid in became vulnerable because the gas station began to open the business. I had to move. I was moving to a better spot where I could not be seen from the street or the manager, until it was too late. I had a big-ass .44 magnum pistol that I had borrowed from Jimmy. It became uncomfortable in my crotch, so I was pulling it out to move it, when I heard the manager whistling while he walked toward the store door with coffee and doughnuts in his hands. Jimmy and Ben had not even had time to get into their positions yet; the manager was ten minutes earlier than usual. Now I was standing to his right, about fifty feet away, when he noticed me. He was reaching for his keys to unlock the door with the bag of doughnuts in his mouth and the cup of coffee in his other hand. I had this long-ass .44 mag in my hand. Our eyes locked, and he realized that he was in trouble. He dropped his keys, and while he was fumbling with them, I started running at him as fast as I could, trying to get to him before he could unlock the door and get inside then lock the door behind him. As he made it into the store and was trying to close the big glass door, I was in the air with a flying dropkick to the door to stop him from shutting it. Then in midair, I realized the door was glass. I pulled off away from the kick with my feet and hit the metal bar with my kneecap. It stunned him and knocked him off balance. I managed to get my arm with the .44 magnum inside, pointing it at him. I was now in terrible pain from hitting my knee, and I told him to "back the fuck up or die right now." He backed up and let me in. I was hurting bad in my kneecap. I grabbed him and told him, "Turn off the alarm right now." He turned it off. I threw him down on the floor and grabbed a floor mat to cover his head. I ordered him not to move as I went back to the door, looking outside for Jimmy and Ben. I saw Jimmy walking around the parking lot, looking for me. I told him, "Get in here." He's surprised I was already in the store. I told him, "Dude showed up early, where's Ben?" and Jimmy's like, "I don't know." I told him, "You don't know? Isn't he supposed to be in position?" We looked across the street, and he's not there. I told Jimmy, "Fuck him, let's do this." We went to where the manger was lying; he's trembling on the floor under the store's floor mat. I was hurting bad. I pulled the mat off him, and I told Jimmy, "Give me your other gun. This one's too loud," so the manager can hear me. I jacked back the chamber of Jimmy's .38 automatic, pushing the safety on without the manager's knowledge. Then I placed it to his head, and I said, "Don't tell me something I'm not gonna want to hear," and the manger cried out, "Oh my god, sweet Jesus, I can't open the safe." This confused me. I knew he's telling the truth, and I asked him, "You're the manager, why can't you open the safe?" He yelled, "I'm the produce manager, not the store manager. That's why I unlock first, to set up the produce." "But your name is Jim." "Yeah, but not Jim that owns the store, check my license." I checked his license. He's telling the truth. Jimmy looked at me. "What do we do now?" We found out the real manager won't be coming in for two more hours after all the cashiers and delivery drivers show up. I told Jimmy, "I'm not doing another job. My leg is fucked up, and we're here, I'm all in. Go out there and find Ben. Tell him to change cars as planned and to sit tight, it's gonna be a long wait. We're gonna tie everyone who comes until we get the manager." Jimmy said, "You sure about this?" I told him, "Jimmy. I'm here and I ain't leaving without the money to help Tony and Dorian." Jimmy said, "I'm with you, Rick, I trust you. I'll go tell Ben." We were whispering all that out of the hearing range of the produce manager.

Jimmy went out to find Ben and told him our plan had changed and what he was supposed to do. I started talking to Jim, the produce manager. I told him straight up, "I want to kill you for making me fuck up my leg, but I'm not gonna. I understand you were just trying to save yourself, but you need to understand what I'm telling you now, what I am promising you now. Today you hold all our lives in your hands, because you are going to have to act normal and let each cashier or delivery driver in as they come and not tip them off that anything is up. I'm promising you that if I see it in your face or hear it in your voice that you are trying to warn them as they come, I will shoot you and them too, dead. You will die today, your coworkers too. Maybe even my friend and I will die today too. It all depends on you, Jim. It's only money. It's not yours, and it's insured. Don't die for it, listen to me. I don't want to hurt you or anyone else, but if I don't get that money, I'm killing you first. Do you understand me? Can you pull it off? Think of it this way, Jim. You can actually save people's lives today."

He agreed to do what I said. Not able to find Ben, Jimmy came back. I had Jimmy get in position and out of sight. I got a bottle of whiskey from one of the shelves for the pain in my knee, and I got in position. I took a swig, and as the first person arrived at the door, I nodded to Jimmy and to Jim and said, "Show time." Jim was great. He let each person in with a smile on his face and a hearty good morning in his voice. As each one came in, Jimmy and I would step out with our guns. I would tell them to "go over to where Jimmy was, cooperate and live, get stupid and die." I was sorry for the inconvenience, but later they would all have a great story to tell all their friends.

Jimmy tied them all up, one by one, till finally the right Jim came in the store, the right manager and owner of the supermarket. He opened both safes; he cooperated fully. I had all the money. I told

Jimmy to go find Ben. Whether he's there or not in five minutes, I was walking out of there with all the money.

As he left the store to go find Ben and our getaway ride, I apologized again to all the victims and thanked them for their cooperation. Just then, I heard tires screeching as Ben and Jimmy came sliding into the parking lot for me. As I exited, I noticed a group of schoolkids standing around outside, doing the same thing I used to do at their age: waiting for the store to open at eight a.m. to buy bubble gum and treats before school. I had a shag wig hairdo on with makeup and a big makeup scar running down my face. But one of my friend's little brother happened to be with that group of kids waiting before school outside the store. When the police would later question the kids, he would say without meaning to say that it was actually me, but that the guy he saw looked kinda like me. The other thing was that Ben had not changed from the first car to the second car we were supposed to leave in as instructed. He instead had come sliding in like gangbusters and flooring it out of there, tires screeching, drawing as much attention to us as he possibly could, making everyone at the neighboring businesses all look up at our car. And that car we were still in was Satin's car, registered to her with a distinguishable different-colored fender on it that stood out like a sore thumb.

We were to meet Satin at the lake parking lot a couple of miles down the road, where we would change clothes and take off our disguises, leaving all that stuff with Satin to get rid of, while we drove off toward San Francisco in the other car. The kid was panicking and telling us he didn't have the chance to change cars because a sheriff stopped him near the store for suspicious behavior and gave him a ticket in Satin's car for a light that was broken in the back. He didn't know what to do, so he just took off and drove on the freeway for a while, while we were inside the store until shift change for the cops. Then he came back and waited for us to come out. I looked at Jimmy as I was reassuring Ben he did good, it was all good, not to worry, but the look I gave Jimmy was one he knew. We were going to have to kill Ben. I wasn't having this panicked idiot throw me in prison. I had too much to lose. I had kept the bottle of whiskey I had been drinking earlier in the store, so we gave him a couple of swigs and calmed him down. I said, "Let's go to Frisco, spend the day there, let Satin check everything out for us with the car. She can let us know if the police question her and if it's safe to come back." In the meantime, we would just have a nice day at this secluded beach in San Francisco.

This seemed to calm Ben down, and once we pulled off the freeway into Frisco, we told Ben to go to this food wagon for us and get some coffee and doughnuts. Jimmy called Satin as soon as he was out of the car and away from us. I told Jimmy, "This guy has to go. You know what I'm risking for this job. Let's take him to the beach, find a quiet spot, get him drunk, and you distract him since he's your little buddy, and I'll get behind him and shoot him in the back of the head." Jimmy offered to kill him instead since it was his fault for raising his hand for Ben and therefore his responsibility. I told Jimmy, "No, it's all right. I'll do it. It's my life in danger, my future. It has to be done." Now that he had a few drinks in him and saw all the money we had gotten, he was talking like a want-to-go-for-it gangster, even apologizing for panicking earlier and getting a ticket. He said he would make up for it. It was his first job, but he didn't just leave us when he was driving on the freeway while we were robbing the store. He came back for us; that should prove his loyalty.

We kept reassuring him it was all good and there would be greater robberies and lots of money in the future. Jimmy and I knew we were talking to a dead man. We got down to the beach. No one was around. It was the end of winter, and this beach was empty. I had known it usually was at this time of year. I had fucked more than one high school–ditching girl there a few times before on this private secluded beach. As Jimmy was talking to Ben, I excused myself to take a leak; it was the signal. Jimmy was to keep him talking and distracted. I would come up behind him and shoot him in the back of the head. We would cover him with sand from the beach and leave his dead body there to be discovered later.

I made the excuse to go take a leak. I took a big swig from the whiskey to steel my nerves for what I had to do. I still had the .38 automatic from the store. I had made sure a round was chambered earlier in the car while Ben was getting coffee and doughnuts from the food truck and had the safety on. Jimmy had Ben turned, sitting and comfortably talking. It was too bad, but once he told us he actually left us there and went for a drive on a freeway while were inside the store robbing it, he had made his bed. When I saw how panicked he was about getting a ticket in Satin's car right next to the store we were in, I knew I couldn't trust my future in the air force and my promise I made to Patty not to get caught. I had to kill him.

I was pissed off at myself for having risked so much because of loyalty to my two friends, Dorian and Tony, and now I had to kill this kid. He was older than I was by a few years, but he was still just a kid trying to be a gangster, because this was what he thought his wife wanted him to do for her. My leg was still in intense pain, and walking in the beach sand was painful as I snuck up behind Ben. I pulled the safety off and eased my gun closer to the back of his head, not wanting to miss and possibly hit Jimmy, who was sitting directly across from him. Just as I was about to squeeze the trigger, Jimmy's eyes went large, and he signaled me, "No, no, don't do it." I was confused, but I pulled back the gun and hid it behind me before Ben turned to look behind him at me. Because of the sudden way Jimmy had reacted and signaled me not to shoot Ben, I kind of stumbled a little because of my knee, and this was the perfect cover for Jimmy's facial expressions and movements signaling me not to shoot, as Jimmy said, "Are you all right? I thought you were going to fall on Ben."

So we played it off, and I was looking at Jimmy like this better be good. Jimmy said aloud, "Ben, I forgot all about Stacy. She's probably worried about you. We'd better go call her and check in. You need to let her know you're all right."

We went back again to the same food truck. We sent Ben again for coffee and for him to call Satin and his wife, Stacy. As soon as he was gone, I was all over Jimmy. "What the fuck, Jimmy. Why did you call it off? Why did you stop me?" Jimmy told me, "I forgot about his wife. She knows everything, and if we come back without him, she would freak out and maybe go to the police."

I was like, "Fuck, who else knows about this?" He assured me, "Don't worry, Rick, we'll split the money. I'll take Ben and Stacy with me and my old lady to Oregon. I'll tell them it's a vacation to celebrate the robbery and to get away for a while until the heat dies down. Once I get them to the river, I'll kill them both and bury them there."

Like I said earlier, Jimmy was a stone-cold killer. I had no reason to doubt he wouldn't kill them both as he promised me he would, and he said, "Besides, I'll keep Ben's share of the money after I kill him, and I'll fuck Stacy before I kill her too. I've been wanting to fuck that fine-ass bitch for a while now."

I made him give me his word he will kill them. I can't have any loose ties. Oh, by the way, we had agreed that no matter what we get, ten grand went to Dorian and Tony, and the rest would be split three ways, Jimmy, Satin, and Me. Jimmy would pay Ben out of his share. We got thirty-two thousand dollars from that robbery, and what I didn't know until later was that Jimmy had robbed each of the ten hostages I had him tie up that day in the store. I never robbed workers. It was against my policy, and so I never imagined Jimmy was robbing these people as he was tying them up that day.

So I took ten grand. That left twenty-two to split three ways. I even told them that out of the remaining twenty-two grand, I was willing to take just five of it instead of my full share, leaving the rest for them. Satin was going to have to get a new car due to Ben's fuck-ups. Jimmy would get seven thousand, and Satin could have the rest of the ten thousand, but she had to buy a new car, new guns, and new supplies for the gang again, even though I wouldn't be with them anymore.

We had a problem. Because Satin had pulled our retainer from our usual bail bondsman, the only way he would bail Dorian and Tony was if somebody put up their house. I told them the problem why I couldn't bail them out even though the bail was only five thousand each, because I had no house to put up with my name on it, and their parents had told them to rot in hell. So I would do the next best thing. I would give the lawyer eight thousand for the both of them; he would represent them both throughout their case for me as a favor. With the remaining two thousand dollars, I gave each of Tony and Dorian's parents the five hundred, 10 percent cash deposit they would have to use to give to a bail bondsman if they had a change of heart and decided to stand by their children and bail them out. With the remaining thousand, I gave each, Tony and Dorian, five hundred dollars on their jail accounts for whatever they needed from the store to survive.

With my five grand, I took Patty to Disneyland one more time. But it wasn't as much fun as the first time. I was still stressing, and I still had Detective Frank Munn trying to gather enough evidence against me to finally be able to arrest me after two years of chasing me ever since my first armed robbery at sixteen years of age.

I had a week before I was to be sworn in and leave for Texas. I threw a great big good-bye party for all my friends with the rest of my money, gave money to my family members, left Patty with some money, and waited to hear through Satin that Jimmy had planted those marijuana seeds on the riverbank in Oregon as promised. That was the agreed-upon signal to let me know he killed Ben and Stacy, and I was all clear.

Satin didn't like the fact that everyone was leaving her behind and alone to deal with the cops over her car being used in an armed robbery. But she had hidden the car and had told the police she had loaned the car to Ben the day before the robbery, and she hadn't heard from him or seen the car since. If he used her car or was involved in a robbery, it had nothing to do with her, and since Jimmy was gonna take Ben and Stacy and kill them in Oregon, there would be no witnesses to tie her to the case.

This was small potatoes for Satin to deal with, and I told her so and that all this shit was her fault in the first place for pulling the money we had all kept with the bail bondsman and lawyer. I told her that I didn't want to hear no sniveling shit, because she too had raised her hand for Ben when I didn't want to use him in this job in the first place. She was jealous too because I was just gonna ride off into the air force and marry Patty and just leave Satin behind in my past.

I should have known better, and for a moment, I thought I should probably just shoot her in the head. Because I remembered that a few of the jobs we had done were done on her ex-boyfriends or business partners that she said had done her wrong. I should have killed that bitch that day, and I knew it. She was dangerous, but instead of killing her, I let her suck my dick for a while. She had wanted me to fuck her again before leaving. If I did this, she would feel better about it all. I told her I couldn't fuck her, not because I was pussy whipped, but because of my knee. I couldn't risk anything happening to it because I was still using a cane to get around and trying to get the swelling to go down before I reported to the induction center that Friday to be sworn in. There was going to be another physical, and I was going to have to pass it that day.

She was telling me that she could do all the work; all I had to do was lie on my back and she would ride my dick. I lied to her the best I could, saying that she knew better than to think that I could just lie there while she had her hot, sexy, beautiful body naked and riding me. She knew I wouldn't be able to control myself with her, and I'd try to get all crazy having sex with her. That's when she told me that just sucking my cock wouldn't damage my knee any more. I tried to tell her to just wait a few more days, let me heal up some more, and then I'd come to see her the day before I was supposed to leave. Then I'd be able to fuck her the way I wanted to before I left for boot camp and basic training. I would still come and have sex with her after.

After what I had seen with her and the change in her, the loss of trust I was feeling with her, I never had any intention of ever having sex with her ever again. I was just trying to keep the peace and keep her from freaking out over Ben and her car. This was the first time we had ever left any kind of evidence or witnesses against us, and I knew something was not right with her, the way she was acting. It was even her fault Ben did not make the change of cars in the first place, which I did not understand. She knew, because of an accident and a different-colored fender on her car, that it would be very recognizable. So why didn't she meet Ben on time to make the car switch and then tell him to just go ahead and use her car?

Hum? Anyway, so I ended up letting the bitch suck on my dick for a while then left her hopefully behind me forever in my past. Now she was calling me every five minutes, it seemed like, about Detective Munn snooping around and threatening her. I kept reassuring her she could handle it, and on the last day before I was to go into the air force, she wanted me to spend some time with her. She knew already that I couldn't because I had planned to spend the day with my mother and family, and it was my last night with Patty. Finally, I got upset with her over the phone, and I jumped in my car and went to her house. I told her good-bye. I thanked her for all she had done for me and with me. I even told her that I loved her but as a friend and not the way she wanted me to be in love with her. I was sorry it had to end like this, but it was over. I gave her a hug and a kiss and said good-bye to her boys.

I actually left her, feeling sorry for her, and I even told her I would see her again when I was done with basic training, but only as friends.

I want to show you just how evil this bitch was and how a young man of seventeen's fantasies of being with and having a thirty-one-year-old exotic stripper gangster bitch can cost him his soul. In my case, it cost me my career in the air force and my marriage and life with my childhood sweetheart, Patty, and it cost me my own mother's life eventually. I should have heeded the warning that "all that glitters is not gold." But with or without Satin, my feet had already been set up that road I myself had foolishly and willingly chosen.

Looking back hindsight is twenty-twenty, everything that I risked, everything that I threw away. I actually thought I was invincible; I could do anything. I had been doing anything and everything that I wanted. I was already a master criminal, and I was just eighteen years old. Looking back now, you can easily say, "Oh, hell no, I wouldn't have been so stupid." But back then, I was stupid. I threw away my whole life. I got them a lawyer, the best lawyer money could buy. I stopped them from actually serving prison terms, and in turn, I put myself in prison. In prison I became something that I never imagined was even possible for me to become, an animal. I remember that I had even made a promise to God. I prayed, "God, if you let me get away with this one, if you let me save them, then I promise that I'll do my best not to hurt anybody in the process. I'll just help my friends. I'll never pick up a gun again. I'll never do a crime again. Just let me do this, because I have to."

I had done it, I had got away with it, I had the money, and I had gotten them a lawyer and gave the bail money to their parents. I did all that, and then I turned myself in to the air force. I had passed the physical and taken the oath and was waiting to board the plane. I was talking with a guy who was reenlisting. He was telling me how much fun it was going to be. I remember the feeling that came over me. I was the happiest I had ever been. I had made it. I was leaving it all behind me. I was gonna get on that plane, and there was gonna be a whole new life for me. I could imagine it all before me, like a dream, but clear. All the things this guy who was reenlisting had described to me about how much fun I was going to have. I was leaving it all behind me, all the garbage, all the evil that I had done. I had made it. Now all that was left to do was board that plane and begin a new adventure, a good and honorable life. I would marry Patty. It had all been too much for me to actually hope for. All my childhood dreams were coming true. As a child, I had visited the Vandenberg air force base in Lompoc, California, with the Salvation Army as a part of a Christmas celebration for poor kids. I had been so impressed with the kindness of the airmen and all the facilities that day that I promised myself that one day, when I grew up, I would join the air force.

I whispered, "Thank you, God, thank you for letting me make it." My name was called over the speakers. The air patrol officer came and asked me, "Are you Rick Riley?" I answered yes while my heart started to sink. I knew right then that something was wrong. There was Detective Munn, who had been chasing me for two years, trying to catch me, standing there. "How did he know where to find me? What does he have on me? Is this just one last harassment before I got away from him forever?" Then he placed me under arrest. The air patrol officer at first told him that he could not just take me. I belonged to the air force now. For a brief moment, I felt relief; he couldn't touch me. The air patrol officer made a phone call to his superiors. When he got off the phone, he looked at me and told me that he was sorry but he had to let the detective take me for now, that someone from the air force would be in touch with me.

I was so angry, so bitter. "God, how could you do this to me? I was Robin Hood. Every time I did something, I gave to the poor, I helped people. I even did this last job to help my friends. I made you a promise. How could you do this to me? How could you let them get me in the end? God, how could you betray me?" But it wasn't God who had betrayed me; it was Satin. She was the one who had called Detective Munn and warned him that I was leaving into the air force that morning. She told Detective Munn exactly where to find me. I would find out later from Detective Munn that she had told him that if he arrested me, she would cooperate against me in the future. This psychotic bitch thought that if I was arrested, I wouldn't be able to leave her, join the air force, and marry Patty. That once I was arrested, the only person I would turn to for help would be her. She would bail me out and have me. What she did not count on, in her sick, twisted plan, was that because unbeknownst to me, Jimmy had been robbing all the store workers as he tied them up while we waited for the real manager to show up to open the safe, that instead of being charged with one count of armed robbery with bail of only five thousand dollars, I was charged with eleven counts of armed robbery with the bail of fifty-five thousand dollars, five thousand for each count. Because she had demanded the retainer back from our bail bondsman previously, and because I was in custody, her credit with the bail bondsman was shit. She had planned to bail me with five thousand from her share of the robbery. So now I was stuck in county jail, waiting for trial. We all believe the only evidence Munn was counting on was they would catch Ben on a warrant put out for him; they would flip Ben to get me. We were confident Ben, by this time, was pushing up daisies on the riverbanks of Oregon, because we believed that Jimmy had taken care of business as he promised. So now, I just had to wait for the case against me to be dismissed due to lack of evidence. This is when I found out from my lawyer, Dominic, who, as soon as he heard I was arrested, offered to represent me for free. He found out about everything that Satin had done against me. When I confronted Satin with this shit, she broke down and confessed everything to me. She loved me and couldn't just let me walk away. She fucked up, but she would stand by me and do everything she could to help me now, to take care of me financially. I knew the visiting room phones were bugged, so I said nothing to give away what I truly intended to do to her the minute I was free, which was to kill this bitch once and for all and be done with her.

Guess what folks. Stupid-ass Jimmy didn't kill Ben and Stacy as he promised. He intended to do it, but he decided to do few robberies in Oregon first with Ben and Stacy helping before he killed them. In the process, he decided that Ben and Stacy could be trusted now and didn't need to be killed. Ben had just panicked; it was his first robbery, and he could be forgiven because apparently he had proven himself worthy during the robberies Jimmy committed with him in Oregon.

In fact, Jimmy and Ben went on a tristate crime spree together while I sat in the county jail thinking that Ben was dead and they had no case against me. Satin had refused to cooperate with Detective Munn after all. The kids at the store who first identified me refused to cooperate also; they said they lied. So now all I had to do was to be patient, but lo and behold, one night in a bar room in Montana, Jimmy and Ben got arrested for a bar room brawl. While in custody, Ben confessed to the police that he was wanted in California, because his wife, Stacy, had left him and went back to California to be with Satin. Ben knew the quickest way to get back to California and to his wife was to waive extradition on the warrant. He turned and he confessed everything against not only me but also Jimmy, but only about the California robbery.

I'll never forget when Detective Munn came to see me in the county jail; he couldn't wait to rub it in and tell me that because of Ben, he finally had me.

Now I will show how sick, twisted, and evil I became. I, from my cell in county jail, orchestrated the complete destruction of two human lives and souls. Today, looking back on it, I regret it. But at the time, I made it happen. I used Satin to destroy Stacy by turning her out into a heroin addict and prostitute and then used Stacy to cause Ben to commit suicide. Then Stacy committed suicide too. I did the job Jimmy failed to do—from my jail cell. My actual plan was that after Ben committed suicide, I would have Satin clean Stacy back up, kick the heroin, and then be with me. Satin knew she had fucked up with her plans to stop me from going into the air force and marrying Patty, and me running straight back into Satin's arms to get me out of jail had backed fired on her.

Satin also knew me and that I could possibly get out and kill her for what she had done. Or worse to her was that once I was out and free, I would cut her completely out of my life. Satin loved me; she was obsessed with me. She would do anything to try to please me. Looking back, I actually think Satin deliberately overdosed Stacy herself, because I had told Satin that I wanted Stacy for myself, cleaned up and off the drugs. Because I wanted to eventually fuck Stacy, I had even had Satin send me pictures of Stacy completely naked in different poses I liked. I was going to keep Stacy around for my own pleasure once I was free. Satin was going to have to accept that and serve her up to me. Stacy was sexy with a big ass and tits, and somewhere inside of Stacy was a decent girl we had turned out and destroyed for our own plans. When I heard Stacy had overdosed after receiving Ben's last suicide letter so soon, I immediately suspected Satin had given her uncut heroin to OD her, making it look like suicide. Of all the murders that I have ever been involved in or committed, these two were the two that I regretted the most. Because they were just two young lovers whose love for each other I used to not only have them kill themselves, but also I destroyed their souls in the process, and because I could have stopped it. I had already taken a deal, but I finished it for the tornado of rage that had been born in me now.

I want to say that today I am ashamed of what I did and how I used and destroyed Stacy to get to Ben, and Stacy killing herself over guilt and shame over what she had become and what she had done and said to Ben that made him kill himself. I had not intended for Stacy to kill herself by overdosing on heroin. But she did kill herself, and I blame myself because I made Satin turn her out when I realized that Ben had ratted me out and was going to testify against us no matter how much he swore to us in county jail that when the time came, he wouldn't actually testify against us. But I knew Detective Munn would threaten him with a prison term if he didn't. And because of not wanting to go to prison and lose Stacy, when the time came, he would testify. The night Ben killed himself, I had Satin order Stacy to visit him and cut him loose, telling him that she had chosen to be a whore and work for Satin, that she didn't want to be with him anymore because he was a weak punk-ass bitch who had ratted and she could not be associated or known as the wife of a rat. Back then, we could receive naked pictures of our girlfriends or whoever in the mail. The night before she visited him, he received a letter from her in the mail, which Satin had instructed her to write. She told him about her new life as a prostitute and how much she loved having sex with so many different men, especially the black men who had bigger dicks than him and knew how to satisfy her better than he ever had. Satin enclosed with that letter pictures of Stacy having sex with two black guys at the same time, as well as pictures with other guys having sex with her. Satin had talked her into taking sex pictures as a means of making money in porno. So knowing Ben's state of mind was fragile and that he had neo-Nazi beliefs and receiving the letter with those pictures, I knew Ben was ready. All it would take was one more push. I ordered Satin to bring Stacy and to have her destroy him the rest of the way by cutting him loose to his face. I called that final move checkmate. The irony of this is that many years later, three guys would be involved with turning out my third wife and best friend and killing her when she tried to leave them to get her life right and return to her children. Two of them mysteriously ended up dying, the other one, the main culprit, is out there somewhere still running and hiding. But karma is a bitch, and he may as well kill himself too, because what had been carved in stone cannot be unwritten, not even by me. I'm sorry to say that even if I could uncarve that stone, I just can't; she deserves justice too. But that's another story; I am getting ahead of myself again.

Chapter 7

My lawyer Dominic managed to work out a plea bargain in exchange for the state to dismiss almost sixteen total felony counts that Detective Munn had managed to keep filing against me every time I attempted to post bail on the charges against me. I had spent almost nine months in custody, fighting the original robbery charges plus all the additional armed robbery charges Munn kept charging me with every time I posted bail. The first time I posted bail, Dominic had managed to get some of the original eleven counts against me dismissed, and my bail reduced to thirty thousand. Satin and a few friends had gotten enough money together so that when I contacted and spoke to Philipeli and gave him my word that if he allowed me to give him ten grand in cash, instead of three thousand, the 10 percent he would usually get, he could trust me without putting a house up as collateral. While he no longer liked or trusted Satin, Philipeli was an old gangster himself, and he told me he believed in me enough to put up the thirty thousand for me. As soon as I posted bail and was released, on the freeway heading home, Munn had the sheriff's department pull us over and detain me until he could get there. He then rearrested me on new charges for new armed robbery cases. That required an additional ten thousand bail, which Philipeli posted once I called him, and told him what Munn had done. Again, I posted bail, and this time, I never even made it off the jail property before Detective Munn showed up to rearrest me on new armed robbery charges. Again, Philipeli, on his own, posted the additional ten grand. I was now on fifty thousand dollars' worth of bail bonds and had four more additional armed robbery cases to fight. It became evident Munn was not going to let me get out of jail. Again, I was getting dressed into my street clothes and was walking out into the jail foyer free. Out stepped Detective Munn with two new armed robbery charges and rearrested me. Up until now, the robberies were robberies I had not personally committed but jobs Tony, Dorian, Jimmy, and his punk had all committed under my direction. This time though, he hit me with two cases I had actually committed, so I told Philipeli not to even bother posting the additional bail for fear that this detective was going to fool around and get lucky and hit me with new cases I had actually done. Robberies I had done before Satin taught me about the use of Hollywood makeup and disguises. Munn might actually find someone to ID me and subsequently convict me.

So I resolved myself to just sit in jail and let my lawyer Dominic file harassment charges against Detective Munn for the way Munn had it out for me. Munn overplayed his hand, because now Dominic had something with which to bargain with in my case. We would drop charges against Detective Munn in exchange for all other cases against me to be dismissed. I would be allowed to plea-bargain for a ninety-day observation to the Department of Corrections. Based upon the evaluation and recommendations, I could either receive county jail time with work furlough and credit for time served. Or if I got a prison recommendation, I would be sent to prison under the Youthful Offenders Act, which entitled me to the lowest range of eligibility for parole. Back then, California still had the indeterminate sentencing law, which meant almost every sentence to prison had a life top. Under the Youthful Offenders Act, I would be sentenced to six months to life, and my crime partner Jimmy would receive a single five-year to life sentence if I took the deal. Unfortunately for me, just before I committed my last robbery, California had passed the new "use a gun, go to prison" law; otherwise, armed robbery could be sentenced to only one year in the county jail. Tony and Dorian would receive the same deal I received for their robbery when Dominic represented them too; everyone knew we were all connected to each other.

Jimmy wanted to take the deal before Ben cracked completely and gave Jimmy up for all the robberies they had done together during their tristate crime spree. Tony and Dorian knew they could end up with a drug program after their ninety-day observation, because they had a drug store robbery, and they claimed they did it because they were drug addicts.

Everyone wanted me to agree to the plea bargain. Like I said before, I knew that no matter how much Ben swore he would not testify against us, he would do anything to get out and be with Stacy again. So I said fuck it, and I agreed to the deal.

So now I was going to prison for a ninety-day observation. My fate was up to chance and dependent upon my staying out of trouble while there and receiving a positive report and recommendation for probation. Even though California had just passed the "use a gun, go to prison" law, the exception to this sentencing law was that a judge could still exercise his discretion based upon a favorable ninety-day diagnostic report.

While I had been there in the county jail, we had heard all the stories from the convicts there about what to expect—violence, gangs, and even about people being raped in prison. I remember all my friends saying, "It's never going to happen to me. I'll get off, I'll kill, I'll be this, I'll be that, nobody's raping me, I ain't getting turned out, I'll be the baddest thing to ever walk a prison yard," etc. The old convicts would ask me, "What about you, super kid?" That's what they called me, super kid. I answered, "Well, I'm learning that nothing is impossible and that anything can happen. I only know one thing for sure, and that's if anyone manages to fuck me, I'm fucking them right back!" They all laughed and told me, "You'll make it, dude." Funny thing was that some of my friends got turned out and raped, but I never did.

I was just so full of anger and rage. Anyway, my second day at the prison in Vacaville, I got a visit from my mother and Patty. Earlier that morning, during orientation, the prison staff had told us that if staff was escorting a prisoner from ad seg, or the hole, these prisoners would be in chains, and we were to get out of the way of the escorts. Staff would holler "escort," and all inmates were to pull over against the wall out of their way.

On my way out of the visiting room, which is on the main-line side of this big hallway corridor gate, if you were coming from the green side, which was reception to the main line, for any reason, you had to check in at the desk at the gate and leave your identification card with them. It was called the green side because everyone in reception wore green-colored clothing; main line wore blue clothing.

As I was going through the gate, I noticed this guy sitting over by the canteen (inmate store). He was just sitting there. I don't know why, but something made me notice him. All the main liners were going to store there, but for some reason, he stood out to me.

One of the things the convicts used to warn us about prison was what they called "the hot ducat." It's a pass calling you to report somewhere on the main line, like to medical or the dentist. They warned us that if someone wanted to get you, they would sometimes pay off an inmate clerk to ducat you to the dentist or to medical, where someone would be waiting to kill you.

Well, what had happened, I found out later, was that the guy I had noticed sitting there on my way to visit had been raped by two members of the Aryan Brotherhood, and after they had finished raping him, they cut his throat and left him for dead. The kid didn't die, and the two gang members had been taken to the ad-seg and were in the hole fighting charges of sodomy and attempted murder.

When I came out from my visit, which was only an hour long when you were in reception, I noticed that same guy sitting in the same place, and at first I thought, "I hope that guy isn't sitting there waiting for me," because I could sense he was there for violence. So I kept my eyes on him as I headed back to the green side. While I was at the gate waiting to get my identification card back from the desk officer, I heard a loud "escort." I looked up to see two guards escorting this big-ass biker-looking dude in chains coming right to the gate where I was waiting to retrieve my prison ID card. I had to actually squeeze myself up against the gate desk to make room for the escort to pass through the narrow gate. I remember the guy being escorted was carrying himself like he was the baddest dude in prison; he had a lot of Nazi tattoos all over his body. Just at the exact moment that I squeezed up against the desk to let him through the gate, the kid I had seen there by the canteen was there. He pushed me aside and started stabbing the shit out of the guy who was being escorted in chains. The kid hit him in his throat and neck and chest. Blood was gushing out everywhere, splattering all over me, on my face too. The guards who were there just stepped out of the way and were yelling at dude to stop stabbing their escort. This kid did not stop until this big-ass biker-looking dude was dead.

Once I got back to my prison cell and was washing all this dead man's blood off my body and face, I was thinking to myself, "Man, this fucking shit is real. All the stories I'd heard about prison violence, it's real." I just watched this guy get butchered right in front of me and had his blood all over me. And I've only been here a full twenty-four hours. So I hit my knees and said a prayer, "God, I know I've been pissed off and I haven't talk to you in a while. I don't even know if you're listening to me anymore. Forgive me my sins, and God I'm only asking one favor, take care of my mother and don't let her die while I'm in prison, and, God, forgive me because I'm gonna do whatever I have to do, even if I have to kill everything that breathes. I'm not gonna be the one murdered or butchered here in prison. I'm gonna make it no matter what!"

This became my creed, I guess, that day, "Do unto others before they do it unto you, if you have to." Later I remembered thinking about what the crime partner of that guy who had been killed, who was back in the hole, was thinking once he heard what happened and about the kid who did it.

So this was my introduction into prison life and death. While I had been in the county jail, all the older convicts, they loved me; they really liked the way I handled myself. They even started calling me super kid because I would fight anybody, any race at any time. I fought some big dudes, mostly black, because that's what was mostly there in the Alameda County Jail, because of Oakland and the rest of the Bay Area. But no matter who, I would kick ass whenever I did fight.

One of the things these older cons used to tell me was that when I got to prison, "the first person who fucks with you, you fuck him up. You make an example of him. You have to beat him down, stab him, and kill him, whatever. But whatever you do, you make sure it's bloody, and it's got to be done in front of God and everybody. This way nobody else will want to mess with you." So this was the advice I went to prison with.

I found out that the kid those two Aryan Brotherhood gang members had butt-fucked and slit his throat, stabbed him up, and left for dead had worked out every day for two years, saved up all his money, and paid off a clerk to send his target one of those "hot ducats" we had been warned about. I had to respect and admire this kid for what he had done.

So here I was, in Vacaville on a ninety-day observation, trying to do good and to stay out of trouble, trying to work and program to try to get a good recommendation. My lawyer had pulled a lot of moves to get me this opportunity, not only for myself but for Tony and Dorian too. I was also trying to protect Tony and Dorian from predators. They were young and pretty; we all were, but my reputation had followed me from the county jail, and nobody fucked with me.

I was programming, and there was this old guy. He was an old white convict in his forties, in his early forties. One of the things too is, when you're in diagnostic and you're in ninety-day observation, they let you keep your personal shoes. I don't know why, maybe because back then they would put your number in your boots, and since you weren't really staying and they didn't want to put a number in your boots for only ninety days, they have you wear your own personal shoes. Well, my personal shoes happened to be a pair of brown-and-white Stacy Adams, a hundred-dollar pair of shoes, you know, superfly style. Anyway, I was always a smart dresser on the streets. So there was this old boy from Bakersfield, I believe, or Modesto, one of those two places, and he worked in the kitchen. He saw my shoes, and he called them fruiter boots, you know. I said, "What the fuck are fruiter boots?" He said, "You know, that's the kind of shoes that gay guys wear," and shit like that. So I said, "Hey, motherfucker, don't be calling me no fruiter boots man." So this dude would fuck with me, man, and every time I came through the chow line, he would be saying, "Hey, fruiter boots." When I went through the chow hall, I'd tell him, "I told you to stop calling me that, motherfucker." Anyway, he got busted for some shit he's got going on in the kitchen, some pruno or something, and they took him to the hole. And so one day, I was going out in the yard. Now the guys in the hole, where you first go to the yard, you can talk to all the guys who are going out into the yard from your cell window in the hole. You could holler out and talk. Well, one of my partners came in and told me, "Hey, man." I forgot this fool's name. "That dude's talkin' shit about you, man, and he's saying that you ratted him out. That's why he's in the hole." So I went out there to the sidewalk there as you go to the yard, and I was yelling at him, "Hey, mother-fucker, what the fuck are you saying?" He's yelling out, "You ratted me out, that's how they knew I had pruno going on." I said, "Motherfucker, you better shut your fucking mouth, you stupid motherfucker. You got yourself busted. I don't even know shit about you." And he's like, "Fruiter boots, I'm gonna fucking kill you when I get out of here!" I said, "All right it's on!" You only did ten days in the hole back then. I went back, and I was thinking, "I'm gonna deal with this dude. I'm gonna fuck him up when he comes out of there." But I got this ninety-day observation. A couple of the older guys were saying, "Hey, fuck that dude. He's a piece of shit. Nobody gives a fuck about what that dude says." And I was like, "Nah, I don't know." And they're like, "Come on, you gotta do good. You got your ninety-day observation." So I was like, "Fuck." I remembered those words in my head from those convicts in the county jail, you know, "Motherfucker disrespects you, you fuck him up." So anyway, I went through the chow hall one day, and he got out of the hole. And I was going through the chow hall, and he's eating at one of the dining tables. Back then, they gave you silverware. They actually gave you forks, spoons, and shit. I was going through the line, and he's talking shit, "Fucking fruiter boots, I'm gonna fucking kill you." So I was like, "Fuck this shit!" So I walked through the line with my tray, and as I walked around to go sit down—he's a couple aisles over—I just fucking dropped my tray. I walked up on him, and the boy stood up. Well, what he didn't know was I've got two forks. I've got them in my hands, and so when I walked up on him, I just started stabbing the fuck out of him with these forks. The forks were bending. They weren't worth a shit, but the first fork I hit him with did stick in his neck and shoulder. He was running around with this fork flapping around in his neck, and the other one was all bent up in my hand from trying to stab the shit out of him. Anyway, so the police, what they would do when there was a situation like that, there's only one officer in that chow hall. So in a fight, he would go out of the chow hall, close the door, lock it, and wait for backup to get there. So anyway, I was beating the shit out of this dude. We're going over tables, into walls. He's trying to get away from me, and he's screaming bloody murder trying to get away from me. Finally, I got him. I cornered him. Everybody's getting out of the way, clearing tables and shit, because we're going right over them, under them, and through them. So I finally got this motherfucker cornered, and he's on the ground, curled up in the fetal position, and I was just kicking the shit out of him. "Here, motherfucker, eat these fruiter boots." I was kicking him with my shoes. You know, I wanted him to just say, "Okay, okay, I'll never call you fruiter boots, you never ratted on me, and I lied." He said everything I wanted him to. By the time the police got there, this guy was just a bloody mess. I was tired; I whipped him so bad I was tired. The fork was still hanging out of his fucking neck. The police were coming, and I said, "Man, get that fucking fork out of your neck!" Anyway, so the police came running inside there. I went to the hole. Great, there goes my ninety-day recommendation. But this dude, the police did not like him. He was a convict. He was no ninety-day observation; he was a regular prison-sentenced convict there. Somehow, they saw it all, and it worked out in my favor. Maybe it was God. I don't know, but I was the victim defending myself against this dude. That's how they wrote it up. I got a break; I eventually went back to court after eighty-nine days of the ninety-day observation. I had done what those old convicts had told me to do. I remember after I had beaten this guy down, everybody treated me like I was a great dude, like I was the greatest guy on the yard. "You need some coffee, need some tobacco, anything you need?" Oh, homie, I had more homies now, I'd earned my respect; it was all good, so I went back to court, and I was still thinking, "Man, this is going to show up there." I stayed there eighty-nine days. Ninety days was the longest you were supposed to stay there. I went back to court, back to the county jail. And now I was an experienced man because I've been around convicts, seen murder, beaten the shit out of this guy, stabbed the shit out of him with forks. I was a little bit more seasoned now. I got back to county jail, and they sent me to the Oakland county jail, and everyone in there was in there for murder. Here I was, for just armed robbery, and I was there on a ninety-day observation return. That was a good experience too. Other than two white homosexuals and an old Portuguese convict, I was the only one in there that wasn't black. There was this guy there, a prison legend named Carnell Knowland, big old black dude. He was like a guerrilla, and these two white dudes, they were good-sized dudes, but they were his punks. He had knocked them out and fucked them. Now this is what Cornell Knowland was known for. You know, he would knock motherfuckers out, and he would pull their shit down and fuck them right there. I'm serious; I'd seen it with my own eyes. The craziest way I saw it is that there was this old Portuguese convict who's there, and I kinda kicked it with him, you know, because we're not black, and I just came back. I was hanging with him because he seemed to know the ropes and everyone seemed to respect him. This guy Carnell Knowland and he knew each other, and they had done time together, so I was thinking they're good friends. One day, Carnell Knowland and he were arguing, and Carnell knocked him out. Now this guy's ugly, a big, fat, ugly Portuguese. He knocked him out cold smooth, knocked him out, threw him on the fucking bed (the bunk), ripped his motherfucking jumpsuit down, and dug up into his ass. He's just fucking away, and I was like, "Oh my god." The whole tank was seeing this shit; there ain't no cops around. I was like, "Wow, this motherfucker, all the shit I heard about him is true, he's sick with it." We used to eat in the common area of the jail tank called the day room. We had metal trays and shit and a big old metal mop bucket with a big old metal wringer, and at the end of the meals, we'd go take the trays up. The cops would come and get them. We'd have to rinse them off and then mop the day room, and then they would take the mop ringer and everything out. Well, I used to work out with martial arts all the time, because I wanted to stay sharp and also I wanted everybody to see I was a bull too, ya know. That old joke about two bulls, the young bull and the old bull, and how they see this bull coming up, a big bad bull fucking all the cows, and he's just going from cow to cow, just fucking the shit out of each cow. All of a sudden, the young bull starts making all kinds of challenging noises. The older bull tells him, "Hey, knock it off, fool. That bull will fuck you up, what are you doing?" The young bull says, "I just want to make sure he knows I'm not a cow, that I'm a bull too." You know, so that's why I was over there working out all the time. I wanted this guy to know I was a bull too. Anyway, so one day I saw him; he's eyeing me. "Oh god." I knew it's just a matter of time. This motherfucker, he's eyeing me. I was young, I was pretty, and I said, "Shit! This guy's gonna try to fuck me, oh shit." So he would hang out in the day room, and he would lean back against the bars, with his two punks sitting there on the bench at his feet. He'd have one leg raised up on the table. So this one particular night, I volunteered to do the washing and the mopping, and everybody's all, "Hey, man, cool." I told everybody, "I'll go ahead and wash dishes, don't trip, I'll put them up there." I told the cops, "Hey, don't trip. I'll do the mopping and all that other shit." So ain't nobody tripping. Carnell Knowland's just standing there against the bars, just leaning back against the bars with his foot up on the table. I saw him watching TV and looking over at me, and I was saying, "Yuh uh huh, this guy's trying to make his move." So I started getting that mop and moving closer to him and mopping, getting closer to him with that big old mop. That mop wringer, that sucker had to weigh thirty pounds. It was a big, heavy sucker, man. One of them old 1940 mop wringers, man. Anyway, so as I was getting closer to him, he didn't notice. He tried to play cool, like he's not watching me, but I knew he's been watching me. So now he turned to the TV; his full attention's on the TV. I was going to go wring the mop out; now I was close enough. I lifted up that heavy-ass mop wringer, and I remembered what my daddy said the first time I had bully problems. Hit him between the eyes and hit him as hard as you can. Well, this big-ass mop wringer was going to do the trick. I hit him upside his head, man. I wasted this dude; he just went *kablam*. And so, I was just beating the shit out of him, because I didn't want him to get back up. All the blacks could have jumped right in, but they didn't. Nobody liked this guy; everybody was scared to death of this guy. So everybody just stayed out of it; even his punks stayed out of it. So I was just braining this guy with the big-ass mop wringer. Blood was everywhere, brains, you know. Finally, I couldn't even swing no more. Now once I was sure this guy's not going to get up, I stopped. Because I didn't want this guy getting up, knocking me out, and pulling my shit down and fucking me. I stopped from a mixture of finally seeing that's he's not moving no more and exhaustion. God, I was exhausted. So I went and I rang the bell for the cops to come and get the mop bucket and shit like that. When the cops came, Carnell Knowland was a bloody mess, unconscious, with his brains hanging out; they knew I did it. I said, "Come get him, come get him out of here." I put the mop wringer back inside the mop bucket. There's blood all inside the mop bucket. So they just looked at me, and they looked at him. They dragged his ass out. Emergency took him to the hospital; the cops didn't do shit to me. It was like, thank you. Another thing about Carnell Knowland was he would beat the shit out of cops too. He would knock a cop out in a minute, so they were happy. Everybody was happy. I was the hero now in the tank, because even the big bad BGFs, the Black Guerilla Family, even the gangsters, everybody was scared of Carnell Knowland. So I took out Carnell Knowland. Now I got this reputation that got me into another gang, another group; I still haven't gone to the La Nuestra Familia yet. I got involved with some revolutionaries, Tribal Thumb. Earl Satcher was the leader, and the reason I got involved was because he was there in the same tank with me. He had come in, and he had heard what I had done to Carnell Knowland. Now Earl Satcher even told me that Carnell Knowland was a bad motherfucker. I said, "Would you have fucked with him?" because Earl Satcher was into martial arts, and we used to spar all the time together. He said, "Yeah, I would have took a fucking piece to him. I'd took a baseball bat." Satcher was big. He was awesome, a big black handsome man, and muscular. He knew everything about Marxism, all the most current political jargon; he was up on it. And he was involved with this group, Tribal Thumb. So he recruited me into Tribal Thumb. He had all these revolutionary white college women visiting me too. And I was like, yeah, hot hairy revolutionary pussy. These women never shaved any of their body hair anywhere. One of my fetishes has always been hairy, unshaven woman. These were now my comrades, revolutionary sisters, willing to do things to ease or comfort us while we were in jail and prison. I was like, "Sign me up, I'm in." The FBI came to see me; they wanted me to infiltrate Tribal Thumb and to burn Earl. They actually wanted me to join and to rat. That ain't happening. You know what I mean? I don't give a fuck; it ain't happening. I ain't no rat, and even if I could, I didn't know enough about Tribal Thumb's criminal activities. I knew they were well-known and respected, accused of bank robberies, police shootings, and were affiliated and allies with the black prison gangs, not just the BGF in California but also even the Black Liberation Army on the East Coast. They were involved in prison breaks too. While I was into politics, I mostly wanted access to all those beautiful non-armpit-shaving sexy-ass sisters. Looking back, I think I got this fetish because of my babysitter Annie and her grandmother, who let me see her naked and committed fellatio on me. Neither one of them used to shave their body hair, especially the grandmother, who was very hairy all over. Even the crack of her ass was hairy. Growing up, I think I learned that once a girl started growing hair on her legs and armpits, it meant she was ready to start having sex. Maybe that's what started the fetish. Who knows?

Earl Satcher and I became cellmates, and not only was he able to convince me to join Tribal Thumb, but we also became very good friends. He told me his whole life story and his goals with Tribal Thumb and eventually the Wellspring Commune. He loved to learn martial arts, and every day we would work out together and spar against each other. While Earl was much more muscular and bigger than I was, I would not have ever wanted to meet him in a battle to death, because he was a killer too. He was very strong, but I was faster and more skilled. Most of our sparring matches would end in draws by points, but I would win more times than he would, and this really impressed him.

We had long talks about the future of Tribal Thumb and the Wellspring Commune over the few years we were comrades. I wasn't his only recruit, and he had told us that we should each try to infiltrate the already existing prison gangs and rise to positions of power and influence—power and influence in the respective prison gangs so that we could manipulate our influence with them to support future revolutionary goals of Tribal Thumb. Also, we were to look for potential recruits from prisoners that we could send out to the streets to Tribal Thumb.

I had a chance of getting released within a few months when Earl first recruited me. Had I been released, I would have been one of his top assets following his orders and being there to do or carry out the things he thought needed to be done. On the other hand, if I was sent to prison, I was to join one of the prison gangs. This was all voluntary and left up to us to decide at the time when that time came. He really wanted to have allies in the prison system because he understood that this was gonna be the best place to find real killers who would not be afraid to pull a trigger for Tribal Thumb should there ever be a need for gun play.

I have to say that the sisters and brothers I met or had a comrade relationship with were good people who bought into the dream of revolution and change in America, dedicated and loyal to the cause, intelligent, educated, and came mostly from middle-class families. There were some soldiers too, like Richard London, Roseann, Betty, Marie, and Wendy, who proved their loyalty, commitment, and dedication to the cause above and beyond.

Sad to say, I was just angry and full of rage, especially after what the FBI did to me. When I finally did join the prison gang and organized criminal organization La Nuestra Familia, it was not for Tribal Thumb, but for my own reasons and new cause.

After Earl Satcher was murdered on the streets over a million-dollar food co-op, the sisters pretty much took over the direction of Tribal Thumb and the Wellspring Commune. Sadly the concepts and training I would give them and my suggestions in changing the rules of membership would cost my favorite sister comrade Roseann her life as she would be the first to be killed for wanting to leave the organization. That's another story, but Roseann was awesome.

The New York Times

U.S.

WORLD   U.S.   N.Y./REGION   BUSINESS   TECHNOLOGY   SCIENCE   HEALTH   SPORTS   OPINION

POLITICS   EDUCATION   TEXAS

2 IN RADICAL GROUP JAILED IN SHOOTING

Special to the New York Times
Published: March 16, 1982

SAN FRANCISCO, March 14— Two fugitive members of a radical
West Coast group who were seized in the investigation into the
Brink's robbery and killings in the New York City suburbs have
pleaded guilty in the death of one of the group's members.

The authorities say they believe the jailing of the two will end the
activities of the Wellsprings Commune, whose members were
involved in a variety of criminal acts including murder, bank robbery
and jail breaking.

The fugitives, Betty Ann Abramson, 29 years old, and Wendy Sue
Heaton, 26, pleaded guilty to voluntary manslaughter charges in the
shooting death of 28-year-old Roseann Gonstin and were sentenced
to three years in prison. Miss Gonstin was killed in 1980 near the
commune's isolated retreat in northern California's rural Humboldt County.

The fugitives were originally charged with first degree murder with special circumstances:
lying in wait. Conviction on that charge would have brought them the death penalty or life
without possibility of parole. Witnesses Lied or Balked

According to Barry Brown, a county prosecutor, an agreement for the guilty pleas was
arranged after it was learned that witnesses had lied or refused to give statements to the
authorities and obliterated physical evidence.

Miss Heaton's sentencing was delayed when the victim's father, Edward Cohen of Miami,
challenged the short prison terms and invoked a new California law, the Victim's Bill of
Rights, which gives family members an opportunity to speak to the court on behalf of crime
victims before sentencing.

The group to which the three women belonged was founded in 1973 under the name Tribal
Thumb by Earl Lamar Satcher, a convict and former Black Panther Party member. Tribal
Thumb and the name Wellsprings Commune were used interchangeably. Rivalry With
Another Group

The group developed a rivalry with another group, the United Prisoners Union, led by
Wilbur Jackson. Mr. Jackson was shot by a Tribal Thumb member in June 1975. In April
1977, Mr. Satcher was shot to death here.

Property that Mr. Satcher had purchased in Humboldt County became a retreat for the
group. The authorities believe it was also a safehouse for fugitives and a weapons training
ground. Sara Jane Moore, who attempted to shoot President Ford in 1975, is believed to
have used the place for target practice.

After Miss Gonstin was killed in a scuffle near the property, Miss Abramson and Miss
Heaton fled. In June 1980, the police raided a San Francisco health food restaurant that
served as the group's headquarters, searching for the two women.

They found weapons and materials for making false identification papers as well as an escape tunnel. Four people were taken into custody, including the man Miss Heaton lived with, Rickey Marcus Blanchard. Two were sent to prison six months later for a botched bank robbery. Another was returned to prison on her conviction as an accessory in the killing of a United States Customs agent in Washington. Hunt for Members Intensifies

After the Brink's holdup, in which two police officers and a guard were killed in Rockland County, N.@Y., in October 1981, the hunt for the commune members intensified. Miss Abramson was arrested at a mail drop in Manhattan in December 1981 where she was picking up false identification papers ordered from North Carolina. She still faces Federal charges of mail fraud.

Her photograph was found in December 1981 at an apartment in East Orange, N.J., rented by a fugitive in the Brink's robbery, Marilyn Jean Buck, who escaped while serving a sentence for a California weapons conviction.

Further investigation led to the arrest of Miss Heaton in New Orleans in June 1982 along with Mr. Blanchard, who was wanted for a California prison escape. Witnesses who saw pictures of Miss Buck said she had been seen with them.

The next month, the police raided a house in San Jose, Calif., and found blueprints of the intrusion-detection alarm system to the armory at Sixth Army Headquarters at the Presidio in San Francisco, entry stickers to several military posts, and various weapons. Her Former Husband Seized

Those arrested were Benjamin Sargis, Miss Heaton's former husband and longtime Tribal Thumb leader, and three women. Mr. Sargis, who was arrested in 1975 in the search for Patricia Hearst and was an unindicted co-conspirator in Mr. Jackson's slaying, was returned to prison as a parole violator.

Agents searched the San Jose house for evidence that Miss Buck might have been hiding there. Spokesmen would not comment on what had been found to connect Miss Buck with the house.

Describing the commune, which drew members from a variety of groups including the Black Guerilla Family, the Black Panthers and the Charles Manson Family, Barry Brown says: "There were a few who were very politically aware and were true revolutionaries. But the organization was inundated with people whose motives were not politically directed."

FACEBOOK   TWITTER   GOOGLE+   EMAIL   SHARE

RICK RILEY

Tribal Thumb

SUMMARY:

Tribal Thumb was a small collective of people who were connected to an eatery called Wellsprings Reunion, located in the South of Market area of San Francisco. The leader of the group, Earl Satcher, was a saxophone-playing ex-convict whom many people saw as the "cult" leader of the Wellsprings group. Tribal Thumb and a few allies in Veritable Vegetables were accused of intimidating members and trying to take over the People's Food System. The dispute escalated into threats of violence and led to several secretly held meetings of the People's Food System to discuss what actions should be taken. An emergency meeting was held in 1977. Called to discuss the expulsion of members deemed disruptive to the organization, the meeting degenerated into a hostile confrontation between opposing sides. Tribal Thumb members and their allies (including two Dobermans), were in the parking lot, reportedly intimidating and threatening Food System representatives against voting for the expulsion of disruptive members. During the break, gunfire broke out in the parking lot, leaving an ex-San Quentin member critically wounded. Tribal Thumb leader Earl Satcher was shot dead.

Tribal Thumb, also known as Wells Spring Communion (WSC) suspected is an inactive group formed c. 1975.

110

Chapter

8

Now my lawyer told me, "Hey, man, you got probation in the bag. They're gonna send you to county jail. The recommendations are good. They said that your partners told them that you did the robberies for them, so they're saying it was a misguided sense of loyalty." Because I had the sense to have my father get my record sealed, he knew a judge, and the judge sealed my record in order for me to be able to get into the air force. So as far as they were concerned, this was the only crime I had on my record. It was looking good. So when the FBI came to me and propositioned me, I told 'em, "You know what, suck my fucking dick. There's nothing you could do for me. I've already got my deal. I got probation coming, and I'm gonna go to work furlough." They said, "Yeah, we will see." I didn't have enough sense to keep my mouth shut. I never should have said that to them, never should have told them that. A week later, I was called down to court, a different courtroom, to be sentenced by a judge who was an ex-federal agent. There goes my probation, there goes all that. I was going to prison. But they sent me this time on something that allowed the judge to call me back. Within 120 days, the judge could bring me back if he changed his mind. Now I didn't ask for it, and I didn't know about it. I found out about it in the courtroom. I fought them, by the way. I was in chains, and I was being held down by cops. I was being sentenced. My family's there in the courtroom, because I was able to get a phone call out real quick to tell them. "Hey, they're sentencing me. Get a hold of my lawyer. I don't know what's going on." I was stalling as long as I could. My girlfriend at the time, you know, my childhood sweetheart, Patty Ely, she's sitting there and watching this. My whole family's watching this, you know, and I was getting sentenced. I bring this up because it's funny.

That night I got a call home. They're all partying; they're thinking I was going to the work furlough, and I was like, "Hey, you were in the courtroom. Didn't you see me? Did that look like I was getting something I wanted?" She finally understood how serious it was, and everything stopped. Everything got quiet in the background. I could hear everybody in the background now. She never was very bright. I said, "I'm going to prison." So I was going to prison. That's how I went to prison, because I wouldn't rat out on Earl or Tribal Thumb. Now when I went back to prison, I was angry. I was pissed off at the world, man. You know, what I mean? I've just been double-crossed, and so I told Earl this was what happened and stuff. I went to prison. Now when I was at prison this time, my first day in receiving and release, R&R, I hadn't even made it to the line yet, my homies were there waiting for me. I had a couple of friends that were regular convicts that were there when I left and were still there when I returned. One of them was my crimey, Jimmy, and it's Jimmy who told me, "Let's go, we're going to kill a child molester." I said, "What?" "We're going to kill a child molester out in the yard, everybody, we're all going to kill him." So I said, "Okay, well, let's go." So I went with him. We went out in the yard. I said, "Well, where's the child molester?" because everybody's grouping up in different little groups around the weight piles like its workout day. We used to have weights, big old dumbbells, and he pointed out this big-ass dude walking the track. They got this guy walking with him, setting him up. He was way at the other end of the track, but as far as he was, I could see this guy was like six foot six, 350 pounds. This was a big old fat boy. I said, "Wow, so what's the plan?" He said, "Everyone will be over here with the weights. We're all gonna get the weights, and when they come around the track—because the track you gotta walk right by the weight pile—everyone's gonna charge him, you know, everyone's gonna stone him with the weights, kill him with the weights." Everybody—blacks, whites, Mexicans, everybody. Here we were, we're going to kill this child molester my first day back. On my ninety-day observation, this guy got murdered. My first day back, we're going to kill this child molester. Can you see where I'm going with this, folks?

I mean, you want to know why or how someone like me could become what I am, well, what I was. I'm not the same guy I was; I am different now. We'll get to that part of the story later. So we went out. We started working out. Everybody's getting their weights, and we're taking some big-ass dumbbells, man. They had hundred-pound dumbbells, and they had fifty-pound dumbbells. They had twenty-five-pound dumbbells, and they had seventy-five-pound dumbbells. Everybody's getting whatever it was they can work with. This guy came around, and the other guy broke off. The guy that was setting him up, walking the track with him, walked him right over to the weight pile. He broke off, and everybody started throwing these weights at him. He's trying to block off the weights, and he's crying. "Hey, what's going on?" Everybody's calling him, "Hey, Chester, you fucking child molester." He's yelling, "I'm not a child molester, you know, I was set up!" That was the last thing he got to say because by then, the weights had found their target. So now people were moving in, and they were actually picking up the weights and hitting the dude with these weights. You know, so we're hitting this dude with these weights. I was there hitting him with the weights. I was throwing weights; I was hitting with weights. And the gun tower was watching all this. Now this was right underneath the gun tower. The gun tower's there, cops were there, they knew this dude was getting killed today, and that's the way it was. They would say, if it's a child molester, they would throw him out there and say go ahead and kill him. I have to say something, man. And I didn't want to. But I had to. That dude, after everybody backed off (everybody's getting away), they thought he's dead, but he's not dead. He's still moaning; he's still groaning. He's fucked up. His brains were spilling out of his head. His face was destroyed, and if by some miracle this guy had lived, he would have been a vegetable, spending the rest of his life in prison. I don't know why, you know. Everybody thought it was for a different reason, I know, but I felt like someone had to stop his misery, you know, how you wound an animal. When I was younger and learning to hunt, they would always say, "Don't just wound an animal, go in there and finish it." Or you step on something and you want to put it out of its misery, kill it as quick as you can. You know? So while everybody was pulling off him, kinda in a circle around him still, Some Hero picked up a seventy-five-pound dumbbell and straddled him, and Some Hero caved in his skull a couple of times just to put him out of his misery. Just until he stopped moaning and twitching. He may have been dead already, twitching, but the moaning was real. Now the whole yard saw this. You know what I mean? Now Some Hero did this as an act of mercy, you know. I felt sorry for the dude. But now, oh my god, I was this vicious killer. Everybody's like, "Oh man, that dude is a fucking killer." I got big respect on the yard now. Crazy, huh? You know, Some Hero was doing an act of mercy, and everybody thought I was the coldest killer walking the yard.

This is when I first really started to get involved with the prison gang La Nuestra Familia. You know, like I said, I'm Mexican Irish with a little Indian in there. So the Mexicans, all of a sudden they wanted to claim me. The white boys wanted to claim me; everybody wanted to claim me, you know. The blacks were my friends because I came out of Oakland; the Asians loved me because I loved them. So these guys, they started getting at me. "Hey, why don't you run with us, man?" They started telling me about the La Nuestra Familia. I'd tell them, "Nah, it's not me, I'm doing my own thing." "All right, cool, you know, cool, man." Nobody was going to fuck with me after they saw what I did out on that yard. I was on the reception side now. In reception, we wore green—green pants, green shirts, everything was green. On the main-line side, you wore blue. The reception side was full. What they would do sometimes when reception got full was they would take some of us from the reception side but put us on the overflow on the main line. Well, guess who got put over there on the overflow on the main line. Me. So I was over on the main line now. The main line was jumping. Here you got war; it's just like the reception side. There you got war too, but it's not as active. This main line's active. You got the Aryan Brotherhood, you got the Mexican Mafia, you got the Black Guerrilla Family, you got the Symbionese Liberation Army, which was just forming, and I fucked with them for a little while too. Because of my involvement with Tribal Thumb as radical revolutionaries, we were going to overthrow the world. Anyway, I had to do something with that anger. I was pissed off. So now, they put me over there, and you got the La Nuestra Familia there too. This was where I had my first run-in with the Aryan Brotherhood, in the gym, over a weight machine they had there; actually, it was over a homosexual. If you want to be honest, that's the truth—a homosexual named Silvia. I worked out. I was a loner, and I ran by myself. Although I had my homies, I always kept my homies at arm's distance. I always loved to work out, and I wanted to work out on the bench press, on the machine. And the time slot that I could work out on, this homosexual actually had that slot, and so I just said, "Hey, can I work out with you? Do you mind if I get in here and get my set?" Silvia said, "Oh yeah, sure, come on," surprised that anybody would want to work out with a homosexual. Nobody worked out with him, I guess; it was taboo. I was still new on the main line, so I guess because I was working out with a homosexual, it was seen as something weak or something. I don't know, but these two guys from the Aryan Brotherhood, they said they were Aryan Brotherhood, anyway, I think they wanted to fuck the punk, Silvia, because they were using these little pressure tactics. What it came down to was over that bench and the time slot, they wanted it. Well, we'd already had our routine down. So I said, "You ain't getting this time slot, now get the fuck out of here, kick rocks." They said, "You don't know who you're fucking with, you know, we're Brand, we're AB." I said, "I don't give the fuck about no little club, get the fuck out of here, kick rocks." So words were exchanged. Now it's like, "Ah, fuck," so the homosexual told me, "Hey, I got a knife, if you want a knife." The homosexual had got involved in the argument too. Now it's me and this homosexual, Silvia, against these two guys who said they're AB. And there's gonna be some drama, right? They underestimated me, I guess. Finally word got to them about who I was and what I'd done because they kinda backed off a little bit, but then we bumped heads again, so I said, "Fuck this shit. We're going to have to get to it because they're going to get to it." And Silvia told me, "I got two knives, I'll go with you." I was like, "Huh?" He's like, "I'll do it with you." I said, "Nah, I'll handle this man, but thanks for offering to back me up. Can I have the other knife too?" So I went out there, and I got into it with these guys. I was not even waiting. I just took off on them, hit them both, ran, and stashed the pieces in the bathroom in the gym over there. Silvia took care of 'em. I got out; the police were already responding and shit. Now these guys were lying there with popped lungs, screaming at the top of their lungs, "Help, save me!" They weren't very good soldiers. So that's how I got into conflict with those dudes. They held their mud; they did not rat. In those days, nobody told. You know, even if you had blood all over you and you're sitting right next to the guy that got butchered, your answer was, "I was watching TV, I didn't notice anything." So I got away with that. The FBI came to see me. I was there like thirty days now, and the FBI came to see me. They called me in; there's the captain of the Department of Corrections, Secret Service Unit, whatever the hell it was called back then. It's ISU now; they've got so many different names. But it's their Secret Service Unit, their police squad. He's a captain; he's there, and there's an FBI agent there. It's the same FBI agent that tried to get me to turn on Satcher and Tribal Thumb. They wanted me to infiltrate them and turn on them. And the agent said, "How do you like prison now?" He told me straight up that I should have kept my mouth shut. I should not have told them about the fact that I already had a deal. So they did this; they put me here, you know?" I was a good guy. I was a good guy, yes. I could still be salvaged. I could still work for the FBI, you know, help them, and they would help me and clear my record and all that other good stuff. What they wanted me to do was they wanted to send me to a camp, and they were gonna let me escape, you know, and have me go back and join Tribal Thumb on the streets. Infiltrate and basically work for them—that was what they offered me. They said, "We sent you here on a hundred-and-twenty-day thing. We can take you back to court at any time, get the judge to change the sentence on you. You can go to the work furlough and escape, or we can send you to camp and you can escape, just work with us."

They wanted to infiltrate Tribal Thumb. Tribal Thumb shot down a police helicopter over Oakland and was involved in a lot of bank robberies, also with the Weathermen, which was another thing, this revolutionary group doing bank robberies and stuff, had ties to the Black Liberation Army, which was some bad, bad dudes. You know, they ran the whole East Coast; they did then. Anyway, so this is why they sent me to prison. Because they figured by now I'd been scared sufficiently enough to where I'd just say, "Okay, yes please, get me out of here." You know, part of me wanted that, I'm not gonna lie. Part of me was like, "Man, freedom." You know? But then, I was like, "Oh, hell no, I can't do that." So I told them, "No!" Now I was pissed off though. I told them, "You played with my life like that? You brought me here, you did this to me? And you expect me now to work with you!"

This FBI and this captain of Department of Corrections, they told me to work with them and I'll be free. I got to escape though. They wanted me to escape, because they wanted me to hook it up where the Tribal Thumb comes to get me and I go with them and I get through their underground and all that. That's the information they had wanted. So like I said, I was angry, and I told them, "You know, you're supposed to be the government. I was supposed to be going in the air force to go serve my country, a country I still believe in." Even though I was a criminal at heart, before, I still believed in America, in the government. And they would do this to me, that they would set me up like this, smash me, put me in prison, and put me in this position because they wanted to use me. So I told them, "Go to hell!" I'll never forget that FBI and that captain. They said, "Well, you're not going to camp." Because I was eligible to go to camp back then. My first term, I was eligible to go to camp, and they were telling me I wasn't gonna get my deal. Again they were telling me I wasn't going to camp. I was like, "All right, whatever, I'm outa here." Sure enough, I got Tracy. "Gladiator school," ain't that great? Ain't that fun?

Like I said, I was only there for thirty days. I still had time to go through all my processing. Even though I was on the main line, I was still RGC. So I still had to be processed, be finished processing. Now, that captain, the security guy, the departmental security guy, he told me, "Look, that incident." They knew about that incident with the two guys, the so-called ABs, Aryan Brotherhood guys, clowns. No disrespect, but those guys were clowns. I don't believe they were real Aryan Brotherhood; the real Aryan Brotherhood is dangerous. It has real killers, not clowns. Anyway, whether they were or not, the captain told me they knew about it. They knew that I did it, even though there were no charges, no 115s, no nothing. But for my own safety, they were going to transfer me to the other RGC center down in Chino to finish my reception, which meant I was going to have to start it all over. So in other words, "We're going to fuck you." You know, aside from telling them to go to hell, I told them to "suck my dick." I said a lot of other things to them, that I didn't give a fuck, to take it and shove it up their ass, and all that other stuff. So they took it quite personally. So anyway, here I go, for "my own safety." I was sent to Chino reception center to finish out my reception, placed in Palm Hall, which at that time was the max, supermax, for all active gang members. I was tossed inside of there, like they set me up to be killed or whatever, I don't know. Well, it just so happened that because I got there so late that night, when they were taking me in, they asked me, "Where you from?" And I said, "What do you mean? I'm from Santa Maria." They went, "You're a Southerner." "Alameda County, that's where I lived, it's in the Bay Area," I answered. "Oh, okay." So then they moved me over the northern side. I guess they had them segregated, separated, or whatever. So they put me up on a tier with active La Nuestra Familia. Even these guys had already heard about me. When I came out in the morning, instead of getting stabbed up by these guys like, I guess, the police had hoped, they're giving me tobacco and coffee, and they were real nice to me, man, real cool, kickin' it, talking to me and everything.

One guy in particular, Crackers, yeah, Crackers, he made the La Nuestra Familia as far as I'm concerned—on the streets, Cracker Vindiola, the Vindiola Brothers, and the Venegas family in Fresno and Bakersfield; the Gabrials and Castros in Salinas; Me, the Rock, and Juanito in the Bay Area and San Jose. Even D. C., whom they say is now the undisputed and only general of La Nuestra Familia, was part of the original push for control of the streets in the seventies and eighties. They were part of the reason we are powerful still today. These are some main guys who made up the foundation upon which the La Nuestra Familia was formed. They were awesome, great soldiers. Loyal, they all were fucked over. Anyway, that's another story.

But so, I was kickin' it with Crackers and everybody there, and they're treating me real good. I was only there for a couple of days, because I came in late at night and it was full, and so they just stuck me in there. I was there not even three days. I think, four days. They took me out; they said, "Okay, there's an opening for you in the main line. We're going to put out on the main line." "Okay, so bye, everybody." I was gone. "Hey, thanks for the coffee and tobacco and the cosmetics and shit. Thanks, guys," and I was gone. So I went to the main line. I was on the main line, and I didn't know anybody there, at all. There's nobody from Alameda County there. And then finally somebody drove up from Alameda County, and it's a black guy. He's a homosexual named Earl. But he was an all right guy, ya know. I still didn't know anybody, so I was keeping to myself, walking the yard. Everybody down there was mostly from Southern California. I was walking the yard one day. I came out, and I saw Crackers, Adrian Vindiola, the NF active lieutenant. He's on the yard, and when I saw him, I said, "Hey, what's up homes?" All right, somebody I knew. He said, "Hey, how ya doing?" I started walking the yard with him. These guys, who turn out to be Mexican Mafia, they're kinda grouping; they're mad-dogging Crackers, and they were glaring at each other. Words were exchanged, "Como vega puto" (eat dick, punk), EME–La Nuestra Familia typical crap. But I was with Crackers, and whatever goes down, I was with him, because that's the way it was. We're walking the track, and I told him, "Hey, fuck those dudes, man, I got your back, man." He explained to me, "Some serious shit could jump off here, man. If you don't want to kick it with me, I'll understand. Step back, they're going to try to stab me and shit like that, and I'm ready for it." I said, "Well then, they're going to have to stab me too." So we're walking the yard that day. The next day, I came out, and Crackers was gone. I guess they put him on a bus; they shipped him. I was like, "Wow, I'm by myself." I was walking the yard. Sure enough, I was by myself, and here comes five dudes, Southern dudes. I found out later that a couple of them were actually EME, Mexican Mafia. Right away they jacked me up; they're like, "Hey, what was it you were doing kicking it with that dude?" But they didn't call him dude; they called him punk and *puto*. And so I was like, "Hey, hold it, man. The homie ain't here to represent himself, to stand up, but I am, and he's all right with me, so all that *puto* shit, you can take that and shove it up your fucking ass. And I hang out with who the fuck I want to hang out with." They told me, "I know you're a first termer and shit dude but we're the EME, and we run this *pinta*." Then again, here I go with my mouth, "I don't give a fuck about your little club." I still didn't understand the depths of these prison gangs. So I walked the yard, and nothing happened. The next day, we got to go to the gym. I went to the gym, and there was a spot over past the weight pile. There's this big old stage. It was way up high, and there was a weight pile where everybody worked out with their weights. But those of us who worked martial arts, we'd go down by the stage. There was a section there where we could work out without the cops seeing it or sweating us. We'd work out martial arts; it was big back then. So I was kinda squatting, watching these two guys work out. Back then, I used to wear my hair parted to the side. Sometimes it would fall into my eyes, and I would just flick my head back to get the hair out of my eyes. I was kinda squatting, watching the two guys, and I was up on the stage. It just so happened that my hair fell in my eyes, and I flicked back my hair to get it out of my eyes; and when I did, I saw one of these guys that had jacked me up in the yard coming at me, and he had a fucking knife. So he's going for my neck, because I was squatting, but I rose up and went to dive out of the way, but he hit me. He hit me in my hip; he got me good in the hip, man. So I was cornered now, and now there were three of them. I was cornered up on the stage, and I was already hit in my hip. I don't know, but I became Samson. I'm telling you, man. I picked this dude up and threw him off the stage on to the weight pile, the weight bench, and he broke his back. I started beating the fuck out of this other guy; the other one, he just took off. So these two guys ended up in the hospital. Now the gym door was open. They had a couple of their buddies keeping the cops and the so-called coach busy in the office. This happened quick; it happens quick in the penitentiary. So I got to get out of there because I was hit. I didn't know how bad I was hit. I hadn't had a chance to examine it, but I was bleeding. I got to get out of there. You know, and these two dudes, I got one knocked out up there on the stage with a broken jaw, and I got the other one on the fucking weight floor with a broken back. I didn't know that until later. So I made it out the door, at the unlock, because they happened to be having an unlock at that time. That's why they made the move then; the cop was distracted with the unlock. The coach, they had pulled with a couple of their homies. So I caught the unlock, I made it out, and I left these two dudes back there, one of them knocked out with a broken jaw, the other one with a broken back. I made it to my cell. I got back to my unit, and I made it into my cell on the unlock. I was able to pull my pants down to see how bad my wound was. I looked at it, man. Now I think I read one too many John Wayne books or Louis L'amour books, because I said, "Ah, fuck, it's just a flesh wound. I just got to close it. What do I do?" They gave us old metal cups back then, these little metal cups we'd drink out of. So I took some toilet paper rolls and made little bombs for fire, and I got a newspaper and I made a handle so I didn't burn myself, and I got that metal cup just as hot as I could get it. Because, you know, in the movies, you see them; they get the knife hot to stop the bleeding, right? Well, I was thinking it's like the movies, so I got this thing hot, and I put it on my wound to shut the wound up to stop the bleeding. That fucker hurt like hell. But I did it; I went back, put the fire on there again, and I did it again. I did it a couple of times. I was sure I got it sealed up; it's all gonna be fine.

Three days later, I was walking down the hall, and my leg went out on me. I fell out. I got to the hospital, and they told me I may have gangrene. They may have to amputate my leg. I was like, "What? Oh my god!" They treated me, and they gave me antibiotics. They were not getting my leg. I was praying now, "God, heal me! Not my leg, please. I'm sorry, forgive me, heal me, Jesus." On the third day in the hospital, recuperating, I got up. The hospital was even divided; they had segregation in there too. They had the maximum security guys with maximum concerns, they had the critical guys, and they had me over here with this infection. That's when I found out that the two guys that hit me were in the hospital, and the one who did hit me had a broken back. I kind of laughed, because here I was on a lesser side, and they were over there on the critical side. That's when I found out that dude had broken his back, and the other guy, aside from his jaw being broken, he had rolled over on his own knife, so he had stabbed himself. Anyway, I didn't stab him; he stabbed himself. He may tell everyone I stabbed him, but he stabbed himself, so that felt kind of good. I think it was maybe a week I was there, and I got a visit from the fucking security squad, and they told me, "Look, we know what happened, nobody's coming forth, nobody's saying anything, but we know what happened, and you just made enemies of the Mexican Mafia, so we have to transfer you, for your own safety." I said, "Well, where are you transferring me? I'm not even through with my processing. You mean I'm gonna go on to prison?" They said, "Well, we don't know, but we're going to transfer you." Well, they transferred me back to Vacaville! Back to the fucking overflow on the main line in Vacaville! So I was on the overflow now, somehow or another. I was there maybe for two days, three days, and they caught it, and they said, "Oh no," and they put me back on the green side. So now, I was back in the green over on the RGC side, finishing my reception. That's a whole other story; I was going to Tracy. Now there was a black guy I used to run with; we called him Young Blood. He was a good dude, and I thought he was bad! You know, he could fight, he had heart, and I thought this guy was tough. They used to post the transfers, where you were going, on the bulletin boards. If your name was there on one of the lists, it told you what prison you're going to, where to go for R&R and all that stuff, turn in your property. So everybody came out of the chow hall. We go look at the latest postings on the board, and I was standing there next to Young Blood. He went up there to read the postings, and for a black man, I watched him turn white when he saw his name and where he was going, and he fainted. I had to catch him. He fainted, and I said, "You all right, dude?" He was quiet, and I said, "What happened?" He just pointed at the roster, so I walked up there and looked, and I said, "You're going to Tracy, so what?" That's how I had an idea of how tough Tracy was going to be. You know back then, Tracy was known as Gladiator School, population, let's say, one thousand inmates, in one-year time. It was on the cover of *Time* magazine as the most violent prison in the United States. There were a hundred and twenty-seven stabbing assaults and nineteen murders in one year. So you know, it was a pretty violent place. This is where I was going. This is where I went. This is where I became La Nuestra Familia.

Visiting with my sister-in-law, Lori, at DVI in Tracy

Chapter

9

So on to Gladiator School. Man, you know, La Nuestra Familia had continually tried to recruit me. One thing I have to say about the La Nuestra Familia is that of all the gangs I had ever seen, and I'd seen them all, these were the most vicious. These guys would kill, they would move, and they didn't care, in front of a cop, under the gun towers. If they had orders to hit, they hit. And they, the majority of them, were all youngsters like me—except for the leaders. The leaders were a little bit older, the few leaders they had at the time. The La Nuestra Familia was just starting to take off as a prison gang. What we had that was different than any other gang was we had a Constitution. Before I joined, there were certain guys there that I respected. Even though they were involved and they were gang members, I had a lot of respect for them. Like Crackers and Hobo, Larry, Art, Poncho, Profit, Yuba, Big Yuba (love ya, Yuba), Black Bob, Macarone—I could go on forever. I came to love all these brothers with all my heart. I would kill and die for them if it had been necessary. These guys were the La Nuestra Familia to me. There in Tracy, and other places too, our paths had crossed, and they inspired me to join them to be one of them—the Vindiolas, the Venegases, the Castros, the Gabrials, the Sosas, and so many more. I knew and respected all of them before I ever became a member. I would kick it with them. They would slip me things, show me the Constitution, and say, "Hey, read the Constitution, check it out. This is what we got going on." I was an outsider, so I figured this was a great honor for them to let an outsider read the Constitution. They had their hit list, and they had their ways; they set things up, their organization there. The way they organized the penitentiary, each block had its structure of organization, and they had their own warehouses of store items for the soldiers. They were really organized; that impressed me about them. But I still wasn't joining any gang. I was doing my own thing, I was dealing drugs there in prison, and I was getting drugs in and dealing them. I had enough sense to know to treat these guys with respect. I remember the first time I went to the lieutenant in my block; I think his name was Smiley, out of Watsonville. I walked up to him, and he had a couple of bodyguards. I said, "Hey, I want to talk to the Smiley." So cool, Smiley gave me the signal to come up and talk to him. I said, "Hey, here," and I handed him some dope. He said, "What's this?" I said, "Well, I'm dealing here, and just out of respect, I'm gonna kick you guys down a little bit of everything I'm dealing." Because I was trying to impress them, I said, "Because if this was my territory, I'd be expecting that if anyone was dealing in my territory, they should be kicking me down." What I was actually doing was covering my ass. They liked that; they liked the way I got at them like that. So in the course of the time that I was there, I was making friends here and making friends there. I was seeing things happen that I didn't agree with. Like my friend Jerry, who got killed, who shouldn't have been killed, though I had stepped in for him and said, "This is my friend." They thought he was an Aryan Brotherhood sympathizer, but he wasn't. He was part of my circle of comrades there in DVI Tracy. When I heard they were gonna hit him, I stepped in and raised my hand for him with the lieutenant on the block. Jerry was on a different block though, but I was assured that the lieutenant could send word over to stop the hit. Anyway, he ended up getting killed because the order to stop the hit didn't get through in time, and I watched him die. He died as the guards were rushing him to the hospital; they had a bloody towel around his neck. Just as he passed my unit door, I saw him, and I saw the bloody towel fall from around his neck. The blood squirted out in a gush, splattering the window in front of me. I looked into his eyes just then, feeling helpless. He died in that moment, as if saying good-bye to me with his last glance. I was so pissed off because I hadn't been able to save him. He had gotten a visit that day, his first visit in a few years from his ex-wife. She brought his two little sons to see him there for the first and last time. I remember he had been so happy and talked of getting back with his ex-wife and kids again.

There were other incidents too, some sick shit jumping off there. I watched guys getting butt-fucked in the shower, turned out, raped, and shit like that. All kinda crap, you know, this was prison reality, all around me. Not just us, but all the different groups and gangs. But I couldn't do anything as long as I was on the sideline. I got close to a lot of the soldiers; I liked them. They had asked me to do this major heroin transaction for them because I could get it, so I said, "Sure, I'll do it." The only one that I was going to deal with was going to be my friend Chato; he's a soldier. Actually, I got the dope, and I gave it to Poncho first, and Poncho would give it to Chato, who would pass it over to Johnny in G wing. We were over in H wing. So I brought the dope back, and I gave the dope to Poncho. I was watching as he's allowed to test it. They just passed a rule in the La Nuestra Familia, by the way. I think it was a bad rule, because the penalty was death. We could have modified it so that anybody who fixed lost rank or some other discipline, but it turned out to be crippling to us. It was that no one was allowed to fix heroin anymore. You know, the old people still did, but if you fixed heroin, you were going to be killed.

So soldiers were not to fix. We lost a lot of brothers over this rule. So I gave the dope to Poncho. He green lights it, it's good, best he ever had, so he sent it with Chato to Johnny. Now Johnny and Chato were homeboys; they're friends. Chato, when he took the dope to Johnny, said, "Hey, look out for me, man, kick me down, right?" Johnny told him, "Yeah, sure, I'll look out for you, homie, don't worry," you know, 'cause they're homeboys. Now it just so happened that I was going to a visit at that time, and I walked out with Chato. I knew Chato had the dope. I watched Chato get it straight from Poncho, and he handed it straight to Johnny. I was watching this because I was going out for a visit; I was walking out with him. So I went on my visit. Johnny got into the dope, and he fucked it all up. He cut it; he fucked the dope up bad. Then he turned around, and he said that either Chato or I fucked the dope up. Johnny did not know that I was an undercover recruit on probation. He thought I was just an outsider and he can just say the outsider burned them. There's an investigation into the dope; I was jacked up about the dope.

Art, the Rock, he was like the second captain there. Larry was actually running that yard. So Rock came to me in the chow hall, and he said, "Hey, what's up, man, you burned us on this shit?" And I was all, "What, what the fuck you talking about?" He said, "Well, the dope turned out to be shit!" The first thing I thought was this was some kind of test. So I told him, "Hey, are you trying to test me or something? Are you testing me to see if I'm weak or what? You know, because I ain't weak, man, and I don't give a fuck. We can get busy right now." And Rock said, "Hold it," because Rock was the one really pushing to recruit me. "Tell me what happened." So I told him, "I gave the dope to Poncho, I brought the dope in, I gave it to Poncho, Poncho tested it, said it was the best he ever had. He gave it to Chato. I walked out with Chato, because I was going for a visit, and I saw Chato hand it directly to Johnny." So there's an investigation, and he said, "Okay, we're going to do an investigation." Now whenever there's an investigation in the La Nuestra Familia, somebody's gonna get killed. So anyway, it turned out that it's under investigation, and they checked with Poncho and Poncho said, "No, the dope was good. It was the best I ever had." Somewhere from Poncho to Johnny, that dope got fucked up, so right away, Johnny put it on Chato; it had to be Chato. So word came down to hit Chato. We kinda looked out for each other. I was thinking about getting into this gang. I mean, because of the Constitution, I saw the potential there. I was thinking, man, with this kind of discipline, this kind of structure, you know? They wanted to go to the streets with this? I was getting ready to go to the streets; it may be a good thing to hook up with. Chato was told, "Hey, they're gonna hit you, brother. The word has come down for us to move the pieces." Now when the word comes down to move all the pieces, that means that one of the brothers is gonna get hit, because they don't want him to know where the pieces are. So good lookin' out, Poncho. I love you, boy. Anyway, so he's the one that gave the heads-up to Chato, and Chato told me, and I remember that, I'll never forget it, man. We're all standing there, like "What are you going to do, Chato?" And I was telling him, "Chato, go fucking kill Johnny, man." A couple of the other guys were like, "Yeah, go hit Johnny." I said, "That's what you got to do, Johnny set you up." "That fucking Johnny, man. My homie, man," sighed Chato. "Well, what do you do?" I said, "Chato, you got to do something. They're gonna kill you." Chato, I'll never forget the look on his face man; he told me, "How do you go to the police and tell them, 'Lock me up, my brothers are going to kill me'?" I'll never forget that, man. You know, and I told Chato, "No matter what, I'll make it right, I'll make it right. But maybe you better go lock it up." So Chato went, and he locked it up. Johnny's walking the yard like he got over, and I was fucking mad. I was not letting this die, and they're telling me, "Let it go. We got it under control." Well, what I did not know was Johnny was getting ready to go home in a couple of months himself. They were going to wait until he got home; they knew what happened. They figured it out that it was Johnny, but they were going to wait until he went home. They were going to kill him on the streets; it would be easier to kill him out there and because Larry, our main captain over Tracy, had been told by administration to cool it on all the killings for a while, or they would lock the leaders up. I mean, we can kill him just as easy in the penitentiary, but nobody would've gotten busted on the streets. That's what they told me later anyway, so I believed 'em. But at the time, I was not letting it go. I was telling them, "No, uh-uh." I didn't know their plan then; they hadn't told me yet. So I was pushing it; I was not letting it go. They're telling me, "Hey, you're starting to rock the boat, man. You're saying shit, and we can't allow that." And that's when I told them, "Look, you guys want me in. This is the terms for me to get in. Give both me and Johnny a knife and let us go at each other on the yard. Let whoever wins be the one who's telling the truth." Here I was again, believing in some Hollywood movie version of how warriors settle a matter to get to the truth. "Well, you don't dictate to us." "Yes, I do. You're asking me to give up my life, you're asking me to devote myself to this. Well, this is what I want. Blood in, blood out. I don't have a problem killing somebody that's got it coming. The one that's got it coming is this guy, because, you know, he was a lieutenant, and if we are going to be in an organization, a criminal organization, loyal to your brotherhood and *Carnalismo*, then we cannot have brothers or lieutenants or leaders who will sell out another brother for anything. One of the things in the Constitution, one of the articles, says, and I quote, 'No brother shall put anything above another brother. No punks, no drugs, no nothing.' And this is what, in my opinion, Johnny has done, so by the Constitution, he deserves to die. And since you guys don't want to seem to do it, I will do it. Give me the knife, give him a knife, that's my terms." Anyway, so my terms were accepted.

So here I was; they had accepted the terms to my becoming a member. In exchange, I must now go out and kill Johnny in a duel of what I thought was honor. Now that it was really going to happen, that night in my cell, I had to search my soul. Was this worth it? I could just as easily lose this duel against Johnny. I dismissed that thought; there was no one equal to me in a fair knife fight, I thought. Then I could spend the rest of my life in prison for killing this piece of shit, and for what? For my friend Chato, who didn't even have the heart to kill Johnny himself. He instead chose to go into protective custody. Here I was, fighting his fight for him. At the time, he was my friend, and I thought it was unjust what was happening to him. Years later, I would find out he was just a piece of shit madly in love with a homosexual drag queen, but at that moment, he was my friend. I watched him cry tears because of the choice he was being forced to make in order to survive and to live.

What the fuck was I doing? I had been running my mouth again, demanding justice for a man who was going to turn out to be worthless. I had talked the talk. Now it was time to walk the walk, or tell them I decided not to join after all, let them clean up their own mess. Back then, when you were placed on probation period before joining, the probation period was meant to give them time to observe you and decide if they wanted to let you in to the La Nuestra Familia. At the same time, at the end of the probation period, you still could say, "No thanks," you had decided this wasn't the life for you after all. The cost of admission was too high; it was blood in, which meant you had to make a kill or at least a very respectable attempt. You either stabbed the shit out of the target, and by the grace of God, the victim lived, in which case, you still get in with the understanding that you still owe a kill.

All this weighed on my mind and heart, all that night after I was told it had been green lighted. Most of all, I would be risking my soon-to-be freedom and release from prison. That is why Rock didn't want to green-light my request, because they wanted me on the streets, where my experience and skills could better be utilized for the advancement of our goals to take over the streets of California. Now because I made it the condition of my becoming a member and because they believed me that Johnny had cut the dope and set up Chato for the fall, they were giving me the green light to have this duel of honor as the price of my membership into La Nuestra Familia. At least this is what I naively believed. In the Bible, it says that pride goes before the fall, when it came down to it; it was now a matter of pride. Like I said, I had talked like a gunfighter. Now it was time; it was sundown, the hour of the gunfighter.

I remembered all those classic westerns. I grew up idolizing the gunfighters who always said, "Get out of town before sundown, or you will die." There is a song by Elton John called "Don't Let the Sun Go Down on Me." It said, "'Cause losing everything would be like the sun going down on me." Going to prison, I had lost everything, my air force career, my new life, and even my childhood sweet heart, Patty, who had warned me that if I ended up in prison, she wouldn't be able to deal with it. Being true to her word, she couldn't handle it. She ran around getting wasted and fucking my friends and had parted ways with me. So I took the name "Sundown" because it meant to me, nothing left to lose. It also meant to me that I was a gunfighter now for the rest of my life.

In the morning, I told the Rock, "Okay, I'm in, let's do this. Give Johnny a knife and give me a knife. Tell his bodyguards and all the Carnales to stay out of it, and I'll show you that I'm the real motherfucker." It was set up for that day, in the afternoon, in the yard. I would be given my piece on the yard, and Johnny would have his knife too; a diversion would be set up. A couple of brothers would start fighting each other way over on the other end of the yard. Except they wouldn't be really fighting, just wrestling and making it look like they were fighting to draw all the gun towers' attention. All the guards would respond over there. They would not stop until given the signal.

Johnny and I would go at each other on the handball court. His bodyguards would not stop me. The Rock himself was on the yard. Everyone was. Whenever a hit of a brother went down, it was mandatory that all the soldiers watched to see our discipline in action. Rock called me over into the inmate minicanteen, where inmates sold sodas and ice creams and other treats to the inmates on the yard for store-bought ducats (inmate money used to purchase items on the yard and to pay for photographs we were allowed to take of ourselves on the yard). Of course, we had our people running that minicanteen. Anyway, he called me inside the store, away from the guards' view, and he handed me a knife, one of the knives I had actually made for the gang. I recognized it; it was a good one. The Rock told me, "You got to be good, you got to be quick." Johnny was supposed to be dangerous with a knife. He told me, "Good luck. As soon as you see all the guards running over to the fake fight, you guys go for it. Johnny's already been given the same instructions." I took the knife and put it under my shirt in the waist of my pants.

This was it; it was showtime. As I eased my way over toward the handball court, I could see Johnny with his two bodyguards. Johnny was leaning against the handball wall, watching the handball players. I thought he sure was confident; he's not even paying any attention to me as I was standing about fifty feet away from him at the end of the handball court. His bodyguards sure were noticing me. For a moment, I thought, by the serious looks on their faces, that maybe this was a setup and they were actually gonna hit me because I kept running my mouth about the injustice to Chato, but then I said to myself, "No, they wouldn't have given me a piece if they were planning on hitting me. That wouldn't make any sense."

Just then, Rock walked past me and said, "Get ready, it's time." Sure enough, a fight started on the farthest side of the yard. The gun towers were yelling for them to stop, and the yard guards were all headed there. I moved quickly to where Johnny was standing near the handball wall. As I was moving toward him, I saw his bodyguards step away. I had never killed a man with a knife before; I had killed a man with a gun on the streets before he could pull his own gun to kill me. I had beaten a monster half to death with a mop wringer before he got a chance to try to butt-fuck me in the county jail, causing him permanent brain damage for the rest of his life. Before I came here to prison, I had beaten down two Mexican Mafias when they came to kill me in Chino. Some Hero put a child molester out of his misery. I had punctured the lungs and ribs of two guys claiming they were Aryan Brotherhood members over a weight bench and a homosexual named Silvia in Vacaville before I came here to Tracy. I had trained myself all my life for this moment, but I had never killed a man in a knife fight. Now that moment was here. I remembered Johnny, at first, when I was about five feet in front of him; he glanced at me as if I were that annoyance who had tried to cause trouble for him over Chato and the dope deal that had gone all wrong. He simply dismissed me as insignificant as he kept his attention on the two brothers' way over in the corner of the yard, fighting.

I remember thinking, "Doesn't this idiot know we don't have much time and we have to get to this now?" So I pulled my knife out, showing it to him, and said, "Are you ready?" At the sight of the knife in my hand and my asking him if he was ready, he jumped back a couple of feet, like he was completely surprised at my being there with a knife in my hand and asking him if he was ready. Fear filled his eyes for a second until he remembered he had bodyguards there to protect him from just such a thing as this. He quickly turned to his bodyguards and ordered them, "Get him." But his bodyguards moved back away from him, and in that moment, I think he realized he was about to get hit. By the way his bodyguards acted, he knew it was sanctioned. He turned back to me, and I remember standing there waiting for him to pull his knife so that we could get to it. In a split second, it all became clear to me that he didn't have a knife. This was not gonna be some idealistic duel of honor as I had imagined and thought it was supposed to be, but that this was my blood-in moment. I was to kill him for what he had done. I remember feeling, for a moment, angry that I had been tricked into this moment. But I saw it in his eyes. Once he realized it was a hit on him, he was gonna run, break away, get away, and I had to move before it was too late. It was as if we were in each other's minds. He started to break away, Instinctively, Some Hero jumped up at him, kicking him full force with a dropkick to his chest. His feet tangled, and he flew backward from the force of the kick. He went headfirst into the cement handball wall, breaking his own neck in the process. Some Hero did not know this at the moment; Some Hero only knew he had to get on him and kill him as quickly as he could. Some Hero jumped down on him and began stabbing him as fast as he could. Some Hero remembered thinking he must have knocked himself out and this is why he wasn't reacting to Some Hero stabbing the shit out of him. Some Hero remembered thinking it odd that there was not that much blood for all the stab wounds he had hit him with. Then Some Hero heard the command in Spanish coming from his bodyguards and from Art. "Basta ya. Basta yas tuvo" (that's enough, that's enough, its over). Art and Johnny's bodyguards were telling Some Hero to hurry up and follow them back into the little minicanteen. As soon as Some Hero got in there, they began giving Some Hero wet towels to wipe blood off him. They had a change of clothes. They took the knife and wiped it off, and for the first time, I noticed the bodyguards handing over their knives too to be stashed and put away in that minicanteen.

Everyone was calling Some Hero "Carnal" as we hurried back outside of the canteen, moving far away from where Johnny's dead body lay. It was as if a signal had been given, and the brothers who had been locked in wrestling holds suddenly stopped pretending to be fighting. The guards moved in to separate them and cuff them to escort them off the yard to the captain's office, not even noticing Johnny's dead body lying against the handball wall as they passed by with the two wrestlers in handcuffs on their way off the yard. We had done it right before yard recall, and though all that only took a few minutes including changing clothes and cleaning up and moving away to another part of the yard, yet it seemed like it was a lot longer; they called yard recall. We were the first to make it back inside from the yard before they finally discovered Johnny's dead body lying there.

One of the things I found out while we were waiting for them to call yard recall was that Johnny's bodyguards were armed because if Some Hero failed to hit Johnny, they were gonna kill him themselves. Because it had all happened so fast and Johnny never offered any resistance, because he was already dead before he hit the ground, and before Some Hero jumped on him and started stabbing him, they never had to get involved. In the official report staff wrote up, which of course, we got copies of, they wrote that it had been an NF housecleaning job and that from the coroner's report, it must have been done by more than one assailant, because he had been hit over the head and stabbed then had his neck broken to make sure.

As far as staff was concerned, as long as it was just an in-house hit, they didn't really care. This is the way it was and why our little prison had made the cover of *Time* magazine as the most violent prison in America. It also turned out that the only reason Johnny had been accepted as a member was because our general at the time was his homeboy. He let him in because, ordinarily, a guy with Johnny's crimes would not have been allowed to join us. He had a couple of sexual battery cases and a manslaughter case for beating down some old man in a robbery burglary. His excuses for the rapes were that he was trying to take control of the prostitutes and that the old man he beat to death supposedly came at him with a knife. It made Some Hero feel better about killing him, but still Some Hero had killed another man, and I don't mind admitting that it troubled me some, my conscience—not because Some Hero had killed him or because he was a piece of shit in my book at the time for the way he was abusing his power in the gang, but because it had not been an honorable duel as I had wanted and as I had been misled to believe by Art that it would be.

I asked Art why it went down as it had, and he told me that they decided Johnny had to go for what he had pulled with the dope deal and with setting up Chato for the fall. Also, because all the leadership and most of the brothers there all wanted me in, Art thought if he made me think Johnny was armed and gonna try to kill me too, it would give me an advantage and make me not hesitate and get it done. Hopefully get away as Some Hero had so that I could still be schooled and prepared for when I did get released. So that I could go out to the streets and set things up for Art so that when he was released, everything would already be in order for him to take over the street regiments.

Now I was getting ready to go home in a few short months. I was to be kept under cover. Although everybody knew I was in, I was undercover. The reason why I was kept undercover was because I was Mexican Irish, and I could pass as a white guy, so I could infiltrate all the whites and find out who was Aryan Brotherhood sympathetic. I could rat them out, and we could hit them, and because I was raised partly in Southern California, I could infiltrate there too. More importantly, they had special plans for me on the streets because of my skills. One of the number 1 things with La Nuestra Familia that everybody forgets is that (and what I'm violating right now, in telling this book, but I have permission from whom it matters. I don't have to worry about that; they already know that I'm gonna write this book, and it's like, "Go for it." You know what I mean?) we had "Omerta," the code of silence. You were never supposed to admit that you are a member of any prison gang, or that there was even a La Nuestra Familia. Your job was to infiltrate, say, "No, I'm not no member, never heard of it," and let them put you on enemy lines, find out who's calling shots there, and hit them. I mean, that's what you were supposed to do; that's the way it was. Sad to say that it's not that way no more.

I remember, I came back in ninety-three. They escorted me with a convoy back to the prison. I was sitting in a holding tank in San Quentin, and I was watching a bus as they unload. I haven't been back to prison in quite a few years. And I didn't know it had flipped so badly, but I was sitting there, and the guards were standing there. Everybody's getting off the bus, and they're asking them, "Well, what clique do you belong to? What gang do you belong to?" And these guys were getting off the bus, telling them, "I'm a southerner," "I'm a Norteno." And I was like, "What the fuck is this shit?" You know what I mean? They're saying this so they can be with their own homies and not try to infiltrate enemy lines or get onto a line and secure it. You know what I mean? I was like, "Man, this would have got you hit before the civil war. That's a protective custody move according to NF rules. You know, you're in violation. What the fuck has gone on? When did this shit flip so bad!" Yet the youngsters who don't even realize what is wrong with doing this have got their chests all puffed out, saying, "I'm a warrior," "I'm a guerrero," or "I'm a Soldier." "Excuse me, motherfucker, you just got off the bus and PC'd! Don't tell me you're fucking soldier." "Well, that's the way we do it now, you know." I said, "Oh fuck. Oh fuck, seriously? Miss me with that shit, get in my path, and I'll kill you. Otherwise, pull up a seat and let me school you about some things, youngster, because I see you got some heart. But in this game, some heart doesn't get it done. You need to use your head too if you want to stay alive. There's gonna be a lot of times when you can't always be with the homies and you need to be superbad and supersharp, and you better be sure." I keep getting way ahead of myself.

Now I was in the La Nuestra Familia, my reasons again, misguided loyalty, you know. Just like I got into prison, misguided loyalty. But I actually believed in the La Nuestra Familia. I did. I still do. I believed in our Constitution, I believed in our concepts of schooling, and I helped to write the majority of our concepts of schooling. It's what we did. I said, "Look, you can't have these guys just getting out and running around just killing everything and anything. You know what I mean? You can't take people who go to prison. The extent of their criminal organization and knowledge is that they did some burglaries, or they dealt drugs, or they did some armed robberies, and all of a sudden, you're gonna put them in positions of power over life and death and your soldiers and the growth of your criminal organization. You can't just do that." We learned that mistake, and so we had to start schooling. You got to school them. You got to teach them. You got to teach them what they have to do, how to infiltrate, how to organize, how to create regiments, you know? Just like we were doing in the penitentiaries and now on the streets. So we created what was called a subdivision. In the subdivision, you start learning how to go out and take over the streets. So this is where we're at now. We haven't yet created the street subdivision. Most of our schooling was word of mouth. I'm coming to that part where I must be schooled. So I was getting out, and I was told by the Rock and by Hobo. By the way, Hobo was my hero and the main influence for the reason I got in, Glenn Holden, I loved him. I still love him, you know. He's the one who finally convinced me to come in; he's the one that kept slipping me all the reports and everything. He let me see what was going on with the money being made in prison itself. Surprisingly, it was a lot of money. You would be surprised how much, so I said, "All right, I'm in, man. I'm all in, come on, let's go, we can do this, we can make this work." I was supposed to get out and establish a regiment for Art. I was supposed to get out and establish a bank for him. You know, because he's going to be following me out. There's soldiers already out there. The concepts of regiments were kind of brand-new. If you look at our Constitution, you sit there and you see where, at that time. Just to have a thousand dollars in the regiment bank was considered something, you know. I would look at that, and I would think, "Well, people who never had nothing would think that looks like a lot," so you'd have to study the Constitution to understand why that was set up that way. To me, a thousand dollars in the bank, that's the bare minimum. I guess they were making it easy on people. To me, you had to have ten, twenty, thirty thousand, you know, just to run a regiment. It got more expensive as time went on. So now I got out, and I was to hook up with the brothers who were out there. The brothers who were out there, let's see. I went to Oakland first. There were, ah okay, one, two, three, four, five brothers that were there. These were good brothers, except for the lieutenant at the time.

Again we're running into the same problem again. I got out, and right away the brothers, they're telling me, "Hey, this is what's going on, this what we're doing." I said, "Well, what are you guys doing?" "Well we're doing a little robberies, and you know, we're trying to extort prostitutes and stuff like that, and we're trying to extort drug dealers and shit." So I said, "Okay, what's happening? What are the problems?" They said, well, like, for an example, there was a brother Chino, a dedicated loyal brother out of Monterey. He told me, "Well, everything we get, we give to the lieutenant. Because right now, that's what we're told, we have to sacrifice. Everything we get we have to give to the regiment, to the establishing of the regiment." He said, "But that lieutenant is just fucking strung out on heroin and burning and ripping everybody off." And Chino told me, "My old lady is selling her ass to pay for our motel." I was like, "What? This ain't the way it's supposed to go down." I was hearing all these complaints from everybody. And also, the major drug dealers, they got at me and they told me, "Hey, ah, what's up with this guy? He is not only collecting kick-downs to the gang, but he is also borrowing dope on front." I keep saying lieutenant because I don't want to say his name, because I already made the mistake of saying someone else's name. I'm gonna edit that. From now on, I'm gonna have to change names, because like I said, murder, they can get you at any time.

Anyway, this lieutenant, for right now, we'll call him idiot, you know. So he's got all these guys doing all this stuff, and he's taking all the money and he's sending a little bit back to the first captain. We had a fucking idiot for our first captain. You know, Death Row Joe Gonzalez, he was a fucking idiot, a fucking idiot. So anyway, he's sending the money back to him, and as long as he's doing that, he thought he's all right. But he's only sending a little bit of money back. Like I said, when you see a thousand dollars, and these guys sitting back in a prison cell collecting it, it seems like a lot, I guess. Death Row Joe was a fucking whino. But he had heart, you know. That's how he got in, but anyway, so he's in charge of everything. And Babo was a bigger idiot; I loved Babo. Loved him, he had heart, loved him, but he was a bigger stupid idiot because he let Death Row Joe just manipulate him, and fucking Joe, I spit on him.

Anyway, so even the connections were getting at me, telling me, "Hey, this guy owes us money, man. We're giving him dope on fronts, and he owes us. We been kicking down, but then he comes in and wants fronts." So I said, "All right." I gathered everybody together, and I said to the soldiers, "Look, we're gonna have to take a vote." I was new to all this, and I was out there. I was under the Rock, and I knew what the Rock told me I was supposed to do. And that's who I was supposed to answer to. And this other lieutenant tried to say that he was under the Rock too. I was like, "Whatever, let's take a vote. You guys want me to take over? Then you're going to have to vote, and it's going to have to be on record why I'm taking over." You know, well, this, this idiot lieutenant, he's all, "You can't do that. It doesn't go that way, you can't do that," and I said, "First of all, we're surrounded by a bunch of enemies. You know what I mean, so this is going to be the number one condition. We're all going to vote, and whoever it decides is going to be the lieutenant. He has to make the first hit." We had a bunch of ABs and Mexican Mafia around us and stuff like that we had to take care of. So I said, "That's the condition, whoever is voted in has to make the first hit." Right away, this idiot lieutenant was like, "Oh, you can't do that. You know the lieutenant doesn't do that. You know, he sends the soldiers." Right away you could see his colors coming out. Everybody was okay, right, of course. Overwhelmingly, the vote was five to one, you know, so now I was the lieutenant. We started making our hits, and I told the dude, "You're stripped. You have no more authority. I'm going to give you a pass, dude, you're strung out. You're not even supposed to be fixing right now. You're strung out, and I could report you on this and we're supposed to kill you, but I'm gonna give you a pass, let it go."

Well, this asshole tried to get at my superiors in the pen and make it look like I was committing acts of treason. Finally, I had enough of it, and I had him hit. Now here I go. I'll go on to tell you about how we established our regiments and what I did to change things. What I did to change things actually really worked and was great. But the reason I'm telling that part is because when I did get back to prison, because he had stirred up all this stuff, saying that I was committing treason and what I had done, and then because I had him hit, you know, you don't spill the blood of another brother without clearance of the general. But I was also taught that in the time of emergency, you had to do what you had to do, but you had better be right. So I was number 1 on the top of our own gang's hit list, because of this action, and when I returned to prison, first they put me with all my brothers. They had them all in West Hall, and there was like a hundred hardcore killers right there, right? I've always said that I'd rather walk into the middle of a Mexican Mafia yard or an Aryan Brotherhood yard with a La Nuestra Familia banner than walk my own yard among my own brothers and have smut on me, because I knew what my brothers were going to do: they were going to kill me.

By the way, knowing I was number 1 on the hit list, the cops called me out of the room and they took me in the office. They showed me the latest confiscated paperwork, because they were always confiscating paperwork, finding it. I knew it was a bona fide hit list, and there was my name right there. They said, "Look, you're number one, dude. We're gonna lock you up. You want to go to protective custody?" I was thinking, "Man, is this a trick or what?" But I looked, and I thought, "No, that's a real hit list." You know? So I said, "No, I don't want to go in protective custody, just put me back in the building." I went back in the building and made the report. I reported to Poncho at the time. It was Poncho in charge at the time. I said, "Look, they took me out. They showed me the latest confiscated hit list, and it's got my name on it, number one on the top of the list." I said, "I don't know what this is about, but I do know that that's a real hit list, and they wanted me to lock up. And I'm not going to lock it up because I know that what I did was right, and I'm going to wait for the investigation. I have the right to an investigation on this. I don't know who put me on that." I found out later it was Death Row Joe who put me on there. Because I had challenged him, so they got to Babo. They said, "Okay, just chill, dude, just kick back, don't trip. We'll get to Babo, and we'll find out what's going on. In the meantime, just go ahead and walk around, don't trip. We're going to investigate this. If everything you say is true, then you got nothing to trip on. If it isn't, then you know what time it is."

So all right, cool. For two weeks I walked around there. I even went out there in the middle of the yard and went to sleep. I refused to be afraid of my own people when I knew what I did was right, and it came back that I was cleared. Two weeks later, they told me, "Hey, stop sleeping out in the yard. You're cleared. You get back and be busy. A lot of people here don't know you. There's a lot of youngsters." Only a handful of people did know me. They said, "We are going to keep you undercover, so stay undercover."

That was when I returned, but let's get back to the first time that I got out. That was when I was establishing regiments. Just wanted to clear that up that I was not in bad standing at any time. I mean, in that time pending, once the investigation cleared me, I was back to normal.

So okay, back to the streets. First of all, I didn't like the way they were running around, you know, like in Salinas. This is how they wanted to organize the prostitutes: they take a prostitute, kill her, and tell the other prostitutes, "Okay, give us your money." Same thing in Fresno. What was happening was we were running around killing whores. It's stupid, and I said, "No, we're not going to do that here. This is what we are going to do." I got at a couple of home girls who were prostitutes, and I told them, "Look, I'm in charge now, and this is what I'm offering you. Any girl that wants to work with us will give us forty percent of your take, but in exchange for forty percent of your take, we're going to protect you from the pimps." In Oakland, there were a lot of pimps, black pimps that were beating up broads and killing them and all that other stuff. "We're going to protect you from that. I love nothing more than fucking up a pimp, so we're going to protect you, and also, if you get arrested, because, you know, it's one of the hazards of the prostitution trade that you are always getting arrested, you just call this number, and you will be bailed immediately. You'll have a lawyer." Back then, we were able to buy off judges. You can't do that anymore. You probably can, but it costs a lot more than it did back then. So, you know, that was attractive. So these broads were coming to us one after the other when they saw it actually working. The broad would get busted and make a phone call, and she was bailed. They were beating down our doors to work with us. They would rather work for us than be out there on their own and have the black pimps running over there and trying to kill them. In exchange, we would protect them, so it worked out good. It was working good. I had them organized; that was the way we set it up. If you worked for us, your name went on the bail bondsman list. At the time, we used our bondsman, and you were on a twenty-four-hour bail list. Any time you got busted, he would go bail you, because we had given him a bunch of money and made arrangements with him that anyone on our list, he bailed 'em. We got it covered; we had it sewed up, and so instead of killing whores, now we were doing business with them. That's the way we should do that, and with the drug connections, it was the same thing. Before, they taught us, for example, to take three drug connections, get them all together, kidnap them, put them in a room, and tell them they're going to kick down then wait for one of them to tell you to go fuck yourselves. The one who tells you to go fuck yourselves, he's not going to do it. You kill him in front of the other two, and you tell them, "Now you're going to pay us." I didn't like that either. You know, there are better ways to deal with it than that. We're going to get into a pretty crazy thing here. But anyway, what we did, we just basically would kick in the door, and I would go in there and I would tell them, "Look, you're dealing, and from now on this is my town. These are my streets, I own the Bay Area. Anything that moves in here is mine, and you're dealing drugs in my town, so you're going to pay me, or you're going out of business. If you're going to continue to deal, then you're paying," and that's the way I did it. I would, like, for example, go in there. Once we got in, then take 'em down, get all their shit, and I would say, "What have you got here?" Okay, if the dude has a pound of dope there, I would say, "Look, you haven't been paying your rent. From now on, you're gonna. I can take all your money, I can take all your dope, I'm not gonna do that. I'm gonna take my share." I would take 25 percent from the drug dealers, and I would leave them the rest of their money and dope. I would take our cut and would tell them, "From now on, this is how it's gonna go." We didn't really get much objection there; everybody kinda got in line there, because they liked it better than losing everything, believe it or not. They would say, "Who you gonna protect me from?" "I'm gonna protect you from me. That's the first place you're buying protection from, from me, and anybody else who comes against you, we are going to protect you from." So that's how we dealt with the drug people, with our connections. That's how we started establishing our protection racket. Then we got into loan sharking too, loaning people money and collecting and stuff like that, and then we bought a bar. We were doing good, we were rolling, and we would make our hits when we had to make our hits. One of the things I had done though, when I had seen the Constitution, one of the things I had seen in the Constitution was the way it was written up, so I said, "Hey, this first captain has too much power. And it seems to me that the general is just a figure head and that the first captain has all the power and there's no checks and balances on him and he's put checks and balances on everybody including the general except for him." And I'd be told, "Hey, you can't be saying that stuff." I'd say, "Nah, that's a weakness, man." "Well, that's Death Row Joe." "I don't give a fuck who it is, that's a weakness."

So Death Row Joe got word of this, that I was bumping the Constitution and I was questioning him, right? So he didn't like me. Let's just put it that way, but I was under the Rock and under Larry and a couple of captains, lower captains. I was producing, man. I was making money. I was making good money for them and robberies, you know. I was good at armed robberies, so I taught these guys. They had them running out there, robbing liquor stores and little mom and pop markets and shit like that. A few hundred dollars here, a few hundred dollars there, and that wasn't nothing. So I taught them how to do real robberies. We knocked off more Safeways, Luckys, banks, even major restaurants, hotels, and stuff like that. Because I knew how to do it. I knew how to go in there, and I went where the money's at. If we're going to do a robbery, I wanted to come out with thirty grand, forty grand, and fifty grand. Those were the kind of robberies worth going to do. We're not going to go rob a liquor store and come out with a couple hundred dollars. That was the first robbery I ever did, by the way, when I was sixteen, a liquor store. I wasn't robbing no more liquor stores. At one point, I thought I robbed everything that had money, anything that made money; I robbed it just to see how much money they had, to learn, for future references in an emergency, what was worth robbing and what wasn't worth robbing. So we were a good, strong regiment. They kept sending me to Salinas too and to San Jose. I was pretty much being moved around, because I was on the run too by now. They were using me up because they knew it was just a matter of time before I was gonna get busted. So I was going all over, and I was trying to teach these guys how we had set it up in the Bay Area. I was helping out in Salinas. Salinas didn't need a whole lot of help; they just needed a little touch up here and there. San Jose needed a lot of help because that's where Rock was going to be going to. That was going to be where he was going to be setting up his regiment. Fresno didn't really need my help that much, other than telling them to stop killing whores. You know, so we're getting organized. That was my first time out, and we finally got regiments going. I want to use an example though, and I'm gonna take a pause here because I got to stop and think about what I'm about to say because I'm sure that there's gonna be police reading this book, so I got to cover myself.

I need to say something here. The thing about La Nuestra Familia, why we were number 1 with a bullet and why we grew so fast, why we were so powerful, is because of our organization, our schooling. The way we schooled, that's what made us, what set us apart from other gang members and stuff. Because we actually schooled, we had classes on how to kidnap, how to extort, how to do robberies, how to murder. I would train guerrilla warfare classes, how to make weapons out of anything. We trained—that was the difference between a La Nuestra Familia soldier and a Mexican Mafia or an Aryan Brotherhood. Although the

Aryan Brotherhood eventually started training too, started catching up, or the BGF, most of them would just get out and kill, you know. Us, we wanted to organize, as long as we had our schooling. Even the police and the FBI, they would say, "Man, their schooling is sharp!" You know what I mean? And I am proud to say I wrote up a lot of that. It was the schooling, but what I want to say is this, we always believed this, that all you needed to establish a regiment was a good lieutenant, a well-schooled, experienced, seasoned lieutenant, and a couple of willing educated soldiers. That's all you needed to go out and build a regiment to start. Because the lieutenant would be the one directing everything, and the soldiers would be the ones doing all the executions and the muscle work. So that's what helped us, and that's what gave us the edge over everybody; it was our schooling. I could probably go into another whole book on our schooling, how important our schooling was. You know, we would get guys that came over from Mexico that couldn't read or write or didn't speak English. The first thing we would do, we would say, "Look, you gotta learn English," so we'd teach them English, and you got to learn how to read and write, so we'd make them go to school. We educated our soldiers—that's one of the things we did. We were strong in education. One of the things that Macarone, out of Stockton, had was he was a good education lieutenant. You know, he was good with that, so we knew we were good at that. We tried to pick the right lieutenants to head our right departments. You know, the teachers, the squad leaders. Teachers, that's what squad leaders and lieutenants were. We would teach these guys who had heart and who were loyal; we would educate them, "This is how you go out there and you establish a regiment. This is how you take over it, this is how you infiltrate," and I've already gone over that; I know that. I mentioned that, but it's really important to understand that what set us apart was our schooling. That was what gave us the edge in our organization, how we organized; that gave us the edge over everybody, and we became number 1 with a bullet.

Like I said, we were not just created to go out and kill people and make money just to send it back to guys that had life, although that was part of it. Because there were brothers who had created us who were never going to get out of prison, and there were some brothers that were going to end up on death row. Like Bobby Loco, Huevo, the true Familianos—dedicated, die-hard, loyal soldiers who were the victims of an abusive person in authority, a piece of shit named Lucky, who was a coward who wanted to be a gangster but who didn't have the balls to take the hit that sometimes comes with being a leader. Sadder still was Lucky was stupid too; he never should have been given any position of rank or authority. I blame him for Bobby and Huevo being on death row for a bullshit kill. They were innocent of committing it, and it was a bullshit kill that went down just so Lucky could act for a while, like he was a gangster. Bobby Loco was one of the most dedicated Familianos we ever produced, and Huevo proved he was too. I love you, Bobby and Huevo. You ever need anything, you just call me. There were some brothers that were going to get shipped all around the country; we had to provide for them too. But our goal was to take over the streets, to establish families, not just regiments, but families. Like I said, *The Godfather* type thing—that was our goal, to take control. In the course of doing all that, I had to talk to a lot of people. I had to deal with the Hells Angels, the Black Mafia, the Black Guerrilla Family, even the EME and AB. I conducted business with my enemies. Because sometimes, there were smart enough leaders in the other groups, who understood. "We could spend all our time running around here shootin' the shit out of each other, but nobody's gonna make no money. Why don't we just pretend we don't see each other out here for a while? You go over there, and I'll go over here. You work there, and I'll work here, and as long as we don't have conflict, we're all right. I don't have time to be running around trying to kill you. You don't have time to be running around trying to kill me. It's about money." That's what it was always about—it was always about money. As long as you produced money, you were all right. And unfortunately, it got to the point where this fucking idiot Death Row was starting to have us kill more of our own than we were killing of the enemies. Well, I can't say that I never did, because I did, but I'll say that I didn't kill my own brothers, not anyone that I loved and had loved me and that I knew were Familia. They were Familianos to the core, you know? But traders, real traders, not just because a guy who should not have never got in got out, he decided he didn't want nothing to have to do with it. You know, to me it was like, "Why the hell are we doing this?" You know, at one point, we had numbers that had reached a thousand. I said, "Why are we recruiting all these guys that we're going to end up having to kill?" Because once you're in and you get the secrets, we just couldn't let you walk away. Especially if you're getting involved in stuff that could jeopardize other people, so, you know, you got to go. Traders, yeah, but people who just walked away, "Hey, do me a favor, right now." Like I would say in meetings and stuff like that, "If there's any of you here that are not really here for the long run, because I'm telling you it's gonna be a hard run, do me a favor and just leave. Just go home, pack your shit and just go, you know. I don't want to kill you, just keep your mouth shut, as long as you ain't pointing your finger at somebody in the courtroom, I'm not worrying about you." That was my philosophy; there were other idiots who were like, "Oh no, we got to kill them, we got to kill them." They would end up being the biggest traders there were. You know an example, like, one time in San Jose, this one clown was a captain, and everybody got busted. So he told everybody, all the soldiers there, "Nobody takes a deal, because if nobody takes a deal, we can clog up the court, and they're going to have to start dismissing cases. They can't take us all to trial at the same time." So he's telling everybody nobody takes a deal. And the reason why he did this was because he turned around and he wanted them to offer him the deal. So when they offered him the deal, he flipped, and everybody that was under him got fucked. So there are examples like that. I think that in any organization, there's gonna be that kind of crap. I hated that, and anybody I saw like that, to me, was a trader. Somebody that would sell out one of his own men. That's my number 1 no-no. You can't do that. And when you put yourself above the regiment or above the brotherhood, the family, then you got to go; that's all there is to it.

Did we have fucked up leadership? Yes, we did. Did it need to be changed? Yes, it needed to be changed. I mean, D. R. had to go, period. Babo had to step down because of what he had done, you know. He had fallen in love with one of the soldiers' wives. First chance he got to have that soldier killed, he had him killed so he could have his wife. That was wrong; he had to step down. Though the soldier did technically fuck up, by the Constitution, you know, he was supposed to be hit. But he could have been given a pass too; it didn't have to go down that way, and Babo shouldn't have taken his old lady. So everybody started talking about needing a change in our leadership. I remember Black Bob being in the hole with him, all of us saying, "Yeah, we need changes." But there was a way to do it, and it was by the Constitution.

Now one thing, when you get in there and you start spilling blood and you start taking human lives, man, it's not just something. Maybe there are some people whom it doesn't bother, but it bothers me. You know, do you do it? Yes, you do it. Does it bother you? Yes, it bothers me. Especially if it's not what you think should be done. You think somebody should be given a pass; instead, they want to kill them. You think somebody could be reeducated, but no, they want to disrespect them. It's crazy. It got to the point where we started killing more of ourselves, each other, than we were killing our enemies. Like I said, that was bad; that was not good. It got to the point where there was a group of us hard-core old-timers. We just said, "No more, that's it." We made a pact. "They try to come for you, we're coming. They try to come for me, you're coming." We had each other's backs; we knew change was in the wind.

Cornejo and Bob, they had things in the works, so they were going to steal the regiment; they were going to steal the family. What they did was fucked up; it caused a civil war to jump off, and like I said, I had sworn an allegiance to a Constitution. I remember the day when they gathered us all together there. This happened after I had returned and had been shown by the police that my own name, Sundown, was on our gang's confiscated hit list. I know I'm bouncing around here, but it's the only way that I know how to tell this story and be faithful to the truth. But back to the streets now, I'll return to this day later in the story.

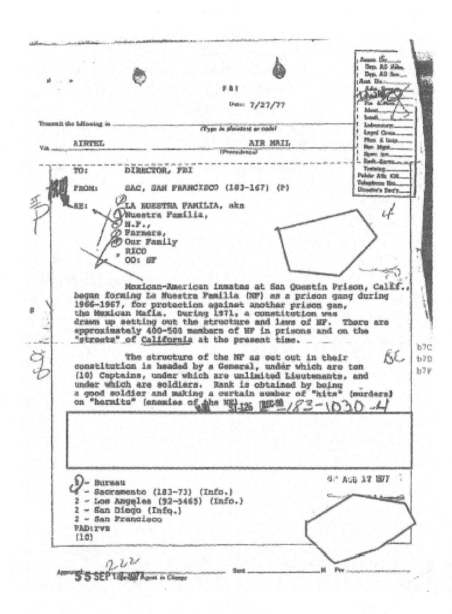

FBI

Date: 7/27/77

Transmit the following in _____
(Type in plaintext or code)

Via AIRTEL _____ AIR MAIL
(Priority)

TO: DIRECTOR, FBI

FROM: SAC, SAN FRANCISCO (183-167) (P)

RE: LA NUESTRA FAMILIA, aka
        Nuestra Familia,
        N.F.,
        Farmers,
        Our Family
        RICO
        OO: SF

        Mexican-American inmates at San Quentin Prison, Calif.,
began forming La Nuestra Familia (NF) as a prison gang during
1966-1967, for protection against another prison gang,
the Mexican Mafia. During 1971, a constitution was
drawn up setting out the structure and laws of NF. There are
approximately 400-500 members of NF in prisons and on the
"streets" of California at the present time.

        The structure of the NF as set out in their
constitution is headed by a General, under which are ten
(10) Captains, under which are unlimited Lieutenants, and
under which are soldiers. Rank is obtained by being
a good soldier and making a certain number of "hits" (murders)
on "hermits" (enemies of the NF).

b7C
b7D
b7E

REC-58 183-1030-4

9 - Bureau   AUG 17 1977
    - Sacramento (183-73) (Info.)
2 - Los Angeles (92-3465) (Info.)
2 - San Diego (Info.)
2 - San Francisco
PAD:rvs
(16)

Approved _____ Sent _____ M Per _____
         5 SEP 1977 Special Agent in Charge

SF 183-167
PAD:rvs

The constitution of the NF sets up a system of banks for handling money obtained from illegal operations. The illegal money is to be funneled into legal enterprises.

NF members have engaged in murders, selling of illegal drugs, prostitution and robberies. There have been over twenty (20) murders linked to NF in the last year.

b7C
b7D
b7E

The following are the "regiments" of NF in the "streets" of California:

1.
2.
3.
4.
5.
6.

Los Angeles and Sacramento have active investigations of NF. Investigation continuing in San Francisco to develop a RICO violation.

UNITED STATES DEPARTMENT OF JUSTICE
FEDERAL BUREAU OF INVESTIGATION

Copy to:	1 - Strike Force, San Francisco
Report by: Date:	11/1/77 b7C
Office:	SAN FRANCISCO, CA.
Field Office File #:	183-167
Bureau File #:	
Title:	LA NUESTRA FAMILIA

Character: RACKETEER INFLUENCED AND CORRUPT ORGANIZATIONS

Synopsis: La Nuestra Familia (NF) was formed in 1968 of Mexican-American inmates and is a California prison based gang of 200 to 400 operating in the prisons and on the streets of California. NF has a written Constitution and By-Laws setting up banks for illegal money to be put in to legal enterprises. The NF is headed by a general and has captains, lieutenants, and soldiers. Rank is obtained by killing enemies of the NF. Three kills are necessary to be a lieutenant, unless you kill one of top ten enemies of NF and then only one kill necessary. NF charging prostitutes to work in Fresno, CA. Alleged the NF attempting to extort money from legal businesses. NF document gives instructions on using children for illegal activities. NF members alleged to be involved in over fifty (50) homicides since 1975. MEMBERS OF THE NF HAVE BEEN KNOWN TO ENGAGE IN VIOLENT ACTS SO MEMBERS OF THE NF SHOULD BE CONSIDERED ARMED AND DANGEROUS.

- P -

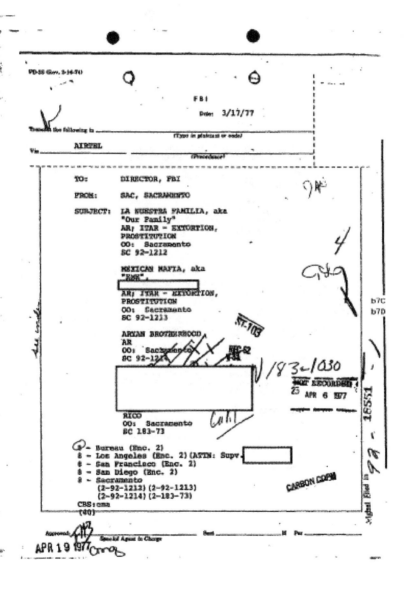

SC 92-1212

Enclosed to the Bureau and receiving offices are two copies each of an article appearing in the Fresno Bee newspaper of 3/11/77 which synopsizes the current problem of the Mexican Mafia and the Nuestra Familia in the State of California.

For the information of the Bureau and receiving offices, Sacramento is instituting investigation of the captioned organizations and individuals, based on the enclosed newspaper article and the following information.

In recent years, there has been an increase in violence and criminal activity on the part of the captioned organizations, which had their origins within the California Prison System. These groups have now spread to the civilian population outside the prison system and have evidenced a high degree of organization. Recent informant information obtained by state and local authorities indicates well organized criminal activity is planned and perpetrated by these groups. Documents seized during local arrests of Nuestra Familia (NF) members discuss in succinct form the intended criminal activity to be undertaken to finance the gang's operations in the areas of prostitution, narcotics, robbery and extortion.

Some examples of criminal activity undertaken by these gangs in the recent past, in the areas of FBI jurisdiction, are as follows:

Sacramento file 91-8130

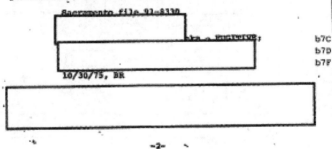

b7C
b7D
b7F

10/30/75, BR

-2-

SC 92-

[California Department] of Corrections, 3001 E Street, Sacramento, California, has advised that he has been following the progress of the MF and the EM for the past four years. He advised these two organizations have increased their membership dramatically and may have as many as 300 to 400 members in the State of California. He stated all of the prison gang organizations are involved in murder, extortion, narcotics and robberies. [   ] has been in recent contact with the state authorities in Texas, New Mexico and Arizona who have acknowledged existence of captioned organizations in their respective states. As several of the members of captioned organizations have been convicted of federal violations and are now serving sentences in federal institutions, recruiting for these organizations will undoubtedly be conducted within the Federal Prison System and in all probability will further the organizations' geographical influence.

b7C
b7D
b7F

-4-

Chapter

10

I'm jumping ahead of myself; I want to go back to the streets. You know, before the civil war, before I came back. With the establishing of regiments, what we did was get the whores organized, the drug dealers, loan sharking, killing our enemies, stuff like that—all that was what we were supposed to be doing. But what I want to show you is we did some pretty organized shit; we were pretty smart, you know. We went from street whores, to escort service. It was very lucrative. So the regiment got up and running in the Bay Area. Now I was sent, like I said, to San Jose and to Salinas. I was kinda being moved about. They saw that I was producing, and that what I was doing was working, so they're sending me everywhere. And also, I was on the run. I had been arrested in a hostage situation in Hayward, California. It was front-page news; it was even on the news on TV. Because of Satin, the headlines said, "Exotic dancer talks Gunman into surrendering." Which was all bullshit. There was no robbery attempt; it was just something that snowballed into a hostage situation. I had sixteen hostages I had taken in a bar because the police forced it into a hostage situation with the newly formed SWAT teams. The first use of a SWAT team in California had just happened down in Southern California, where the Symbionese Liberation Army, the SLA members, had all been killed by the police and barbequed by the fire created in the house. So I had the unique honor of being only the second time in California police history of them using the newly formed SWAT team. It was big news for a few months, and then they captured Bill and Emily Harris, who had the heiress Patty Hearst with them. The irony of that was Bill Harris became my cellmate for a while, and I got close to the remaining SLA members. Bill and Emily, Russell Little, Joe Romero, our paths had crossed, and we all became friends for a while. It's funny. I was in jail with Sonny Barger of the Hells Angels, in prison with Donald De Freeze, the SLA leader, and Joseph and Russell of the SLA in San Quentin. Anthony Bottoms, the leader of the Black Liberation Army of the East Coast; Steve Browning, who inherited the leadership of the BGF, whom I loved, he was my friend. He had the BGF meet me in San Quentin as I got off the bus, to protect me from the Mexican Mafia there at the time. Anyway, I escaped after they arrested me and was back to work again on the streets for a few more deadly months. They wanted to use me up, and D. R. had made one mistake. The lieutenant that I was put up under was a good lieutenant; he was loyal, and I'm not gonna say his name because, like I said, murder can get you at any time. His wife was visiting D. R.; she was the runner, and she would take the instructions and orders from D. R. straight to him. He would in turn pass it on down to us. One time, we were told—well, let me show you something. There were things I did, because D. R., every time something came down, he used me up. And when D. R. flipped, he tried to betray me. Stupid idiot, he had me do all these hits and he had me do all this stuff, but the only one who could actually say that I did this stuff was D. R. and this lieutenant or the runner. So later on, when RICO came in, they started hitting us all with RICO; they had to prove a chain, of a continuing conspiracy, criminal conspiracy. Well, D. R. had this lieutenant and his wife killed for stealing some money; he claimed they had stolen some money. The truth is that D. R. stole all the money; he used our money to support his friends and family while brothers were sacrificing and were sometimes broke. D. R.'s people were all driving around in brand-new cars and living in new houses. When stupid-ass Babo finally woke up enough to ask D. R., "Hey, where's all the money? I'm reading in the newspapers about all these crimes we're committing, so where's the money?" D. R. lied against my lieutenant and set him up with his wife to be killed and barbequed in a car fire. They were killed and burned up in their car. So all the stuff that D. R. could have told on me, and he tried to tell on me, could not be collaborated. Because he had killed the two people who could have said, "Yes, Sundown did all this stuff that D.R. says he did."

So that's why they couldn't get me on that stuff, and believe me, they tried. I believed that we were a noble thing. Because we're out there, and we're trying to establish regiments and families, look out for each other, take care of our brothers in prison, and look out for our families out here. Anybody disrespects anybody in our families, we take care of it. Our families have needs; we'll take care of it. Be self-sufficient, that's what we were doing. Well, I was given a little squad to work with, a couple of soldiers to carry out stuff. This one time, they wanted me to go to this drug dealer, a major drug dealer. I mean, this guy was big, he was from Mexico, and his stuff was coming up from Mexico. Now that was back when the Mexicans in Mexico, the Mexico Mexican Mafia, organized Mexican groups back there; they were trying to establish in California. But the problem was that the Californian Mexican Mafia controlled Southern California, and La Nuestra Familia controlled Northern California. So anything that they did, they were going to have to go through us, to pay us. So we're going to go to this guy's house. We knew this guy was big. He's major; he's got a wife, a teenage son, and a teenage daughter. He lived in a real nice house. This guy's moving major weight, and he had major money. We got to take him out, not kill him. We're gonna go in there, and we're gonna tell him, "Hey, you're gonna work for us now. You're gonna pay a percentage now." So I was given a couple of guys to work with, and it just so happened that this other brother was getting out. What would happen when a brother would get out is, usually they would have someone meet you, and if there was time, there would be some prostitute there to suck his dick or give him some pussy, if that was what the brother wanted. Sometimes they'd even just have the whores pick them up, depending on what was going on. This time, we had to pick him up, this brother who must have had something on him or something. Usually, when you had some question mark on you, you were going to have to put in work to clear that question mark off you. It usually meant that you're going to have to kill somebody to prove your loyalty, to reestablish your good standing, stuff like that. When they tell you to pick this guy up and take him with you and use him, you kinda got an idea he is in trouble of some kind. Well, too, there's also the other thing too, that this guy could be the one that they're sending in to replace you.

When I had got out, I was told the first time, "Hey, go out there and check on the regiment that's out there. Make sure it's running right. If need be, I want you to take over the regiment, but mainly I want you to start establishing a regiment ultimately in San Jose for me." But the one in the Bay Area, like I said, had its problems, and I had to step in and take over. Then I was sent over to start working in San Jose, Salinas, and Fresno. So I was told that, hey, since I was so good at this, I was given a squad to take and represent the NF and to go talk to this guy. This was what I did; I was the best at it. But they told me to pick up this brother. And we'll just call him Lupe. Okay, so we went to pick up Lupe. He's gonna go with us. Now this brother had been down for a while; I think he'd been down for ten years. He's an older guy. He was like in his late thirties. He's older than me at the time. When we picked him up, because we're going on this job, we're told to take him with us, and I was like, "Well, this guy hasn't been schooled yet, I haven't worked with him." "Take him with you, all right." So, you know, you follow orders, so okay, I took him with me, and they're like, "If anyone has to be killed, make him do the hit." So here we go, if it goes sour, he's the one that has to kill. They wanted him to make whatever kill that has to go down.

We're not going there to kill, but if it turned to that, we would make him do it. Okay, so he must have something on him. Now I knew he's not being sent out to replace anybody; he's just being sent out to clear up his name. We picked him up, and the first thing that he's talking about was, "Hey, man, I've been locked down awhile. I want to get my dick sucked. I want to fuck. Where's the girls?" and shit like that. And I told him, "We ain't got time for that right now. You're gonna go with us, and after that, you can go get your dick sucked all you want and fuck all you want and party all you want." I gave him a briefing on what we're going to do; I briefed everybody. We've already cased this place; we cased the guy's house, and I said, "Look, this is what's in there, he's got himself, his wife, and he's got two teenage kids, a son who was seventeen and a daughter who was fifteen, some dogs, and some shit like that. So we're gonna go in, and this is how we're going to take it off." Everybody had their role to play. We spent a couple of hours briefing. We went to look at the place. We're going to wait tell it got dark to hit it and shit, and this guy kept saying, "Don't we have time to, let me go pick up on some pussy?" I said, "You ain't going nowhere, you're staying right here." We're getting ready, we hit the place, and we got in, so now I told these guys to get everybody together. We got them all together; I got the guy, the target we're going after. He's a border brother, what we call a border brother. A border brother means he's from Mexico. He speaks some English but not that good. His wife, she was fine, very fine; she spoke English and Spanish. His son and his daughter, they both spoke English. His son was, like, seventeen, like I said, and the daughter was, like, fifteen. We went in there, we gathered them all together, and we got them inside the main room there. Now we caught these people in bed. So we got this guy, and he's in his boxers. I got the wife; she's in this sexy-ass see-through baby-doll thing, right. This woman was sexy; she had these big-ass fucking tits, big-ass dark nipples, hairy-ass bush, and big nice butt. She was fine. We caught the son, and this guy had on some little leopard jockey shorts. We called them come-fuck-mes in prison because nobody wears those except for the homosexuals, but they were little jockey shorts. I guess he thought he was a playboy or whatever, and he had a T-shirt on also. The daughter, she was in her little pajamas. She had a pair of panties and a pajama top. So we got them in there all together now. What you have to understand is that when you go in and you're doing this kinda stuff, there's a sense of power. This overriding power, because you're in here and you could kill these people or you can do anything you want with these people, you got to be careful. Because that has turned bad sometimes, and I'm gonna give you an example.

Remember, my job was not to just go in there and take everything he's got; we're not there for that. We wanted him to work for us, we wanted his connections, and we wanted his drugs. My job was to go in there and impress upon him that he needed our protection. You know, and of course, I would take the customary 25 percent of whatever he's got there. He wanted our protection from us and from other gangs that were doing the same thing. He's gonna work for us because, let me explain something to you, the way I believed, the way we believed, especially me, was that this was the jungle and we were tigers and I was the biggest, baddest tiger in this jungle, as far as I was concerned. And if you were in my jungle, you were going to pay rent. Or you were going to answer for it; that's just the way it was. I hate to say this, but I was God. God forgive me for saying that, but that's how I felt—on these streets, I ruled. Whatever I say goes when I've got that gun in my hands. I was there to represent, and I was there to convince this guy that he wanted to work for us. So we wanted it to go smooth. Well, now, like I said, his wife, I mean, she may as well have been naked, you know, and his teenage daughter, god, the girl. If she was fifteen, she looked like she was twenty-two. And I got this guy, and my guys were like, "Man!" Everybody was just, you know, we're guys; we're checking the wife and the daughter out right. But this Lupe, he's really like, "Hey, are we gonna fuck these bitches. Are we gonna fuck them?" I was like, "Man, shut the fuck up. We ain't here to do stupid shit like that." So I told the soldiers, "Hey, take them kids and take them in the other room and hold them there and don't do nothing to them. Don't hurt them, just hold them there. All right? I'm gonna talk to the father here and the wife." I got one of my soldiers with me, and we're talking to them. I was trying to show them that we're people of class, we're sophisticated, we're like the Italian Mafia, you know, we're bon a fide. "You need to work for us. You see how we got in here. We can come back anytime. We could have killed you." I was doing my usual spiel. "As long as you work with us, we'll protect you. If you don't work with us, then we're gonna kill you. That's just the way it's gonna be," and I was also telling him I wanted all his drugs and all his money. I wanted him to produce them; I wanted to see what he's got. This guy's playing stupid. He started trying to clam up, and he ain't giving nothing up. His wife was like, "Hey, tell them, man, give it up." Well, what I had to do once I saw that this fool wasn't cooperating and playing stupid, I told the brother with me, "Go bring me his daughter." So he went in there, and he brought me his daughter. Well, he left Lupe alone with the boy, right, guarding the boy, and he brought the daughter to me. I told the father, "Look, do you want us to take turns raping your wife and your daughter in front of you before we cut your throat and kill you? Because that's what we will do." The wife right away, she's like, "No, no, no, not my daughter. Not my daughter, not my son. Rape me, you guys can do anything you want to me," and she's telling him, "Give them the stuff. Tell them where the stuff is!" This guy was still playing stupid. We grabbed his daughter, and we laid her down and said, "We're going to do this in front of you. You get to watch, and then I'm gonna kill you." We weren't really going to do this, but that's what made him break. So he's all, "Okay, okay, okay, okay," because his wife was threatening him now. She's like, "If you don't tell them, I'll kill you." So we got all his drugs, got all his money. It's all there, and it's a lot, you know. I was telling them, "Look, sorry the way it had to go down, but this is the way it goes." We took our cut, and we told him, "Look, we're going to represent you. I want to do business with you, and if you try to go to anybody or anything like that, we're just going to kill you. This is just the nature of the beast, you know. You're from Mexico, you're over here. You've been getting away with this all this time. Now it's time to pay the piper." So I took mine; the brothers were like, "Hey, the wife's offering to let us fuck her, let us fuck her," and I was saying, "Nah, we ain't here to do that. What kinda reflection is that on us, you know? We're organized businessmen." Well, all this time, I didn't know what's going on with Lupe in the back room. We got our money and everything, and we're getting ready to peel up out of there, and I told them to go get Lupe and bring the boy. So the brother went and he came back and he looked at me and he kinda pulled me over and he said, "Hey, Lupe ain't coming out." He didn't tell me what he's doing, but I knew something's not right. So I said, "All right, hold these people." I went inside there, and I opened the back bedroom door, and there's Lupe. He's got this boy, and he's fucking this boy in the ass, this seventeen-year-old teenage boy. He's butt-fucking him, and I was like, "Oh my god, oh my fucking god." So I was telling him to get off him. "What the fuck is wrong with you? We're not here for that!" He's telling me, "Man, I ain't had no pussy in a while. Man, I been locked up ten years. I'm almost done." I was like, "Get the fuck off this dude!" Then this asshole reached for his fucking gun. He had the nerve to raise it up at me and say, "I'm gonna finish, man." I was like, "Dude, we're leaving. You can stay, but we're leaving. You better be done." Just then, all of a sudden, he's finishing, and he's like, "Ahhahhah." He finished fucking this kid, man, and got up and wiped his dick off with the kid's underwear and pulled his pants up. "Oh man, I needed that. All right, brother, sorry, brother, you know it's been a long time. Let's get the fuck out of here." And I was thinking, "Oh fuck," so I told the kid before I left, "Don't tell anything to your father. Don't say anything to your father. Don't tell anybody what happened here, because then, I'll have to come back and kill you all." One of the things that this asshole Lupe was trying to tell me while he was having sex with the kid was,

"He wants it, he likes it. He's a little puto, you know, see." This guy was sick with it, man. He's fucking the kid on his side, and he's jacking the kid off at the same time he's fucking him, and the kid had a hard-on, you know. I was like, "Maybe the kid is a little faggot. Maybe that's why he had the little panties on. I don't know, but this is not what we were here to do. And this motherfucker never should have pulled that gun on me." So we left, we got out of there, we took off, and we got a lot of money and a lot of dope. This was a major connection. This guy had money; he had drugs.

The problem was, we got in there and represented ourselves as this organized gang, like the Italian Mafia, you know? How's it gonna look that we're just fucking perverts out of prison, butt-fucking boys, right? So I said, "Oh fuck, man." Even before we're leaving, I was thinking, I may as well just go in there and kill everybody and just take everything, because this guy ain't gonna work with us. If he finds out that his kid was just butt-fucked, he's probably gonna use everything he's got to try to get back at us, you know. He might go side with the Mexican Mafia. I was like, "Fuck, let's just get the fuck out of here," and so we left. You know, everybody knew what went down, the soldiers, the rest of the squad, and this guy's telling us not to tell on him. He's sorry, but you know, he was horny. I should have thought about this earlier. Earlier, Lupe had even mentioned, "Hey, I'll even settle for a punk. You know what I mean." I didn't trip on that, but later on, he's in there fucking this boy. And he pulled a gun, you know. He didn't really point it at me. He lifted the gun up and said he was gonna finish, so I was thinking, "'Well, he shouldn't ever had done that." So, the long and short of it is, it's a done deal, man. He was even telling this kid that he had the best ass he ever had and "I love you and I'll be back to see you" and all that other shit. I don't know what all went on there. I just knew that this was not a good reflection on us. We were not a bunch of guys that go in there and rape boys and shit. So I got to deal with this dude. I was gonna kill him. I was gonna kill him for what he did. I was gonna kill him because he raised that gun at me. But you know, this was one of Death Row Joe's boys. So you know what was I gonna do? I got to be careful about how I do this. But this guy's got to go.

This is embarrassing to me; it's an embarrassment, and I don't want people thinking that's what the La Nuestra Familia is. I'm thinking, you know? He had the girl back there too, not to justify it, and I'm not saying it's right or wrong or anything like that, but if it were me and if I were that horny and that crazy, I think I would have fucked the girl. You know? Not the boy, or maybe because we pulled the girl out and left him with the boy, I don't know. I mean, that's just sick. And this is not what La Nuestra Familia is.

We got orders, I think about a month later, to hit this other brother, one of our brothers. It's like, "Hey, take him out and kill him," and again, Death Row Joe said, "Make sure Sundown does it and make sure he takes Lupe with him." They wanted Lupe to do the killing. The brother they wanted us to kill, he was an all right brother. He just got tired and said, "Hey, I'm not with this shit." I guess it just wasn't what he really wanted to be about. He said, "I'm done. I'm not gonna do anything, I'm not gonna tell, I'm just gonna do my own thing." He was told, "No, you're not going to do that." So we got orders to hit him. I was curious as to why this loyal brother said no more. Because I knew he had killed for us, and he was loyal. They wanted me to get him to come out of hiding. They knew that he would trust me and that I could get him. I got at him, and I asked him, "What's up, brother? Why are you doing this?" He told me why they wanted him hit. While I had gone to Fresno for a while, they put this Lupe in charge of a mission because Lupe knew the target: a Mexican Mafia associate who was dealing in our territory. There were three targets, two dudes and a broad. They were to kill all three of them. They went in and took control of the targets and the house. They got all their dope and money, but before they killed them, Lupe decided he wanted them to rape the broad in front of the boyfriend; also, the broad had a baby in the house. She was actually worse than the two Mexican Mafia guys as far as preaching pro-Mexican Mafia in the town, and she was one tough bitch. That night, she offered to let each of the brothers fuck her. She promised them the best fuck and sucking of their dicks they ever had. And even if they wanted to fuck her in her ass, they could. She told them she would give them each a good fuck with no resistance in exchange for not killing her baby. He said she was fine too, so they went ahead and fucked her. Lupe didn't want to fuck her; he wanted to fuck one of the guys in the ass before they killed him, for revenge because one of these dudes knew Lupe. He was calling Lupe a puto who got turned out in the county jail and now was clowning them and the Nuestra Familia for having homosexuals in their gang. He was calling Lupe a faggot who loved it in his ass. Lupe shot him because the dude kept telling them that they were taking orders from a faggot. After Lupe killed that dude and then watched them take turns fucking the broad, Rudy even confessed that he fucked her too because it was just all crazy there, and everyone else was getting their dicks sucked and fucking her and enjoying it. She was like no broad he had ever seen before. She knew she was gonna die, but she had heart and all she kept asking each brother as she was fucking them was that since she was giving them the best sex they ever had, she only wanted each brother to promise her they would not kill her baby. Rudy said he felt like shit for fucking her too, and she told him she didn't trust Lupe not to kill her baby after they were done with her and killed her too. She made him promise her that he would protect her baby from Lupe after they killed her. That's when he said he knew he couldn't kill her if ordered to. He promised her he would save her baby no matter what. He said he was still hiding her and her baby with some of his family in another town. He knew he would get hit for letting her get away. Lupe wanted to fuck the other guy in the ass, and he made two of the brothers hold the guy down while he tried to fuck him in the ass. He said he was showing them who the faggots were. But Lupe couldn't finish or something. His dick wouldn't stay hard or some shit. So they just killed him. Lupe gathered all the dope and money and left Rudy and the other brother there to finish fucking the broad with orders to kill her after he finished. They were to kill the baby too, to really send a message to everybody who ruled this town. Both Rudy and the other brother didn't want to kill no baby, so Rudy told the other brother to just go out to the car and wait for him. That he would take care of everything. The other brother agreed with him that it wasn't cool to kill no baby and that Lupe was nuts. He didn't want to be killed for disobeying a direct order though. That's when brother Rudy told him, "Just tell them I told you to wait in the car because I wanted to finish fucking the broad, that I said I would take care of both the broad and the baby."

They agreed on that, and while the other brother waited in the car as he had been ordered to, Rudy got the broad and her baby and walked them out the back door. He took them to his sister's house to hide them from Lupe, and that's when he decided no more. He didn't sign up for this kinda shit. The problem was that this broad was a real enemy; she was a diehard mafia runner and associate and had set brothers up in the past. When Lupe reported it to D. R., he left out the sick shit and denied he said to kill the baby, that Rudy was a coward who didn't kill the broad as he was ordered. Lupe gave all the dope and money straight to D. R.'s runner to cover his ass.

Just then, after he told me the story of what happened, Lupe rolled up on us and pulled his gun on Rudy and told me, "Good job, bro. We got him, let's take him out to the fields." Now, I did not want to hit this brother. Like I said, I was not about hitting my brothers. So we went. We got Rudy, and we went and we pulled over. The brother knew we're going to kill him, man, so he told me, "I don't want to die, of course." You know, but he knows it's his time and we're going to kill him. So he said, "Hey, can I say a prayer first before you kill me?" I say, "Okay, go ahead and say your prayer." So he's saying his prayers now. Lupe was the one who was supposed to pull the trigger. So while Rudy's saying his prayer and as he was finishing praying, I don't know why, but that was the perfect time, you know. Lupe told me, "We should fuck him in the ass first, hahaha. He's a traitor and a coward, and we should make him suck our dicks and take turns fucking him in his ass before we kill him. Hahaha."

I shot Lupe. I killed him. I shot him dead. The other brother, Rudy, that we were supposed to take out, he was just in shock. He's still on his knees, praying. He was in shock that I had turned around and shot the shit out of Lupe. So I told the brother, "Come on, get up. I'm not gonna kill you, man." So I took him, and I told him, "Look, I love you, man. I know that you just couldn't take no more of this shit. Lupe is not what La Nuestra Familia is about. He's just a piece of shit that slipped in. If you want, I'll go to the leadership for you and explain what Lupe did and how he ordered you guys to kill a baby. I'm sure they will understand and be grateful that we took Lupe out. But they're gonna still want to kill the broad because of all the shit she had been talking against us for the Mexican Mafia and for the shit she did against some of the brothers." Rudy said, "No, D. R. won't care. He will still want me hit, and I'm not gonna give up the broad to be hit because she's not the same broad anymore. She's changed after that night. All she wants to do is go to church and raise her baby safely." I asked him, "What's up with you and this broad? You got feelings for her now or something?" Rudy admitted that he and this broad are together now. They will never go to the police or turn about the killings of the other two dudes that night. They just wanted to be left alone and just take their chances. Rudy said the only reason we got him that night was because of me. He only came out of hiding because it was me asking for him, and he trusted me. I told him, "From now on, don't trust anyone, not even me." Then I told him, "I'll give you a ride back into town where I picked you up, but once you get out of the car, go, disappear, man. Don't come back, because what I'm going to say is that we went out to hit you, that you were ready for us. Lupe was supposed to have shook you down and you had a piece on you and you shot him, okay?" "All right, all right, all right. Hahahah!" He was just happy to live. Crazy shit you do, you know? I don't know, maybe because he was kneeling praying. I don't know, maybe because that sick-ass Lupe said we should butt-fuck him first, you know, and he was serious. He wanted to fuck this other brother in the ass. I was like, "What kind of motherfucking animal have I got here? What the fuck are we recruiting? I had planned to get rid of him anyway at one time, so it might as well be now. They wanted a dead brother—they got one."

I'd like to say something here too, you know, when brothers did start turning and testifying against other brothers. There were these three lieutenants, ex-lieutenants, who were testifying, soldiers and lieutenants, and they kept asking them about me. And they would tell them, "You could ask us about anybody, anything about ourselves, but we will never tell you anything about Sundown." You know, so I still love those guys. The guys that they did turn on, they were pieces of shit too, as far as I was concerned. Turning is wrong, but at least they never turned on me. And I mean it, they really said that, "We will tell on anybody, but we will never tell on Sundown." You know, they couldn't get anybody to turn against me. Could you turn on someone whom you knew loved you? I mean really loved you, and you knew they loved you because you loved them too? Thank God they couldn't and didn't, and they know who they are and I still love them. They were soldiers; they paid their dues. They just didn't like the way we had turned when we turned in on ourselves. It was like a monster had been released, and it had to have its share of blood, even if, sadly, too often, it had become our own.

Back in prison now, and before the civil war. I think one of the things that broke us was, like I said, we started killing each other. In the beginning, we understood that this was not to be just another prison gang and that we were to become an organization. Based along the lines of the Italian Mafia gangsters, we grew up watching and idolizing in Hollywood movies and novels. We were not just Northern gangsters; we were made up of Southern and Northern prisoners, with whites and Puerto Ricans and Indians and even Asians who proved their worthiness by killing to become a member. We warned anyone and everyone if they chose to become a Familiano. There was no turning back or just walking away once you were free from prison. In fact, it clearly states in our Constitution that once you are released from prison, you will be expected to really put in work and make even more sacrifices for the betterment of the organization as a whole. So don't join just because you want recognition, respect, and protection while you're inside a very violent prison environment. Because once you get released, there was no just walking away. You would be killed as an example of how serious we were about our goals of becoming the most powerful criminal organization and family in all of California and eventually the United States. This was our discipline to remind every member and even our enemies of just how serious we were. We understood that there had to be a limit and a goal for us to strive for, to be free from having to keep killing and risking our lives and freedom too. So we made it a rule that once a Familiano had put in twenty years of loyal active service and had reached the age of fifty years old, then he could go into an honorable semiretirement from active duty and service and would only be called upon for active duty again in an emergency and state of war. There in West Hall, I told you about these lieutenants who had turned, and they had had enough. The straw that broke the camel's back, I believe, was Payaso. There was a seventeen-year-old boy who had got in to the La Nuestra Familia in Y. A., when he was sixteen. What we were doing recruiting sixteen-year-old kids, I do not know. You know? But he's a kid! You know, so here he was with all these men, and we're older. Now, *Payaso*, it means "clown." The guy who's running the regiment at the time, interestingly, is K. C. He's the direct link between Babo and us. D. R.'s broke. D. R.'s turned, and so we didn't have any more captains now. All we had was the general and our security lieutenant, K. C. Babo fucked up; they were being hit with cases when D. R. turned. RICO came, all these prosecutions came, and all these murder cases came. So they were so busy fighting their murder cases that they lost sight of what they should have been taking care of. They should have appointed the right captains; they waited too long. And so, well, they had K. C. Interesting thing about K. C. is that K. C. was my kid. When I came back, I met him in Vacaville at the reception center; he had got in at Norco, the CRC rehabilitation center. So he didn't know anything really, but he was holding down the line there, trying his best and doing his best. And so I got there, and I started schooling him. Right away I was schooling him, what to do, you know, so I was giving him schooling while I was there and I was telling him who's to make hits, how to make hits, how to recognize enemies. I spend the time schooling him, then I was transferred. I went to San Quentin. He went to Tracy. I made the route: I went to San Quentin, I went to Folsom, I went to Soledad. I was making the rounds, because that's what they do with me. I go to one penitentiary, I get on line, I catch a case, I get in the hole, and they transfer me. I get out, I catch a case, I get in the hole, and they transfer me. Finally, I made it to Tracy, and K. C.'s in charge there. So I got it made; K. C. loved me. You know, so just stay undercover, just stay down, and stay undercover for now. Don't admit to who you are and what have you as far as that still went. "Omerta for me." But everybody knew; that was the worst undercover thing you ever saw. Because they wanted to try to preserve me, you know. Because like I said, I looked like a white guy. I could pass for a white boy. I could grow my hair long, and I did. I could grow a beard, and I could just infiltrate the whites. They tried to keep that cover for me. K. C. was okay. K. C. was decent, but I guess he wanted to flex his muscle; he wanted to make his bone. I don't know that he ever did, but this kid was always horseplaying, and like I said, we had strict discipline; we didn't play. And if you get told don't horseplay, don't horseplay. Well, this kid, he's a young kid; he's seventeen years old. He's horseplaying, so K. C. told him if he keeps horseplaying, he's gonna have him killed. So, well, the kid, he's seventeen years old. He's a kid; he's goofing off and horseplaying. So K. C. got permission from Babo to kill him. That day, that kid was butchered right there in front of God and everybody. All of us were to watch this; he was butchered, ten feet from me and my feet. There was a change there. I felt it, you know, because a lot of us older guys, we were just pissed that it had come to this. It wasn't so much the killing; we were used to killing. But we were killing this kid for being a kid, for horseplay. You know? That's when guys started turning; guys started leaving. "If this is what we've become, I don't want nothing to do with this," they would say. That's when, I think, we said, "What the fuck, you know, now we're killing kids." K. C. eventually would get hit, and the irony of it was, he hated the Vindiolas. I don't know why, and he did everything he could to try to, you know, discipline Indio Vindiola, because Indio called K. C. white boy and was always complaining that a white boy was in charge of the Mexican La Nuestra Familia. But Indio knew that Nuestra Familia was not just Mexican, neither was it ever about North and South. We were a professional criminal organization, not just a gang. Indio just had no respect for K. C., and like all Vindiolas, he spoke his mind.

Indio Vindiola, this brother, is a warrior to the bone, as were all the Vindiolas. He's just like me; we're not gonna be broken. That's when they started trying to ease the Vindiolas out. One way they would do it was to give you shitty missions, give you discipline up the ass, and hopefully you get discouraged and leave. Well, when the time came to hit K. C., and they put my brother-in-law in charge, who do you think they put on K. C. to hit him? Yeah, Indio. Hahahahahahahahahahaha! Oh, man, I remember that day because the miracle is that K. C. lived, because K. C. was inside the yard shack that was his little office. That office was also used for other things too; that's where guys would go to get their dicks sucked by the homosexuals we had there for sex, for guys who were into that kind of shit. In the yard shack office, you could fuck them in the ass or what have you. You had to put in a request to Loco, who was in charge of the homosexuals, like a pimp. K. C. was in there. Indio went in there, and Indio fucking butchered him, man. When they dragged K. C. out, I swear to God he looked like he was decapitated. His neck was hanging, and he lived, and then he turned. He lived, and he lived to turn around and come back to be a witness in nine murder trials. That's how it worked, you know. It was smart to put Indio on him; Indio got payback.

I want to say something for K. C. anyway, even though he ended up turning rat and shit, but an order had come down to hit this other Indio, not Indio Vindiola, but this other Indio. We were going to kill him. He had a prison wedding and family visit coming up, and K. C. let him have it. He just got married to this pretty young Mexican girl. She was gorgeous, and two of her brothers, they were outsiders; they were out there on the yard with us. So this Indio, he got in there, he married this broad, and they let him go out on this family visit. You know, it's his honeymoon; they let him have his honeymoon. He probably stayed up all forty-eight hours having sex. He came back in covered in hickeys and shit, so he's exhausted. When he came back from his honeymoon, we butchered him out there on the yard. I mean butchered him; we butchered him. Not me, we, I say us, La Nuestra Familia. Man, the bloodcurdling screams. I never heard nobody scream like that. This was the one thing I remember, screams. You could hear them in the parking lot, I think, man. He was just running and screaming, and the two brothers they had on him, they were chasing him and hitting him. He was down and screaming and crying, and Bozo had to make the hit because he had smut on him, so Bozo looked over at K. C., and Bozo's like, "Do I finish him or what? Do I go for more?" and K. C. nodded at him, like, finish it, you know. Bozo walked over, picked up his head, cut his throat, and planted one in his heart, and so the job's done, quiet him up. But that was probably the worst I ever remember. I mean, this guy was supposed to be a warrior; apparently, his colors came out. I mean, he was running like a bitch, screaming, blood everywhere, bloodcurdling screams, but it was a legitimate hit. We're going to be locked down for a couple of days, so everybody's on their way in, grabbing what they got to get, because they're gonna be locked down for a couple of days. And the animals that we had become to show how indifferent we were to this kinda shit by now. Everybody's like, "Hey, give me some chips, give me some this," getting their supplies because they're running in. And "Hey, give me some smut magazine" and "I want some hard-core magazine so I can go jack off for the next couple of days." You just killed one of your brothers, man, and you're going to go in here and do this kinda shit, you know? Guilty as charged. I was just as guilty; I did the same shit. But that's the way it was, you know? That's the way it was. But K. C. did let him have his honeymoon before he killed him. So maybe that's why K. C. lived. I don't know.

Maybe one of the reasons I'm alive today is because when Rudy, that brother, was kneeling and praying, he was praying to Jesus. Maybe because I didn't kill him, maybe that kinda gave me grace, when I turned around and killed Lupe. Hey, I'm telling you folks. This sick motherfucker really wanted to fuck this guy. We're going to kill a brother; he wanted to make the brother suck his dick and then fuck him in the ass and then kill him. You know, what kind of sick shit is that? Unfortunately, this is the nature of beasts sometimes. In every gang or group of madmen and armies, some animals slip in. These kinds of mad dogs must be put down, like in the old days, when a dog had rabies. I mean, that's not La Nuestra Familia; that is not what we are about. But in every organization, when you recruit crap, you're gonna get shit like that. But then let's look at Rudy and the other little brother who was with him. Even though they took advantage of the offer to have sex, they were not down with killing the baby or the woman. Instead, they saved her and her baby. Even though this woman was an active enemy and they were having sex with her, they had to respect her as a mother who was sacrificing herself for the promise that her baby would live. Even though she was a female gangster and wasn't afraid to die, she used the only thing she had at the time, to offer herself, to become human, in their eyes, not just an enemy. The funny thing is that I ran into her and Rudy years later. They had gotten out of that whole criminal life, they had stayed together as husband and wife, and they were going to church and living a different life together. They said that they were praying for me too.

Anyway, we hit K. C. This is still before the civil war. I want to cover this because, what we did do, my brother-in-law now steps in. He's in charge, and the regiment is running smooth; shit's starting to get a little bit together. Babo and Fig, everybody's fighting murder beefs and shit. One of the things that we did do, because it's like, we said, "Look, were recruiting all these guys and we're gonna have to kill half of them." That's ridiculous, so we got to change this. Numbers don't mean anything, because in the end, the storm comes. We knew RICO was coming; we knew the prosecutions were coming. We knew we were going to get scattered out across the United States, in the federal penitentiaries and shit. And I remember Hobo telling me, "Yeah, the tree's gonna get shook." He would tell me, "Just stay faithful, Down." He said, "Tree's gonna get shook, man." In the end, out of a thousand, if we only had maybe fifty solid brothers left, that's all we need. So all these guys were cannon fodder. You know what I mean? So that's what we shot for. If we could get a family of fifty solid soldiers, well educated, trained, and seasoned. I'm telling you, we trained, we schooled, I personally taught soldiers how to kill, I taught 'em how to be soldiers, I taught 'em how to kill with their bare hands and with weapons, I taught them how to do all this stuff—how to kidnap, how to rob, everything, took 'em and showed 'em. We educated, we came up with the Northern Structure, and we put Ricardo London, my old Tribal Thumb comrade, to run it. Ricardo was with us now; he was an undercover member of La Nuestra Familia as I once was undercover. As far as I'm concerned, Ricardo made that structure; he was sharp. The Mexican Mafia had created the Southern Government for the same reason. There was a riot in Tracy where they ended up locking us all up. That's how we all ended up in West Hall, what have you. There's so much I'm missing here, and I'm bypassing quickly. There were murders that happed that I'm not gonna talk about, but anyway, what we finally figured out, because the EME, they were locking them up too. But what the EME was doing, through the Southern guys. I have to give this to the South. These guys were raised on this stuff; they're breastfed on gangs, you know. It's natural to them to represent and to be in that gang lifestyle. Northern Mexicans were not so much raised like that, because you know, the big cities versus the rural cities and stuff like that. So we had to literally train them. But what the Mexican Mafia was doing is, they were pushing the Southern Government shit. You know, and while they're in the hole, they were using their Serranos, Southern guys, Southern Mexicans, to do their dirty work. So we figured out, well, we got to do the same thing, so we created what is now called the Northern Structure. Now the Northern Structure took off; we never imagined it taking off the way it is now today. We decided on three categories. First of all, anyone from Northern California would be part of the structure whether they wanted to be or not. Just by virtue of being from Northern California, you were classified as a category 1. When you were a Northerner who was a sympathizer to our cause and to the La Nuestra Familia, you were category 2. Category 3 were guys from Northern California who put work in for us, made hits for us, sold drugs for us, and controlled main lines for us. From the category 3s we would draw new members, recruits to become a Familianos. We drew some of our best and most loyal from category 3. They were young, full of heart, and had a willingness to learn and to become a part of what the La Nuestra Familia was really meant to be: a family. A family of warriors, a family that offered men who had nothing left to lose, a reason to be proud, a reason to go on sometimes, because you knew you belonged to something feared and respected by anyone who had any sense. They outnumbered La Nuestra Familia and everybody else. But still, they are just what you call the minor league. Like in the pros, you got the pro teams, and you got the farm clubs. The structure was created as our farm club. We had the three levels. This structure got turned around and all this stuff, but that was the framework we laid. We put Ricardo London over that right there in West Hall, teaching the outsiders there, the Northern boys there. Ricardo was sharp, a vicious, vicious man. He's changed now, but in his day, Ricardo was as vicious as me—that's vicious. So we put him over it, and he was teaching 'em and schooling 'em. We started giving them things to do, giving them concepts, that later became the bonds and what have you. So we created that; that was our farm club. This way we can watch them progress through, and by the time somebody's ready to become a member, we had been able to watch him and say, "Okay, this guy is a member." Instead of just recruiting just anybody like we had done, you know, trying to keep up with the Mexican Mafia and ending up having to kill half of them. So that's how that got formed, everybody running around wearing a read headband and everything else. They probably didn't even realize what they're fighting for; same with the guys with the blue headbands. But you know, Southerners were used by the Mexican Mafia, and Northerners were used by the La Nuestra Familia. Because most of the leaders are locked up, but of course we got our undercovers here and there too. I'm getting into an area that I really don't want to go too far into. Let's just say that's what it is, and it is what it is. That's where we created it, there in Tracy; I sat at the table that created it. So I kinda feel responsible for a lot of this crap that's going on. I always do. I feel responsible. I look around at what's going on now with it, and I'm like, "Man." You know? That's a part of what I was a part of. I helped create that, so I'm guilty.

THE THIEF ON THE CROSS

The Familiano's Creed
By Sundown

If I lead, follow me
If I fall behind, pick me up and push me
If I betray you, kill me
Que Viva La Nuestra Familia
" Long live Nuestra Familia"

EXAMPLE
History of
Violence

'148 slain by prison gangs'

SACRAMENTO (AP) — The state attorney general's office believes prison gangs in California are responsible for 148 killings in a 2½-year period, more than 100 of them on the streets, the Sacramento Union reported Sunday.

said a

This is the period from when I became a made member and was on the streets the first time in our initial push for control of all of Northern and Central California.

THE THIEF ON THE CROSS

Gang link seen in 3 gun deaths

FRESNO (AP) — Authorities have linked three shooting deaths in Fresno County to extortions by members of Nuestra Familia, a Mexican-American gang.

The bodies of Tina Arevalo, 26, and Luis Gonzalges Jr., both of Fresno, were found in a vineyard near Kerman, west of here Saturday.

The same day, Francis Enriquez Castillo, 23, of Fresno was discovered slumped against a wall in west Fresno. She had been shot five times.

Police said Miss Arevalo and Miss Castillo both had complained of extortion attempts.

Miss Arevalo had told police that Nuestra Familia members demanded money to let her work as a prostitute, officers said. Miss Castillo had reported extortion attempts against herself and other women in west Fresno, they added.

The three Christmas Eve killings raised the number of slayings blamed on Mexican-American gangs to 26 in Fresno County

Example of
Extortion of
prostitution
Trade

RICK RILEY

2 stabbings linked to gang war

FRESNO (AP) — Law enforcement officials have linked the stabbings of a Fresno brother and sister to the narcotics war between rival, Mexican-American gangs in Central California.

The Fresno Bee reports unnamed officials said the Wednesday night stabbings were in retaliation for testimony given by one of the victims at a preliminary murder hearing of an admitted gang member.

██████ ██████, 19, had testified recently at the hearing of ██████ ████████. A known member of the Nuestra Familia gang. Miss ██████ and her brother ██████, ██, were stabbed repeatedly by about six assailants in front of their residence here.

She was reported in serious condition and her brother was still listed as critical. No arrests have been made yet in connection with the stabbings.

██████████ has pleaded guilty to being an accessory to one of 11 Fresno-area killings authorities have at-

Example of hitting any witnesses against any N.F. member

174

Example ✗ ✗ ✗ ✗

3 slayings, drug link eyed

FRESNO (AP) — Law enforcement officials are trying to determine if three men slain execution-style are the latest victims of a feud between Mexican-American gangs.

The bodies of the three, all residents of Sanger in southeast Fresno County, were found face down yesterday along a vineyard road in that area.

Each had been shot in the head, Fresno County sheriff's officers said.

Deputies reported they had not established a connection between these killings and a struggle for control of narcotics in Central California between the Mexican Mafia and Nuestra Familia. However, officers conceded such a link is a possibility.

Authorities have blamed eight other homicides in this area since last fall on the warring prison-spawned gangs. All but one of those victims were Mexican-Americans.

Tire tracks were checked at the entrance to the roadway for clues after a worker found the bodies. It was unknown whether the three were killed at that location or dumped there after being shot somewhere else.

The victims were identified as Moses Garcia, 22, Alexander Pena, 26, and Leon Diaz, 22.

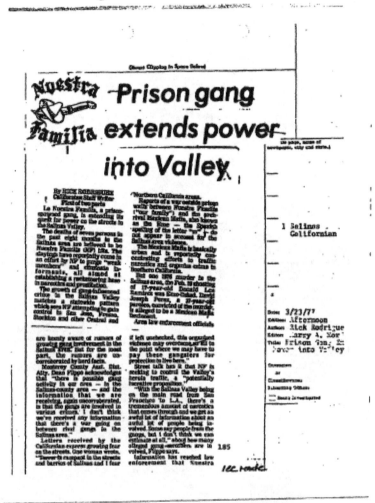

Prison gang extends power into Valley

By RICK ROBINSON
Californian Staff Writer

First of two parts

News
www.newspapers.com/image/#19013442

Independent Press-Telegram (Long Beach, California), Edition - Page
Printed on May 7

San Jose hub of drug cartel by prison gangs

SAN JOSE (AP) — An intensive six-week undercover investigation has pinpointed San Jose as the hub of one of the state's largest prison gangs, the San Jose News reported Friday.

The newspaper said an undercover officer it called Robert Jones had identified the group as the Nuestra Familia, which he said operates in and out of the state penal system.

The paper said "Robert Jones" is a fictitious name used to protect the identity of the narcotics officer.

JONES said the group was made up primarily of Mexican-Americans and has been forming an organization based in San Jose to control prison narcotics traffic and other prison activities throughout the state.

Jones said recent efforts by the group grew out of plans made by Nuestra Familia members while still in prison. Organizing was carried out by members after they were released from custody, he said.

"They are organized to the point of having a complete power structure with a constitution, by-laws and amendments," Jones said.

Since Jones and another officer were assigned to investigate the group in early October, 17 persons all of them suspected members -- have been arrested on a variety of charges ranging from sale of heroin to robbery and burglary, Jones said.

In the last week, four persons believed to belong to rival prison gangs have been stabbed by alleged Nuestra Familia members at Santa Clara County jail, the newspaper quoted Jones as saying.

JONES explained that rival gangs, including the Aryan Brotherhood, the Mexican Mafia, and the Black Guerrilla Family, compete with Nuestra Familia for leadership in prisons throughout the state.

He said the group had plans to purchase a legitimate business in San Jose with profits from local drug sales. He said property and drugs recovered since the investigation began now total in the thousands of dollars.

MICRO
HOLI

Soldiers in Bay Area

EXAMPLE / Regimen

Alleged 'gang' clues lacking

HAYWARD — Police have exhausted their leads, and no additional charges will be filed against seven alleged Nuestra Familia gang members arrested ~~Tuesday, said authorities said~~

At the time, police felt they could connect the defendants to several area robberies, murders and assaults.

defendants will be bound over superior court on charges of sawed-off weapons and posses property allegedly found at th ~~blank street~~ balls for the

The defendants and their t ~~named Gutierrez~~, also known as 28, transient, $6,000 bail; ~~Pedro~~ known as ~~Hector Gallegos~~, 26

The Argus (Fremont, California) Edition — Page
Printed on May 7

Example of power

Murder suspect linked to gang

FRESNO (AP) — A man police say is suspected of being a member of a Mexican-American gang has been booked for investigation of murder.

Gapino Rodolfo Lopez Jr., 26, of Parlier was arrested at a bar here in connection with the Sept. 12 stabbing death of Jose Ruiz Beltran, 33, of Fresno.

Beltran, stabbed in the chest outside a bar, was one of up to 23 Fresno County homicides linked to Mexican-American gang violence in the past year.

Police said Lopez is believed to be a member of La Nuestra Familia. Beltran reportedly was killed for cheating a member of the prison-spawned gang on a drug deal.

EXAMPLE/ HOME CLEANING

Slaying suspect caught

CALEXICO) (AP) — A Fresno-area man wanted in connection with one of 12 recent, gangland-style slayings there has been arrested on a murder warrant by border authorities here.

Alfred Sosa, 34, was booked for investigation of killing Gilbert Roybal Feb. 1 in Fresno, police reported. Bail has been set at $100,000.

Two Southern California men and a Visalia man had already been arrested in connection with Roybal's murder. Police say all four men in custody and Roybal were members of Nuestra Familia, a prison-spawned Mexican-American gang.

Chapter

11

I believed in the La Nuestra Familia. I really did. I still believe in La Nuestra Familia, the original La Nuestra Familia. I even believe in the new La Nuestra Familia. I believe in Tibbs and Pinky no matter where the government sends them. These brothers are La Nuestra Familia, the best of what came out of the original La Nuestra Familia and the new. These brothers, especially Tibbs, will put in work no matter where they are. They will never lie down, and for the true Familiano, he will always believe. He has to; it is in his heart, and it is his source of strength. He cannot deny what he has suffered and what he has learned and what he has become or the sacrifices he has made.

I do not want to give glory to all this nor do I want to make it sound like this is a noble profession that anyone should pursue. Because this profession is only for those who have been to hell and back and for men who truly have nothing left to lose.

But we believed it was at that time. As I said in the beginning, we were, all of us, Pancho Villas and Joaquin Murrietas with a dash of Michael Corleone. We were brothers; we had a brotherhood. Not to sound gay or nothing like that, but, man, we loved each other; a lot of us really loved each other. We had a strong love and a strong respect for each other; we called it *Carnalismo*, or "Brotherhood."

A belonging to a secret society of special soldiers, warriors, guerreros—this was our strength. When you are there and you are alone and you're in an enemy camp, you are representing, man; you're representing all your brothers. You are representing what you believe in. You're out there, and that is what makes you vicious. That is what makes you fearless. With the schooling, the training, how to make a weapon out of anything, there was no excuse for you to not be able to defend yourself, to get off. But it was a sense of brotherhood, that comradeship, you know? We believed we had a goal. It wasn't just that; we were gonna get out there and support the guys in prison. It was that we were going to establish a family, like the Italian Mafia we had seen in movies. We were going to do this for real. I think Hollywood had a lot do with us; we grew up with all these gangster movies, you know, *The Godfather* and all that. So "Hey, we can really do that, let's really do that. Let's find the kind of guys that are as equally committed and guys that are loyal, that have heart and that are intelligent." So you do things and you go through things together, both in prison and on the streets. I can't stress enough how valuable and important it is to a man who has nothing left to lose how much of a sense of pride that you were part of something and that you represented something that was vicious, feared, and respected, you know? That was abused of course. It got abused, like anything. Power corrupts, and absolute power absolutely corrupts. Were there cases of that? Yes, there were. There's a lot still to go with this story, but I want to say, there are guys that I will always love. I will love them, I will lay down my life for them, and I will defend them, because those are my brothers, and that's what made us strong. But that's also what kinda screwed us over also, because we started having idiots getting in the wrong positions of power and setting up these same guys that you loved. This is when your sense of loyalty was severely tested, and the more powerful we got, the worst we got, I think. Fucking Death Row. I will kill him ten thousand times. Babo, you fucking idiot. God bless you, Babo. Love you, man, but you were stupid. And some of our leaders were completely stupid, like I said. So Death Row Joe (D. R.) had it out for me. Every hit or job, it seemed, that came down the road, he wanted me in on it. I was like, "Man, what the fuck is going on? This guy wants me to do everything, you know?" He was just trying to break me; he hated me because I exposed him, and sure enough, he did in fact eventually turn on us. He fucking wounded us bad.

I produced. I produced money. That's one thing I did do, and people that had to be killed got killed, let's just say that. Unfortunately, many people that shouldn't have been killed got killed too; that's my one regret. Anyway, I just want to say, Carnalismo, it doesn't exist anymore, not like it did once. Brotherhood, it just doesn't exist like it used to. Maybe it will come back; maybe it makes a comeback, who knows? If it ever does, watch out, America, you can't stop us. You can't stop anybody that has that. You cannot. You can put us in strip cells, you can beat us down, you can feed us juke balls, you can give us baths with water hoses, you can give us baths with tear gas, and you can threaten us with a million years. But as long as we're doing this—because we believe in this and we love each other and there are guys that we love that are doing this with us—you can't stop us. You can never stop that.

When I came back, I had all the knowledge of all my experiences since I became a Familiano, in prison, on the streets, in the county jail, and then back to the prisons again. I saw how dedicated and devoted I had become, even more so to this cause that I first picked up behind the gates of hell. I learned from all the mistakes I had made and those that I had witnessed by everyone else. I decided, finally, this really was gonna be it for me. I would do everything and devote everything to help to fix the broken pieces, to reeducate all my people, all my brothers, to be a family, both inside prison and on the streets. I began to study the law so I could help my brothers beat murder cases and learn how to try to manipulate and cripple the system with lawsuits and convict and about revolutionary unity. I brought in Tribal Thumb resources and assistances. I communicated with all the various groups, gangs, gangsters, revolutionaries, bikers, even the Indians and the Asians.

To cement this idea and dream of mine for La Nuestra Familia, I married off different members of my own family to my Familia brothers that I loved and believed in and who believed with me in La Nuestra Familia as a family. But still, bullshit was going on with some of our newer and older appointed leaders. This bothered me, especially when it's not what you think should be done. You think somebody should be given a pass; instead, they want to kill them. You think somebody could be reeducated, but no, they want to fuck them over. You think somebody should be respected, and they want to disrespect them. This, I had the greatest problem with. In any organization, there will be jealousies and also fear of how deadly, seasoned, and experienced some of the soldiers truly had become and to have one among you who could very well kill you. For some leaders, this became their secret dirty little fear, because they had gained their positions and ranks by doing some dirt. While they may have seemed to have gotten away with doing dirty against made, respected, seasoned brothers who could someday come back to get them. Even Black Bob, who represented what a true Familiano should be, did a little dirt. I know, because he did it to me. I don't think he even saw it as dirt until that day we finally bumped heads in that visiting room. I believe he realized it, and that's why he saved my life that day. It is crazy. It got to the point where we started killing more of ourselves than we were killing enemies. That was bad; that was not good. It got to the point where there were a group of us hard-core Familianos, we just said, "No more, that's it." We made a pact. "They try to come for you, we're coming. They try to come for me, you're coming." We had each other's backs; we knew change was in the wind. Cornejo and Bob, they had this thing in the works. They were going to try to steal the regiment. They were going to steal the Family. What they did was they fucked it up. It caused a civil war to jump off, and like I said, I had sworn an allegiance to a Constitution. I remember the day when they gathered us all together. This was the main body, West Hall. Tracy had always been considered home, the school, the college, where you went to get schooled. Anybody that came out of Tracy, you knew was schooled. Another thing too was that they had recruited so many young guys, new guys, that this was what was helping them, because these guys had not been around. They had heart. Yeah, they were young killers. They were down for the cause, but they had not been there all the years and had not seen everything and all the work that everybody had put in. These were the guys that they were going to count on to support them when they made their move to grab the Family. I remember they called us all together for a big junta (a *junta* is a meeting). So we were all there, and there's like eighty of us there. We're having a big meeting, and Cornejo's standing there like he's somebody, big old fucking cow. Anyway, he had the nerve to call us cows when he was telling us, "I'm going to be leaving you, cows." You know what I mean? Talking to us like we were supposed to think like this was, oh, hahaha, funny. "Yeah, I'll cow you motherfucker." They were telling us that Babo was no longer in control; he already locked it up and turned. Babo's stripped, Fig's stripped, and they were removing

Hobo's captaincy. Hobo had just been made Captain. Now Hobo I love. I was like, "Wait a minute, what's going on here?"

From now on, Bob was going to run the penitentiary, Cornejo was going to go out and run the streets, and that's the way it was going to be. There was going to be no more Constitution. I remember there were about fifteen of us there out of those eighty brothers. We all just looked at each other like, "Shit, they're doing it. They're going to try to steal it." We were just watching each other like, "Ah, fuck!" The meeting broke up, and a few of us got together here and there. We said to each other, "We just committed treason, you know. We just committed treason according to our Constitution. As a whole, we all just committed treason." Like I said, I was one of those fucking idiots who were loyal to the core. I was loyal to the Constitution whether Babo was wrong or not; that was not the way to do it. Setting Hobo aside, that bothered me too.

I went, and what I did was trick Bob, but Bob had enough sense to have bodyguards all around him, youngsters, so I managed to get him alone. I said, "Bob, can I talk to you?" We went over by the tire volleyball thing. We were sitting there. We squat down to talk. There's nobody there but me and him. "Bob, listen to me, you know I love you, brother, but we just committed treason, and you need to know I have a knife on me right now, and you're not going to get up from this tire until you explain to me what the fuck just happened. Don't fucking move, don't jump, don't scream, because I'm going to hit you. I need to know what the fuck just went on, brother." Bob was great. Everyone loved him, so I gave him that respect. He told me, "Sundown, follow me. I am the Familia, remember when we used to talk about it? Remember how we used to say we needed to change, we needed to have new leaders?" I said, "Yeah, but not like this. What about Hobo? What's up with that? Why is he being stripped? Hobo better not be in any danger, Bob. I'm not gonna stand by and have that." Bob said, "No, don't worry. Hobo's all right. We just don't think he's ready yet. We will give him back his captaincy in a little bit. We're not going to hurt Hobo." "Okay, Bob, you better not, I'm telling you. You might as well kill me right now." I asked him about a few other brothers, and he said they would all be all right. The Vindiolas, they got fucked over, you know? They had helped make the Familia, and each one of them, one by one, got fucked over, kinda driven away, you know? Used up and driven away, and that bothered me. Bob was telling me, "Follow me, I am the Familia," I was like, "Man, this guy really believes this shit."

I understood that, because I tell people too, "I am the La Nuestra Familia." There's something when you say that. It means to the death I will represent, motherfucker. So I understood what he was saying. But I told him, "Bob, I took an allegiance to a Constitution, and you know we've done a lot of shitty shit. We killed a lot of people, man, because of that Constitution. Brothers have died over it. Now you're just gonna tell me there is no more Constitution? Well, if there is no more Constitution, then there is no more La Nuestra Familia. I took an oath to a Constitution, and that's why I got you here right now." "Follow me, Sundown," he repeated. I knew he was sincere, and I too agreed with Black Bob that if any man ever was a La Nuestra Familia, it was him; he was a good leader too. But I had sworn an oath to that Constitution. I had sacrificed my life, my future, my family. I had spilled blood; I had done some ugly shit because I had given an allegiance to that Constitution. I had been faithful; I fulfilled my oath. If there was no more Constitution, then I was free. I can walk away with no shame. I did not quit; they quit on me. All those of us who shared this belief, who shared this oath, all of us were free if we wanted to be. We left it at that. I said, "I follow the Constitution, Bob." I knew my days there were numbered. The thing is, they knew too that we had a pact there with some of the top soldiers. They didn't want to cross any one of us. There was no way they wanted to send some young fucking untested, un-fucking-proven young soldiers. I didn't care how much heart they got at us. We're gonna chew them up; they had to be very careful what they did. But now we had a civil war. Babo, Fig, and Casper, our leaders, were never gonna just lie down and accept this. No more than Tibbs or Pinky would ever accept just being kicked to the curb after having given and suffered so much.

They knew they could not just hit us. They already knew whom they had to get rid of. So one by one, they started trying to drive us away, me, for example. We used to have a thing called the pony. In that pony was an envelope with instructions for the day and the latest news and stuff. It would have who was on discipline; we had discipline. Our discipline was severe, from taking everything you had to taking your life. Anyway, if you got in trouble, you usually just had to write an essay about what you had done and shit. We would want a good essay, like, "I want ten thousand words on this, and I want it by this time. And I don't want *and the* and *the the* and *and and*. I want you to think about what you did, and I want you to write me a ten-thousand-word essay, and I want it in double mini." Which is hard writing. You're not gonna be allowed to have this or that, your TV is taken from you for so long, and you're restricted from participating in certain activities and recreations. It's just like the military. The pony would say who was on discipline, like he's not allowed to smoke. So we take his tobacco, we take his coffee, and we take his recreation. It would be a brother, say, a good brother like Taco. "Taco's on discipline for sleeping during the day." That wasn't' allowed. We're not allowed to sleep during the day. So the discipline would consist of a) loss of tobacco, b) loss of coffee, c) loss of day room privileges, and that would be it. Most guys were A, B, and/or C—that would be it. Well, me, when I would pop in the pony. It would be all the way up to H, I, J, K, L, M, N, O, P, you know what I mean? It was to the point where I was out there scrubbing toilets on the yard with a toothbrush. Because they figured, just keep disciplining. Eventually he will just get tired and go away. Well, I wasn't going nowhere. They took my visits too. They started taking visits because they were afraid that Babo and Fig and the other brothers in the other regiments were going to get word back to hit Bob and Cornejo. So they took my visits, but the reason they took my visits was because of my wife I was married to at the time, Netty Lou. Bob had a girlfriend that was visiting him; he eventually married her. All the wives kinda knew each other. I guess this broad now thought she was the NF general of all the wives or what have you, because she was with Bob. She would try to pull shit with the wives. My wife told her one day in the bathroom in front of the other wives, which I had no idea that this even happened, "She would beat all the brown off her fucking ass and that she didn't run shit. She wasn't in the fucking gang, and she couldn't tell her shit." All the other wives loved my wife; they were like, "Go, Netty, get her, get her." Anyway, what happened was that bitch, Bob's old lady, went and cried to Bob, you know? "That bitch disrespected me." Shit like that. "I don't want her around here!"

So that is why they took my family visits. I didn't find out until later. I wasn't tripping, take my visits, I don't give a fuck. But at the time, my wife had just had an incident with her ex-husband. He came and kidnapped my stepson, his son, JC. So she was falling apart. We had a family visit scheduled, and I wasn't going to be able to take it. But I had the right to go to one visit to explain to my family, "Hey, I'm not going to be able to come out and visit for a while. I'll let you know when and all that." Well, it just so happened that my ex-gang bitch Satin had sent some little young broad up to see me one day. It was like a quarter to three. Visiting was from nine to three, so it was like a last-minute thing. I was out there and visited for like ten minutes. I didn't expect it; it wasn't my wife or anything. So it was, "Hi, hi, good to see ya. Bye." You know? So my wife showed up to see me a few days later to visit me. They called me out for a visit. There is a lot more in here too. There was a fucking piece of shit named Bobo. Bobo was conducting an investigation on some misuse of money over a lieutenant who had the regiment before, who was my brother-in-law. Anyway, I had tried to strangle him in the day room because he said something in this investigation report of his that I never said to him about my brother-in-law and a couple of other brothers there whom they had under investigation at the time. Bob and they were there, and I was called in as a witness. He started trying to say some shit that wasn't true, and I fucking went off. They had to hold me down because I was gonna tear his fucking head off his shoulders. I said, "You fucking piece of shit, you don't be putting my fucking brothers' lives on the line because you're trying to get yourself a position. I'll fucking kill you, man!" You know, so Black Bob and the other brothers there were saying to me, "Calm down, Sundown, calm down." Well, that person, he and I, it was on. I was going to kill him, and he wanted to try to get me killed. He knew it, I knew it, and we both knew it. Well, when all was said and done, they made him the security lieutenant as his reward.

So we were out there this day, and I was playing basketball. My name got called for a visit. I went and was getting ready for my visit, and this piece of shit Bobo came over and said, "Hey, where do you think you're going?" I said, "I'm going to visit." He said, "You lost your visits." I said, "I know, but I'm gonna go out there and let my old lady know. I got that right to go out there and tell her." "You already had your visit," he answered. I said, "What are you talking about?" He said, "Remember, they called you for a visit the other day." I said, "No, that wasn't my visit. That was a surprise thing for fifteen minutes." "You're not going for a visit." He got all puffed up in the chest like he was ordering me and I'd better obey. I said, "You know what, you try to stop me, motherfucker!" He was enraged, like how dare somebody talk to him that way. But he got the fuck out of my way! I lived up on the third tier; Bob was down on the first tier with all his bodyguards around him. He's waiting to get called out on his visit too, so I went up, and I started getting dressed. Well, they sent my squad, because I had been demoted down to squad leader. But they sent my whole squad up there to tell me, "Hey, Sundown, they sent us over here to tell you you can't go on your visit. We're supposed to stop you." I said, "Who sent you, Bobo? Man, don't even trip, just get out of my way." They said, "Well, what are we gonna do, man?" and then Dennis told me, "Go see Bob, go to Bob." So I said, "Oh, fuck it, man." I went down to Bob. "Bob, let me talk to you." He had his bodyguards with him, and he said, "What?" Well, now, Bob's scared of me, I know. Something's in the air, but he went and talked to me. I said, "Hey, that fucking Bobo tried to tell me I can't go out for my visit. You guys have done everything in the world to me. I don't give a fuck. But I got to go out there and tell my old lady. Her ex-old man just snatched the kid. I got to go out there and calm her down. I'm just gonna go out there and let her know, then I'll be back, I ain't going nowhere, man." So Bob said, "Go ahead, man, go on your visit." That relieved my squad from having to have to hit me. So I went out to the visiting room. Now one of the things too is that I used to work in the visiting room. I used to run the visiting room. I decided who got family visits and all that other shit. When I ran the visiting room, I had weapons out there. I had money out there for emergencies for family members and shit. That was one of the ruling body's moves against me. I was forced to leave my job. That was one of my disciplines; they wanted me out of the visiting room. Because everybody liked me, right? So I went out for my visit. My wife was sitting there, and she had my son Ricky with her. Ricky was about nine months old, I think. I knew shit's gonna jump, and I told Bobo to suck my dick, get the fuck out of my way. I was sitting there with her, and I was trying to explain to her, "Hey, shit's getting thick here. Don't worry, it will be all right. I'm not going to be able to see you for a while." What happened? A couple of other brothers started getting visits, and Yuba— love you, brother—he was out there. The regulars started showing up. Well, Bob's old lady showed up. Now when Bob's old lady showed up and they started to visit, next thing I knew, Yuba signaled me to go to the machines, so I went to the vending machines. "Hey, Down, I don't know what's up, but they just told me to tell you your visit's over." He went, "What's up, brother?" I told him, "You just don't trip, stay out of it, okay? Just stay out of it, brother." He said, "All right." Because Yuba loved me, man. I loved him, and he loved me. So he went back with his old lady and sat down. I went back to my old lady and sat down, and I went on with the visit. I told her to hand me my son, you know. What they didn't know was that I went into the bathroom and got a piece that I had hidden in there, and I brought it back out with me and I had it with me. So I was holding my son, and the next thing I know, they got a couple of other brothers coming toward me to tell me visit's over. So I handed my son to my wife and looked at the other brothers, and I told them, "Stand down." They said, "We were told to tell you your visit's over, brother. We don't know what's going on." I said, "All right, don't trip, brothers, I got the message, thank you." They went and sat down. I said, "Fuck this shit, man!" Bob was sitting there with his old lady, and they're kinda huddled up, you know. So I walked over to Bob's table, and his old lady was sitting there, that piece of shit. Because now, my wife told me what happened; she told me about the fight in the bathroom with Bob's old lady, you know? I was like, "What? That's why they took my fucking visits away?" I went straight over to Bob's table. I had my piece on me. I just told him straight up in front of that broad, "Bob, you put this bitch and my bitch over us? You put personal business between them and that fight between them just so your old lady can make all the other wives fear her because she can have their visits taken away with their husbands? That's what this is all about? That's *commadre* shit." Bob just looked at me, you know, and I said, "Bob, you send another brother to me to tell me my visit's over, and I swear to God, I'll cut your throat right in front of this bitch." I showed him I had a knife on me. It was on; that was it. It was over; we had just tore it. There was no way that I could be allowed to live now. I went back to my table, and everybody left me alone, right? So I was gonna have my visit. Our visiting room, the visiting yard, all the whole setup, everybody in West Block could see us; they could even talk to us. That's the way it was set up. I was walking the yard, and all the guys that knew what time it was were like, "Sundown, you're fucking crazy. They're gonna kill you." I was walking with my wife and my son. I was stopping and waving at everybody and talking to everybody. "Yeah, fuck it. I know this is my last visit, so fuck you, Bobo." We went back in. Now

I've got to get my wife out of there. I got to get her safe, so I told her, "Look, visiting's over at three, the van will come every hour." I said, "At two o clock, you're leaving. I want you to just get on that van, go home, get the kids, go to San Jose, and stay with my mom. Stay there until I call you." She's like, "What's going on?" "Don't worry about it," I told her. I didn't want her to worry too much. I thought I was going to sneak her out at two o'clock, right? Usually, all the wives stay until visiting is over at three. Because it's at that time that all the extra kissing, touching, and grinding goes on. So I told her to catch the bus. I was gonna go in at two. When I got up to go, and my wife got up to go, all of a sudden, everybody else was leaving the visiting room too. All the other Carnales were leaving with me. There were like five of us in there. The only brother that stayed in the visiting room after that was Bob and his old lady. Now, usually, when we're all going back from the end of visit, we're all there joking, clowning, and shit, and the officers are searching us down and shit. But this time, when we went in there, it's complete deadly silence; it's a race to get back. The cops were picking up on it. Something's up; something's not right. These guys were usually clowning and joking, but they could sense death was in the air, you know? We headed back; it's a race. As I was going into the unit, we got into the gate, and it just so happened the officer working there at the gate was a good officer. He liked me and shit like that. I told him, "Hey, can I get up in my room real quick?" Ordinarily, they just tossed you out in the yard; that's what they were supposed to do. They were supposed to just toss us back from the visit out on the yard, where everybody was exercising and stuff. That's where I was supposed to be killed, so I asked, "Can I get up in my room and change clothes? I got my visiting clothes on. I want to change first." He said, "Yeah," so he let me. Now he's not supposed to, but he let me. The other guys went out into the yard, and as I was going up, I saw the tumbler with the pieces being passed out the window. I saw this other Rocky passing out the pieces. He didn't know whom the pieces were for, who's going to be hit. If he'd have known it was me, I don't know if he'd have done it. I know how it goes down. We had a lot of brothers on cell arrest; you had to stay in your cell all day in a strip cell as one of our disciplines. There were about five brothers around me on strip cell status still in their rooms. I went back to my room and told one of my neighbors to tell a couple of other brothers there what was going down. I told him what happened in the visiting room. He was asking me, "What are you going to do?" I told him, "I'm going to handle my business, man." I made it back; they fucked up. I got my big-ass sword. I was ready to go out. I was not going out like no punk; I was killing, you know what I mean? "Send somebody for me, motherfucker. I'm going to show you what a fucking warrior is!" So I was strapped, man, and I came back down the stairs. The cop started to open the door to let me back out in the yard. I was ready. I was getting ready to go out on the yard, and as soon as they opened that door, the goon squad swooped. Cops came from everywhere. "Riley, get down!" "What?" "Get down." I was frozen right there on the stairs. I didn't know if that was God or who looking out for me, you know. I went down. They picked me up and put me in cuffs. They took me. "The warden wants to see you."

They took me to the associate warden's office. I was sitting, and the associate warden came in. Now they didn't know that I got a fucking knife on me when I went, because they didn't bother to fucking search me. They just put me down and put handcuffs on me. They were afraid of me; cops were afraid of me. I was a vicious motherfucker. I ain't gonna lie. I would beat a cop in a minute. So they respected me. I said, "What's up?" He said, "We just got word you were going to be killed. You have been on a list. We've been watching you for two weeks now. That gunman has been watching you every time you've been out in the yard. We got word they were going to kill you right now. So I'm trying to save your life. I'm going to give you a chance."

They had the fucking SSI guy, the gang guy from Sacramento there. I was like, "What the fuck's going on here?" I said, "How the fuck did they get word? Everybody left with me. The only one left in the visiting room was Bob." You know, so who the fuck told the police that I was about to be killed out there? I wasn't gonna get killed though. They probably would have a few brothers on me, but I was gonna get busy. Whoever they sent was gonna get chopped up, you know? They said, "Well, we got confidential information that you were about to be killed. We saved you. If you would have made it to the yard, you would have been killed." I was racking my brain. What do you mean? Did my wife say something? I'll kill that bitch if she said something. No, she never said nothing. So anyway, the guys over there offering me a chance to debrief. "Fuck you, I ain't debriefing shit!" Okay, well, no matter what. You're not going back. We're putting you over in the hole." That's the same thing they did to the Vindiolas. I said, "Ah fuck, they're gonna take me to the hole." So he gave me a phone call. "You might as well call your wife, if you want a phone call." They were trying to be nice to me. "You want coffee? You want cigarettes? You want a phone call?" So I called just to make sure my old lady had gotten ghost and went to stay with my mom. I spoke to my wife, and she told me she called my mom but couldn't get ahold of her, but not to worry, she would be on her toes and my cousin Roxanne, Manos's wife, was living with her and had a gun and had her back. Not to worry, once she gets ahold of my mom, she will leave and stay with her until I tell her different. This snake bitch, the whole investigation that got me into this shit list with our new security lieutenant Bobo, was partly her fault for gossiping and jealousy over some wives having extra money. There is even more to be revealed real soon, this story about this backstabbing bitch. They're getting ready to take me, and I said, "Hey, you know, before everybody panics and freaks, I have a knife on me." I gave it to the associate warden, and he said, "Don't worry, I'm not gonna charge you." And shit like that, because I could have stabbed him or the SSI guy. But I gave him the knife; I was going to the hole. I went to the hole, and Shadow Vindiola was there and a couple others. I got kinda squeezed out the same way. Everybody wanted to know what happened. So I told everybody what happened. Before I left my cell to go the yard, I wrote on my wall, "Midnight train to Georgia," so anybody would come by and see that, you know, that song by Gladys Knight, "He's leaving on that midnight train to Georgia, going back to find," you know. I told the brothers there good-bye. Now I was in the hole. I was trying to figure out what went wrong, who fucking said something. It took a while to find out. But Bob was the one who told the police to have me locked up. Bob saved my life, thanks, Bob. I know it was you. He told the police to get me off the yard; they were going to kill me. See, even in war, even in madness, we loved each other. We had respect for each other; we were just going different directions. I was going, staying where I was. I was going to Babo, Fig, and Casper and everyone else you know. I was staying with the original La Nuestra Familia. You guys just stole the big body, okay, but we're gonna have a civil war now. We still have soldiers loyal to us.

But before I finally made it to San Quentin, the day before I was taken off the yard and placed in the hole, there had been a story on the

TV news station about the discovery of a woman's body believed to be in her late twenties, early thirties, murdered execution style and left in a field in a town right next to Tracy prison, where I was.

The news report had drawn my attention. I didn't know why, but I waited for the news to come on again later that night in my cell. Same limited information was reported, but I just felt drawn to that story, and I didn't know why. Execution style, outside the prison, it sounded like maybe it could have been us.

I was in the hole, devastated about what was going on with my family, La Nuestra Familia, when the guards took me out for a visit with the local police there in one of the offices in the hole. They introduced themselves and told me that they were investigating what they thought was a possible execution-style murder of a woman whose body was discovered in a field between Tracy and Manteca. I told them, "Yeah, I saw that story on the news, what's it got to do with me?" They said, "We are not asking you to rat or tell on anyone, we're just trying to identify her so we can notify her family. We have been able to find out that some of the locals have seen her before. They think she comes to visit someone here at the prison. We know you used to work in the visiting room, and we would like to show you some pictures. See if you are able to at least give us her name, then we can let this poor woman's family know about her." Like I said, I had been drawn to this news story and I was curious about it, so I said, "Okay, I'll look at the pictures, and if I know her, I'll let you know who she is so you can let her family know, but that's all I can do." They said, "Fine, thank you very much. We have to warn you that these are field photos of her." I said. "Yeah, don't worry. I've seen my share of dead bodies." They laid the pictures down on the table before me, and I saw the dead face of my mother.

I looked in her dead eyes, my beautiful mother. My mother was beautiful, lying there looking up at me. I said, "That's my mom." One of the officers, I guess, thought I was joking or something. He started to kinda laugh. He thought I was making a joke. But when they saw how serious I was, all of a sudden, I don't know, I kinda went into shock. Because all of us sudden, there were phone calls going off and everything else. "Shit, we got a situation here." Now they got doctors there; they gave me a shot. I was just in shock, you know. I was looking at my dead mother, so now I was trying to find out what's going on, what happened. I was thinking, "They killed my mother?" All I knew was, all I could think of was, "That's it, I'm killing cats, dogs, chickens. I'm going to Bob's ranch." Because I'd been there, where his family lives. "I'm gonna kill everybody—his mother, his father, his brothers, his sisters, his wife, their grandchildren, their cats, the dogs, the chickens." Everybody's dying, you know what I mean? So I was sitting there in the hole with that, you know?

I guess other people found out too. Bob sent word to me, "Hey, Down, we had nothing to do with this. We don't have anything to do with it. This is not us." Other groups started getting at me too. Because whoever killed my mother, I was getting close to going home again, I only had like a year left, I think, so somebody was going to die. There was going to be some death. I was coming out, and so even my enemies got at me to tell me, "Hey, condolences, man, we didn't have nothing to do with this," you know, so I was like, well, who was it then that had to do with this, you know? Well, it turned out, like I said, that my ex-gangster bitch Satin, who was obsessed with me, the bitch was involved with my mother's murder, so was her oldest son, the one who idolized me.

What happened was, Satin had hooked up with some dude, young dude, youngster named Billy. She had put a pistol in his hand; she had him doing crimes and all that other shit. Anyway, my mom, it turned out, had been dealing drugs for the Hells Angels, you know, pretty major drugs. I didn't even know; Mom had been keeping this secret from me. So she was dealing for the Hells Angels, major drugs. What happened was that Billy had tried to get a front from my mother; my mom was still staying in touch with this bitch Satin even though I told her to stay away from her. I told her I didn't want her hanging around with her, but mom would go over there, and so one day, my mom went over there, and she had a couple of my soldiers. You know, dudes loyal to me, with her. They went over there to visit. This Billy asked my mom for a front or something like that. Mom, she didn't like him, so she told him, "You know, I don't know you. I gave you a little taste because you're with her, but I don't know you, and I'm not gonna front you anything, and no, I'm not gonna tell you who I'm dealing for." He got a little disrespectful, and the brothers who were with her, they put him in check. Mom had to tell them, "Nah, leave him alone, it's okay, let it go." Well, that little asshole, I didn't know about this shit, this all came out later, a while later. Biggest part of what he and Satin were doing was they were ripping off drug connections and things like that. My mom had gotten in a fight with her husband that she was with at the time, Carl. She had decided she was leaving him, so she had packed her suitcases, and of all the places she went, she went to Satin's, and she did this in the middle of the night. You know what mean? So she didn't have backup or anybody with her, you know, one of those women. Listen, women, stop doing stupid shit. You get all fucking pissed off and emotional, and you don't think, you know, stop to think, okay?

Anyway, my mom went to Satin's, and while she was there, I guess they got high. I didn't know that my mother was smoking PCP. I didn't know that. And this guy was smoking PCP; they were all smoking PCP. Well, somehow or another, this guy convinced my mother that he wanted to go buy a pound of crank. My mother didn't feel comfortable going with him, so she said, "Well, I'm not going with you alone." So Satin said, "Well, here, Deron, go with them." Her son, like a stepkid to me, he was just eighteen. My mom said, "Okay, if Deron rides along, I'll go." This could get deep and long, and I'm not gonna go into it because too many people got hurt, and there are too many people still hurting over this and still so many people who are gonna be hurt over this. So what happened was, long and short of it, somewhere on the way, Mom got hip that this guy didn't have the money or that something wasn't right. So she had tried to stop in Tracy to go see my wife who lived in Tracy at that time. Mom went there, knocking on the door about eleven o'clock, kept knocking on the door. Well, my wife did not answer the door because she was inside fucking some guy named Tony. She wasn't about to answer the door. Had she answered the fucking door, my mother would be alive today. If Netty Lou hadn't have been in there sucking some other guy's dick and answered the door, my mother would be alive. Netty confessed later that she knew it was my mother, except in Netty's version, she looked out the window and saw it was my mom, as my mom was already leaving, and the only reason Netty didn't get up and answer the door was because it was already so late. She had been in bed already asleep plus the kids were asleep, and she didn't want to wake them up. She stayed in bed rather than answer the door to my mother, who was trying to bail out of the situation she found herself in with this dude Billy. Netty said my mom knocked on the door for a long time, but she was just too tired and sleepy. I was told by several of her friends that the lying bitch was in there getting fucked by this guy Tony. They had been having sexual relations together for a long time while she was married to me. I knew Netty Lou was weak when it came to dick. She couldn't help it; she was a nymphomaniac as a teenage girl when I met her. I knew what I was getting when at the last minute I changed my female Tribal Thumb comrade Marie's name off the marriage certificate and put on Netty's name. It was just three days before the wedding, at the time, all I cared about was the sex and getting conjugal visits regularly. Once I was released from prison that time, Netty Lou knew that I had found out about her activities. The one thing Netty had always known about me was that if she was completely honest and confessed what I already knew, that I would forgive her. Because one thing all my women knew was to be completely honest with me no matter how ugly, and I will forgive. She confessed the truth to me. The only reason Netty Lou is alive today is that she was the mother of my children. Especially for my stepdaughter Olympia's sake. She was heartbroken, and seeing her crying for her mother who had abandoned them, asking me for her mother, broke my heart. I rode the bus all the way back into Tracy to find Netty. I found her at the Shamrock bar; I took a handful of pictures of the kids to her and told her to get her ass back to my children. Otherwise, her head would be hanging on the fucking telephone pole. That's another story. Anyway, somehow or another, this guy Billy said he's got to take a leak. So they pulled over in this reservoir area by Manteca, and the car got stuck in the mud or something. They all went out and started pushing the car. Mom's pushing the car on the passenger side. I guess Deron's pushing from the back. Dude's in the driver seat, pushing there. So when Mom went to get back in the car once they got out of the mud, dude picked up a sawed off shotgun and shot her. She went flying back into the field. Now I'm unclear here. I never knew this part until twenty years later. I thought that was it. But I found out there was another shot. So either Deron took the shot or Billy went up there, made sure, and shot her again. I think he made Deron shoot, because Deron was scared to death after that. I didn't know what happened. I do know Billy killed my mother though; this all came out. The Hells Angels, they took this piece of shit, made him think they were hiding him out. Until he figured it out, they were holding him until orders came down to kill him. They were gonna take him out and kill him. He crawled out of the bathroom window of the house they were holding him in. He then flagged down the police and turned himself in for my mother's murder and asked for protective custody. The dude's cousin, or something like that, was a prospect for the Hells Angels, when the Hells Angels found out about this dude.

But the reason why this guy did it was because this bitch Satin, who idolized me, she would always put him down; that's what she did with men. She would tell him he couldn't fuck like me, he had a smaller dick than me, he would never be as bad as me, you know. She had posters of me around her house. He could never measure up to me and all this shit, and when my mom wouldn't front him and shit like that, and also he wanted to be in the Aryan Brotherhood someday. So in his little demented mind, he thought that if he killed my mother that somehow or another, the Aryan Brotherhood was going to say, "All right brother, come on in."

Four arrested in murder of S.J. woman

HAYWARD — Three South County men and one woman were arrested between Saturday and today on murder warrants in what detectives suspect was a "drug-related homicide."

San Joaquin County Sheriff's deputies arrested Wayne Garro Espinas, 27, of Castro Valley at his home Saturday. He was charged with murder, conspiracy and possession of a shotgun.

Deputies arrested Deron Lee Baker, 18, also known as Ron Baker Jr., this morning at his Hayward home on charges of murder and possession of a shotgun. His mother, Sylvia Lee Enos, 46, is custody in Santa Rita county jail on a parole violation, was arrested Tuesday on a murder warrant.

The third man, William Franklin Wainwright, 24, of Hayward, turned himself in to Pittsburg police Tuesday after learning of a warrant for his arrest. He is charged with murder, conspiracy and possession of a shotgun.

The four are suspected of shooting Mary Inez Robbins, 44, of San Jose, according to San Joaquin Sheriff's Commander Dave Derkson.

Derkson said that four said Ms. Robbins, also known as Mom Mary Robbins, knew each other. Ms. Enos and Ms. Robbins were close friends, he said.

Ms. Robbins' body was found Aug. 12 in a rural area outside of Manteca. A farmer discovered her body in a cornfield about 1 a.m. Coroner's deputies say she was killed about 11 p.m. the night before.

Derkson said the woman had been shot twice with a shotgun — once in the chest and once in the neck.

Derkson said the group apparently met in Hayward on the night of the murder, then traveled to San Joaquin County, where the shooting occurred.

Derkson said it appears the shooting may have resulted from a drug deal. He declined to elaborate.

Ricks Mother
MARY. INEZ Robbins

Sylvia Lee Enos
AKA Satin Doll

Mom and Me

Me & Mom, see how you can talk to prisoners in the yard.

Chapter

12

The civil war, okay, so Cornejo, Black Bob, and a few lieutenants had managed to steal the main body regiment of La Nuestra Familia. But the old tried, true, and proven members, we still had our regiments in a couple of penitentiaries and in a couple of the cities in California, and we still had some of the best of our leadership. One of the things I mentioned earlier in one of my rabbit trails was that there were actually three factions of the one La Nuestra Familia, not just the two sides of us battling over control of California. But now courtesy of the federal authorities and organized crime prosecutions and later the governors, from out of the state transfers of La Nuestra Familia leadership, there is also now the Federal Faction.

I've enclosed news articles in this book, which illustrate this very fact. Let me say this, once you get up there in position of command and leadership, and you have life sentences that you received while giving your all to this organization, men like this, they are never going to just let go. They're not gonna just say, "Uh, awright, okay, just take the organization, you know, all the blood we spilled, all the sacrifices we've made, uh, awright, take the organization. Just tell us to kick rocks, thanks, we'll think kindly of you." That's not going down. I was torn, you know? I never wanted to kill my brothers; that's not what I am about. I was never about that. Did I do a couple? Yes, I had to. But in all honesty, the brothers that I did kill, they were no good. I know, I know, who was I to judge? But I'm telling you, they were no good. We had a code; we had a belief of what we were and what we were about. Those of us who were true Familianos, Black Bob, Fig, even Cornejo, everybody thought that what they were doing was right. Sometimes when everybody thinks that they are right, wrong decisions are made and we have to live with the consequences.

In San Quentin, I finally hook up with Fig, Casper, and Babo, and everyone else that were there. But even there, I was told that they too are rewriting the original Constitution, to which I had sworn my allegiance. Because they agreed, as did the mutineers, that the Constitution was obsolete and that due to changing times and circumstances, the Family needed to change too. Here I am like a dinosaur and old gunfighter; time had passed by, and I was only twenty-nine years old.

The Department of Corrections transferred everybody to San Quentin, both sides, to let us go at each other and settle our family squabble. While I was there, Hobo, Tibbs, and a lot of brothers who rode with Black Bob and Cornejo would get at me. "Hey, Sundown, come back over here with us, you know. Leave Fig and Casper and them and come back to us." I was telling them all, "Nah, I'm here, but I haven't decided if I'm even gonna be involved with anybody yet. I'm just stepping aside and watching what's going on." Now our generalship has fallen to Fig. It's funny because Hobo was actually running the prison regiment for them, and Fig was running the remaining original body. Both brothers were crime partners when they first came to prison together, on a stolen car sentence. They were just eighteen years old, and together they killed a member and shot collar of the Aryan Brotherhood, and each ended up with new life sentences to go along with their membership in the fledging newly formed La Nuestra Familia prison gang. Fig would go on to receive seven more additional life sentences for seven more murder convictions for being a loyal soldier and lieutenant of La Nuestra Familia. Here they were both pulling for my soul, loyalty, and commitment to their cause. Hobo had been my hero, one of the main influences over my decision to become a Familiano. Fig won my respect for his loyalty and for the price he had already paid for being loyal and a good soldier, so had Casper. The Department of Corrections had designated us Nuestra Familia 1, Fig's side; Nuestra Familia 2, or Black Bob's side; NF1 and NF2 for short. If you have a problem with this label or designation, take it up with the State of California.

NF2 kept sending their younger new recruits to try to hit Fig or Casper. They did not want Casper to live and make it back out to the streets on parole to Salinas. Just like Tracy was considered our home in the prison system, Salinas had always been considered our home too, but on the streets and with the street regiments. Fresno had been like a second home for us also, until Crackers Vindiola organized all the Mexicans from Fresno into their own group not bound any longer in loyalty to anyone but themselves, because of the dirty way that not just Crackers but all the Vindiolas had been fucked over by us. They called themselves the F14s at first and eventually blew into the new and powerful Fresno Bulldogs gang. I was there that day when the NF2 tried to squash the rebellion there on the upper yard of San Quentin. Everybody was digging shotgun pellets out of their bodies for a while there, from all the shooting from the gun towers. One man died that day, not from a knife or beating by any of the over sixty guys on the yard that day, fighting and stabbing each other, but rather died from shotgun pellets in his throat from the gun towers. Two things happened that would affect the future of the prison system in California: one, a new prison gang was born, and two, shotguns were no longer allowed or used in the prison gun towers. They would be replaced by the more controlled mini-14 assault rifle. No sooner than they started using mini 14s to respond to incidents, I would be shot by one on the lower yard of East Block there in San Quentin, saving Fig's life from two of my once own loyal squad members and soldiers, Ricky and Pinky.

Before that day, NF2 had sent youngsters to make the hits against NF1, and every time, it ended up as an embarrassment for them. Like I said, you can't send the inexperienced against the most experienced and expect to be successful. No disrespect toward the youngsters they sent, but they never stood a chance. They were humiliated a lot of the times. One example is, one time NF2 wanted to hit Crackers real bad because as I've said before, the Vindiola boys, they are soldiers and not afraid to talk shit to you if they don't like you. Any Vindiola I've ever known could back up anything they said. Also, Crackers had convinced all the Fresno boys to turn against NF2 and to have an allegiance with NF1. So they slipped some hacksaw blades down to one of their more loyal and eager young recruits who lived in a cell on the tier Crackers swept up and kept clean as part of his inmate job assignment. Crackers loved to get drunk and then talk shit to the NF2 members on the tiers above him.

This youngster managed to cut his cell bars so that he can sneak out of his cell and stab Crackers when he was drunk and an easy target. On that day, this youngster came out of those cut cell bars and managed to stab Crackers by sneaking up behind him, because Crackers would be the only inmate free on the tier at the time where he was working. To this youngster's credit, he had managed to stab Crackers a couple of good times in his kidneys and his back before Crackers sobered up enough to realize there was someone else loose on the tier with him and trying to kill him. Once Crackers realized he was being hit, he turned around and took the knife away from the youngster who was stabbing him, and all the track star and Michael Jackson came out in that Familiano wannabe, as he tried to beat it, beat it, beat it, running up and down the tier, yelling for the cops to come save him. By the time the guards got there, Crackers had caught this kid and was on top of him, with the kid's knife up against the youngster's own throat. Crackers told that kid, "I ought to just cut your throat and kill you right now, right here, you piece of shit. You didn't have the balls to face me," and then Crackers spat on him. The guards had been yelling at Crackers, "Don't do it, Vindiola, he's not worth it. Everybody heard him screaming. You don't have to prove nothing."

Crackers had been reading the Bible secretly lately; he looked up toward heaven and said something like, "Are you watching this? You owe me one." Then Crackers told the kid, "You ain't no gangster. This ain't the life for you, you need to find another career. You just remember that I let you live." Crackers got off the kid, walked over to the guards, handed them the knife, and collapsed to the floor.

That youngster had hit him pretty good with a good knife. They took Crackers to an outside hospital. As they were taking the youngster away, I told him, "If Crackers dies, I'm gonna kill you. I'm gonna hunt you down, and I'm gonna kill you. You had the chance to go out to the yard with us and handle your business. You took the punk way out."

Crackers lived and came back and was back to work on his same job a week later. Crackers was tough. You know, that youngster was just following orders, and if it had been anybody but Crackers, that youngster might have made his kill that day instead of getting clowned.

Before I had made it there to San Quentin, I had been in Soledad prison. A court order had come down saying it was illegal to house two men to a cell together in San Quentin, Folsom, Tracy, and Soledad administrative segregation units, or as we call it, in the hole. So the state had to release hundreds of active hard-core gang members, from all the gangs. The Aryan Brotherhood, the Black Guerrilla Family, the Mexican Mafia, and us, the whole NF, so they tossed us all out together at the same time onto the Soledad prison main line. That was exciting, I guess. Who's on one of the first buses there? Yeah, yours truly. The picture I have chosen for the cover of this book was taken there, at one of the very first unity meetings in the chapel, between members of each warring prison gangs. I wanted nothing to do with anyone there, except for a very chosen few that I'd even associated with or even talked to. An old comrade from my revolutionary-thinking days was there, an old convict I loved name Jose Prendez.

I used to work out with my boxing and martial arts there on the yard. I would draw a big circle ring in which I would work out, and it was understood by everyone on that yard that you'd better get permission to approach me when I was working out, or else it would be on, even my friends or so-called homeboys. Only Jose could approach me or enter that circle anytime. One day, he came to me and told me that these two monks from the streets were trying to form a unity group from among the inmates there to discuss cultural heritages and common concerns shared by prisoners there. Jose wanted me to come with him to the very first meeting being held. I tried to tell him, "Nah, no thanks, not my business nor my concern." I was just doing my own time and just wanted to be left alone as I was still dealing with my mother's death.

Jose was persistent. He reminded me of the time when we first met in the Oakland jail and I went out my cell into the day room to fight the police there over some new guy whom they threw in our tank. He was going through methadone withdrawals, and they were refusing him medical attention. I told the whole tank that it was nothing personal against anyone there, but unless they got that man some medical treatment, I was gonna refuse lockdown at day room recall. I was taking that day room hostage, and there was probably gonna be some fighting between me and the cops. That would mean tear gas they would have to deal with, and maybe everyone would be locked to their cells for a day or two as punishment, but I was gonna do what I felt I had to do. I wasn't asking anyone to go out there with me for this new dude nobody even knew. That night, the oldest man there, old man Jose, told everybody, "I'm backing Sundown." He was going to refuse to lock up too, and he was gonna fight these cops with me. I tried to talk Jose out of standing with me, but the old convict stood toe-to-toe with me that night against the Oakland police officers. That worked at that jail, and we got that dude medical attention. Then after it was all over, I ended up slapping the shit out of that dude for selling and trading his medications we had sacrificed and fought for to get him. Go figure.

Anyway, "Okay, Jose, just for you. I'll go check it out, but I'm not making any promises." I told him. He is dead now, died of old age in prison, but he was my friend even if he had killed his wife and got rid of her body. They never did ever find her.

I'm telling this part of my story because while at that prison, while I was in the hole from a case I caught there, I met a female correctional officer, Ms. Hill (Mikey), who left her job to be with me. I was waiting for a visit with her when NF2 made their move against Fig and what happened that made me decide to stay loyal to La Nuestra Familia, with Fig, Casper, Cricket, and everyone else that was still on our side.

Even before Soledad, like I said, my mother had been murdered with a sawed-off shotgun, and her body had been left in a field. Fortunately, her body was discovered the next morning, so it did not suffer decomposing or being ravaged by wild animals. My mother was a beautiful woman, as you can see from the pictures I've enclosed in this book. She had taken such good care of herself that she was originally thought to be in her late twenties or early thirties.

They put me in a strip cell that night after I had learned that she had been murdered and left in a field near the very prison I was in. I was enraged. I did not know who was responsible yet, but I knew that I was not just gonna kill whoever had done it, but I was gonna destroy them. I was gonna kill them and their whole family tree. I was mostly really pissed off at God. I had prayed that he wouldn't let my mother die while I was in prison, and she not only was allowed to die but also murdered and dumped outside my prison. I'll never forget it in that stripped cell with nothing but four walls and a hole in the ground to shit and piss in. They had put me in a strip cell for my own safety and for the safety of the staff, because they didn't know how a man of violence would react, I guess. It was late at night. I clenched my fist, and I looked upward, as if trying to see through my cement prison roof into heaven itself, and I screamed at God. "I wish You would come down in the flesh so that I could kill You and You would know my rage and pain too!" Suddenly, I heard a voice answer me, "I did, and you did." And there on that cement prison wall, I saw Jesus Christ on the cross, being crucified, as if He were actually there on my wall. I remember staggering backward, raising my hands up, and falling to my knees. Sorry for accusing God, all I could say was, "I'm sorry, God, I'm sorry. My war is not with You. I see, I see, but, God, forgive me. I am at war, and I'm going to kill whomever I have to, God. I'm sorry, forgive me. My war is not with You. I don't want war with You, God. It's not Your fault, I know, but I have to do what I have to do."

You know, I know who I saw that night on my prison wall. You would have thought that after such a vision my life would change, that I would change, but I couldn't. It hurt too much inside of me. There was madness all around me, and I was still in a manmade hell. I did change that night. I think I became more merciful in a way. I began to feel compassion and pity a little bit more for the prisoners around me. I think, looking back, that this is why I said yes to my friend Jose and attended the first ever attempted meeting of all active gang factions there in a chapel at Soledad prison. It was not a religious group or program; we met in the chapel only because it was the only place big enough for all of us to be in comfortably.

I remember sitting and listening to the monks, Brother William and Brother Jim, but especially Brother William, speak to us about what kind of a program they were hoping to create there. All the convicts and gang members there were all quiet and noncommittal. Jose was elbowing me to speak, to say something, and I was like, "What do you want me to say?" Jose was one of the original Mexican Raza Unity called Venceremos. It was big in the late 1960s while Cesar Chavez was beginning to try to organize farmworkers and peasants to unite and form a union and boycott. In the prison system, Venceremos was trying to politically organize, first, Mexican American prisoners, but all prisoners in struggle against the prison authorities. Here Jose saw something; he saw that for the first time in his experience, there were active members and representatives of all the active prison gangs together in one room.

Jose whispered to me, "Talk about all this shit going on here with conditions and the staff and each other." When the courts told the California Department of Corrections that they could not force double celling of inmates who are in the prison holes, the CDC responded by throwing all known active enemies onto one big overcrowded, over-populated, rundown prison, hoping that we would all start killing each other and then show the courts by all the violence that the courts should stay out of their business and just leave the running of the prisons to them. Let them do whatever they wanted to control us.

We did have a few in-house cleanings by the different gangs when everyone first got there, and now a few officers had started getting hurt. So the prison staff was concerned too about the violence being turned against them. They were allowing these two monks to come in to try to help quell the violence. I looked around me, and I counted how many men responded to the monk's invitation for the first meeting; the monks called it Discovery.

There were thirty-five men there including Jose and me. Jose would not stop elbowing me in the side. So I spoke up, then I stood up and turned to face everybody else. I remember telling everybody that the reason I came to this meeting, aside from my friend Jose's pestering me to come, was what I read on the posters that the monks had put everywhere. It said, "We are looking for men not afraid to discover each other's heritages and cultures, etc. etc."

I said, "Looking for men, well, I'm a man and I'm not afraid. You guys here, you had the balls to come here, so I guess that makes you men too." I knew everyone there would go back to their people and groups in the prison and let everyone know what went on, what this program was about. So I addressed the reality of our common fates and situations and our conditions, the reality of what the mucky mucks who ran the Department of Corrections wanted us to do to each other. They wanted to hopefully benefit their own objectives, which was more restrictions and control over us. Then I challenged everybody to be real, to be honest, and to try to work together through this program and opportunities it promised to bring about. That we need positive changes in our surroundings and conditions, because these monks would bring in college students and professors, free people, to these meetings whom we could try to win over to support our common cause for better prison conditions. But we have to agree not to go at each other for the administration's benefit, but to only go at each other when there was no other recourse but to deal with a matter in that way. I told them that I wasn't expecting us all to come together, hold hands, and start singing "Kumbaya." Just respect and no bullshit—these would be the only rules of this group we were agreeing to join together, yellow, white, black, and brown, north, south, east, and west. Just be a man and represent your own people like a man. Everybody left, and a second meeting was scheduled for the next week. We would see if everybody stayed away or came back for the second meeting.

The following week, there were over a hundred prisoners there. That was how the Discovery program took off. For a while, we did what had never been done before. Instead of everyone exploding and killing each other as before, we had semitruce, a semipeace. I'd like to think that it was my speech alone that caused such a great turnout, but the truth is that it was the two nineteen-year-old college girls, Francine and Charlotte. They were drop-dead gorgeous girls who came with the two monks for our second meeting and then for the next few months. Busloads of young college students, girls and college professors, even employees of the prison, free people who worked at the prison, would come and attend too.

For a while there, at Soledad State Prison, it was like sitting on a powder keg and trying to stop everybody from giving off sparks and blowing us all up together. I forgot to mention an incident that occurred there at Soledad, about a week prior to that first Discovery meeting. We had night yard there, and upon unlocks, admittance, and releases off the yard back to the prison housing units, everyone would have to line up, and it was that whole lining up period that was gonna explode one day soon. It was just a matter of time; as everyone, especially the younger inmates, would start lining up, there would be saving places in line and people cutting to the front of the line, a lot of jostling and overcrowding.

I remember one night I had finished working out and Jose and I were going to get in the back of the line. Some Northern boys up front saw me and hollered. "Over here, Sundown, cut in line here. We got a spot for you, homie." I yelled back so that everyone crowding and pushing in line could hear me. "Nah, no thanks, homies, I don't cut in lines. I don't like it when people cut in front of me, so I don't cut no lines." I went and stood with Jose toward the back of the line to wait our turn to get in off the yard.

There was a female lieutenant; she was an Indian, I believe, and she was all of five foot three and two hundred fifty pounds. This woman was crazy; she had heart, and everybody called her Goon Squad Rosie. She had a reputation of just running headfirst into inmate stabbings and hits or inmate riots. She was the first one there whipping ass, swinging her stick, and spraying tear gas; she was fearless. She would go on to become a warden over a prison in Centinela, but this night, she messed up. She was out overseeing the yard unlock, with all the cutting in lines and the pushing and shoving, which mostly youngsters would be doing, trying to rush the gate to get in first off the yard so they could make it to the showers first.

This one night, Rosie got pissed off, and she was refusing to let her guards let anyone in until everyone settled down and got in in a quiet, orderly line. She was barking out orders, and all the inmates weren't paying any attention to her. She was right; these unlocks needed to be done better, more orderly, but what she did next was nuts. Rosie gave an order for her yard gun towers to open fire with live rounds into the overcrowded lines of inmates ignoring her and telling her, "Shut the hell up, bitch!"

I remember thinking, "Did I just hear this crazy bitch right?" I looked up at the guards on the roof tower pumping their shotguns and getting ready to just open fire. I grabbed Jose and told him, "Let's get away from here," and just then, it sounded like duck season had just opened up. Shotguns started exploding and spraying pellets everywhere; even her own guards caught pellets. Everyone was scattering away and lying on the ground because they were being ordered to by the shotgun-shooting guards. There was a moment of dead silence as people lay down everywhere on that yard. It was a miracle that other than a few stray pellets, no one had actually gotten killed or seriously injured. The night air was filled with the choking stench of gunpowder everywhere. That was a strange moment of quiet, when, I don't know why, but I jumped up and started screaming at this lieutenant Goon Squad Rosie, "Are you fucking crazy, bitch! You want us all to go home tonight? We'll hit them fences and go home, and you can explain to your superiors how you let over five hundred inmates go over the fences at one time! You might stop a few of us, but the rest of us are gonna escape! You had better tell your officers to put them guns away, and you had better beg us not to all leave tonight all at once! Right fucking now!" Suddenly, as if everyone else found their own voices, each man started standing up and repeating the same things that I had just said. From every group out there—yellow, black, white, and brown, north, east, west, and south—that night we all had one common cause and enemy courtesy of Goon Squad Rosie.

Goon Squad Rosie realized she had messed up bad; the gun towers had used up their ammunition, and it was nighttime. That end of the yard was the weakest point of their fences' security, and had we all actually decided to hit the fence under the cover of night, she would have had "some 'splaining to do, Lucy," but worse than that, she had just united every prisoner on that yard at that moment. Even her own officers who caught pellets in their legs and arms from the shotgun ricochets were telling her off. We had a situation she had not counted on. She tried to tell us all to calm down and line up, because now she had to get us all off that yard before it got much later and darker outside.

Everyone was now looking to me to be the leader and the spokesman. I told her the only way that everyone would cooperate with her orders was if she guaranteed no one would receive any disciplinary actions written up against them for this incident, which she created. Now no one would be able to take their showers due to all the time that had passed. She, as the watch commander, which is like acting warden, would have to agree to extend the prison lockup an extra hour to let everybody get their showers and run around getting all their last-minute shit everybody usually did before lockup and count, which meant the institutional count was gonna be late.

She had no choice because as I was telling her all this there on that yard. Every one of the prisoners' respective spokesperson were chiming right in behind me—white, black, yellow, brown, Northerners, Southerners, Aryan Brotherhood, BGF, Crips, Mexican Mafia, and Nuestra Familia members. So she agreed that if everyone lined up and came off the yard, she would delay lockup by one hour.

So now, I was telling everyone there, "Hey, let's line up. If this is what everyone here wants, because I ain't calling no shots here." All of a sudden, everyone was saying, "Yeah, okay, that's good," and telling all their own people, "Come on guys, let's line up." For the first time since

I'd been there, everyone lined up like it was a military drill. This scared the staff, I know, because we all united together.

As we were going in, people were coming up to me and saying, "Good looking out!" "All right, man!" Even my enemies were nodding their heads in gestures of respect. It was like I became popular all of a sudden. This was not necessarily a good thing, because now prison staff had their eyes on me. Anyway, I think this kind of gave me an acceptance there; even some of the guards were nicer to me. It gave me respect whenever I would stand up to speak at those Discovery meetings. I remember speaking to the second meeting. It was evident a lot of people wanted to try this Discovery program, see what we could accomplish together with some outside help, and we agreed, "Look, if we're going to do this, this is what it's gonna be about. It ain't gonna be no bullshit. We're gonna address the issues we're facing here. You know they're telling us here to go ahead and kill each other. Ordinarily, we don't got a problem killing each other. But when the police want us to kill each other, we need to step back and say, 'Hold it,' step back and say, 'We aren't killing each other for your benefit.' You know, so let's work this out first."

So they started having people come, and the group grew. We started having college people come. We met a lot of girls, and of course, the guys wanted to see the college girls. We even had the people who worked there in the prison coming in on Discovery night. It would be a packed Catholic chapel, and speakers would get up and speak about, you know, black heritage, Mexican heritage. I even spoke about white heritage, about the Irish. Even though I was running as a Mexican, I had been labeled Mexican, because I can go as Mexican, or I can go as white. A lot of times, I get mistaken for Italian or Indian. I do have Indian in me. I'm proud of Indians. I love Indians. They're my people. I'll get to that later, but it became a good format, and we started having peace there, and we started dealing with the stuff. And the staff, they saw that it was keeping officers from getting hurt. So that's the only reason that they were behind it. There was a group that they took me in to be part of, the MAC, Men's Advisory Council. These guys were supposed to be representing the inmates. They asked me to join that thing, and I really didn't want to, but I said, "Okay, I'd go in there." So I went into the first meeting with the associate warden. All these guys were going up there. They're supposed to be representing the inmates, and they're going up there asking the warden to sign off on room moves and to squash 115s and shit, for themselves. For their little homies and shit, and I was watching this whole thing and I saw the associate warden really pretty bored about this. He would go on to be the Director of Corrections for a while. He asked me, "You got anything to say?" and I said, "First of all, I'm not here about anything about me, about a room move for me or squashing a 115 for me," and I was looking at everybody. "You know, I thought we were supposed to be in here representing the inmates, the convicts. My understanding is, I represent the guys in blue, you represent the guys in green, and we're just trying to keep peace." So this guy liked me. "Hey, finally somebody's stepping up." That's where I was. As long as guys were real, I was willing to be real, and we had peace there for a while. We actually had the La Nuestra Familia, Mexican Mafia, Aryan Brotherhood, Black Guerilla Family, and Crips start coming in then, and the Bloods, they started coming in then. Peace, you know, it was possible, because we were dealing with shit, you know. What happened was, the staff wasn't responding quickly enough to some of the demands that we're asking for. So everybody was all pissed off and shit. I would tell these guys, "Hey, look, there's gonna come a time when all you quiet guys, you're the ones I'm talking to back there. Because I know you're real. You're not up here, standing up here and talking and stuff like that, but just your presence shows me that you're some serious guys. So I'm not gonna be here long. You guys are going to have to step up and take over and make sure that this continues on the path that we set it on." I guess I was predicting the future, because on my birthday, we have kinda a semi lockdown. I wrote up this list of demands of what we wanted, and I got my knife. And because I was on this committee, I was able to go see the associate warden. So they let me go see the associate warden. I got past all the security, and I got into his office. Nobody's checked me out, searched me, pat me down, you know. I got inside there, and I read the list of demands to the associate warden. Then I took out my knife, and I just touched him on the shoulder with it, and then I set it down in front of him, and I said, "That's just to show you that we can and will get you, you know, if these things aren't met. Everybody's ready to blow right now, and they've sent me in here to tell you that this is your last chance. You want to save your cops, you had better do what we said. You know, I want to save guys in blue, you want to save guys in green." So they took me around from block to block, and I got to pick out who gets out, who comes out to take care of everything, to get the laundry to everybody, to get the food to everybody, and all that other stuff, and who's going to be representing who and all that other shit. Then they took me from block to block, and I got it done. It took like about four hours to do that, and they told me, "You know we have to lock you up, and we're going to have to charge you." I said, "Yeah, I know, and that's what we're trying to tell you. We don't care, we don't care if you put us in the hole. We don't care if you charge us, we are serious." So I went to the hole. This is where I met my wife, one of my wives. I'm telling this because eventually it would lead me back to San Quentin, because of her. I think they got wind of it, but she also had my back when I was on that yard. She was up in the gun tower with that shotgun. Hahahah! God help anybody that I couldn't whoop, because she would shoot them. Hahahahaha! Funny, huh? Anyway, she was a dedicated die-hard cop. She wasn't one of those off welfare and all that stuff and just getting a job. You know, but what happened was, the lieutenant that was there thought he was somebody. He was in there with me in Tracy when he was an officer. Now he's a lieutenant there, and this was the famous O wing in Soledad. So the day I went in the hole, they had a special meeting. They called all the officers together, and she said she'd never forget it because the lieutenant told her about me. He's telling all of them about me. He said, "This man is treacherous, treacherous, treacherous!" She said he said it three times. This lieutenant, he was her hero. She had never seen him look that shook up about having somebody in their hole. He didn't want me on the tier without three or four officers around me at all times or whenever they escorted me anywhere. I was a martial artist and all that other stuff. Instead of scaring her away, she came running down to my cell to check me out, like, who's this guy? She said, turns out that I was the nicest guy in the whole hole; I was the nicest guy in the whole prison. That's how I ended up with her, Michaelleen. I fell in love with her, and I married her. But she was not the first or the last female correctional officer that I was intimate with. I was in Tracy when they first started hiring females to be guards there at Tracy prison. One of the very first women to be hired to work at the all-male prison in Tracy, Duel Vocational Institute (DVI), became a drug runner for us. Our main captain, Larry, was over the whole prison and Nuestra Familia there. Larry took advantage of some information given to him about this female correctional officer by one of the local Tracy members of the La Nuestra Familia. His name was Pretty T. When this female correctional officer first came to Tracy, she was every prisoner's fantasy fuck. She was tall, chubby but curvy, and a natural blond. On the streets, she would have been a six, but here in prison, she was a ten times ten. In those days, the female correctional officers did not wear pants like they do today. They wore a uniform, which had a skirt. On this big, thick, beautiful blond bombshell with thick thighs, it looked like a miniskirt.

Pretty T recognized her from his hometown in Tracy; he told Larry that he used to have sex with this broad and her husband on the streets. Pretty T was an older convict who had no qualms about having his dick sucked by a punk or even fucking them in the ass. That was what he was used to from his many years spent in prison. This female officer's husband was a bisexual freak who would let you fuck his wife if he got to suck your dick or got fucked in the ass first, then he would enjoy watching his wife have sex with the other guy too. They were hippie, free love types, but the husband was also a drug addict. Pretty T sold dope to him on the streets; he told Larry that the husband would be willing to have his correctional officer wife bring drugs in for us as long as we paid him with drugs. This was what we as an organization looked for, an opportunity to get drugs in and cash money out. Larry worked it out, drugs were exchanged, and the female correctional officer would bring drugs in for us in exchange for drugs for her husband and a line of credit from our dealer on the streets, and Larry was having sex with her.

The best, safest, and most private way to make the handoff was in my area of the prison where I worked. I alone worked in and had access to it because I was the food manager's clerk. Next to the warden, the food manager, back in those days, had just as much influence as the warden. Back then, the food manager gave all the contracts for the prisoners' food to the local merchants. Because I did all the ordering, checked all shipping, unloading, and storage, plus distribution of all the food that came into the prison, I had juice. There was a long, almost tunnel-like corridor between the front corridor of the prison and where she was stationed. It led to a very private bathroom used only by her. Next to the bathroom, which was also one that I kept cleaned and stocked, it's one that I was assigned to, was the food manager's office and his clerks area, which no other inmates were allowed access to unless escorted by me.

So the way it worked was, on Saturday mornings, Larry worked in the main kitchen area. My office was in the back of that. I would let Larry inside of my office; the female officer would meet him in the very private bathroom. She would give him the drugs she smuggled in to the prison, then they would have sex while I guarded the door. She and I had to have conversations and exchanges because she would arrive first, and then I would go get Larry. They would go into the bathroom and do their business. Larry would leave first, and she and I would exchange pleasantries, but she would also flirt with me, really strongly, and I used to worry because I knew who and what Larry was, and I wasn't yet on probation or a member. I didn't want no problems over any potential jealousies over this broad. I did, however, masturbate to fantasies of having sex with her, as did every other prisoner there at DVI. She knew I know what's going on, and this one time, they put Larry in the hole on a Friday morning, so she would have known not to meet Larry. That Saturday morning, I did not expect her to still come back there, so I was lying on the floor, cleaning underneath the food carts, when I heard her walk in the back entrance as usual. I slid out from underneath the food cart, still on my back, still on the floor. I was about to tell her, "Hey, what's up? Larry's in the hole, didn't you know?" But before I could say a word, she stood over me with both of her legs spread wide open so that my head was between her feet, and I looked up and was being treated to a clear view of her natural-blond pussy. She had the whole crotch of her panty hose cut out, and as I was stuttering to her that Larry was in the hole, my eyes were locked in on that hairy fat blond pussy. Between looking at her pussy and glancing up at her face looking down at me, I saw she was teasing me and enjoying it. When I told her, "Hey, Larry's in the hole," she told me, "I know, but I still have this package for him, and I can't keep it on me. I think I'm under suspicion, so I'm gonna give it to you to give to Larry's people, okay?" Then she unstraddled my head and told me, "Come on, let's go." In other words, she wanted me to follow her. The look on her face and the way she just stood over me told me there may be a chance for sex with her if I do.

We went into the bathroom, and it's big with big bathroom stalls and doors for privacy. I was just following her lead. She pulled me inside one of the stalls, hiked up her skirt, and placed one foot on the toilet seat, giving me full, unhindered access to her pussy. She was slowly rubbing her clit, and she told me to help her get the package out of her pussy. You know, feel around in there with your fingers for the string tied to the condom full of dope inside of her.

Now I was more afraid of Larry than I was of being discovered by the authorities, but this was prison, and I have not had sex in a couple of years. This woman was my ideal fantasy, not just because she was a female officer and the proverbial forbidden fruit, but also because I love big, fat, thick, juicy blond women with big, fat, thick thighs and big asses, like a black woman.

I rubbed her pussy and fingered it while searching for the end of the string inside of her, to get the drugs. She was oohing and aahing and dripping wet. I finally found the string, and I pulled out the condom packed with heroin. I wrapped it in a piece of toilet paper and shove it in my pants pocket. She started attacking my belt and zipper, telling me that since I was stepping up for Larry, I might as well get rewarded for it. She knew that I knew her and Larry were having sex sometimes back here and how Larry mainly would just want to have his dick sucked by her. However, between attacking and sucking the life out of my penis, she was playing with herself, telling me that she knew I wanted her. She saw it in my eyes every time we would talk, that she wanted to feel my hard cock inside of her. She leaned over the toilet seat with her hands and presented that juicy ass of hers to me and told me to stick it in her, hurry up, we didn't have much time. She could sense my fear and hesitation, I guess, because she told me not to worry about Larry. She would never tell him or anyone else. She just wanted me to "give it to her good, baby." I did just that. I gave it to her good, like ten tigers unleashed.

So we had sex, and I gave the drugs to Hobo, who was the Nuestra Familia lieutenant on my block. They were really grateful to me for doing this for them since Larry had gone to the hole. They would get back to me about maybe wanting me to continue as the go-between for them and the mule. A mule is someone from prison staff that we have turned out to bring in stuff for us.

The next Saturday, no one had said anything to me about continuing as a go-between, yet she came back to my work area and this time just signaled me to meet her in the bathroom. I went and I followed her in. This time she reached up inside of herself and pulled out a big balloon full of marijuana, wiped it off with toilet paper, and handed it to me. I told her no one had gotten to me yet about this, to be expecting this, and she told me, "Oh, that's not for the gang. This is for you. It's weed. I remember you told me you liked to smoke weed, so I brought this in myself, just for you. Now get over here, let's hurry up, we don't have a lot of time." She started unzipping and unbuckling my pants, kissing me, telling me how she had been thinking about me all week long and couldn't wait to be with me again. It had been a long time since she had been fucked so good.

Larry stayed in the hole for three more weeks. Hobo and Rock had gotten back to me, telling me how they would be really grateful if I would continue to be the middleman between them and this female officer. Michaelleen was not the first female correctional officer I had been intimate with, nor had she been the last one either. Two of these women were my counselors, both of them I came to love too. Each one blessed me when I needed blessing most. I will not say who they were.

I was much younger then. I was a handsome, well-built man back then, and one thing I realized about female officers and all female staff was that underneath those uniforms, they are still just women. They have real feelings and emotions, desires, needs, and weaknesses too. It's funny when I returned to prison after having been married to Michaelleen. The gang coordinators and security people came to interview me. They told me straight out, "We don't care about what you do as far as gang activity is concerned." They just wanted me to assure them that I was gonna leave all female officers and staff alone, not be involved with any of them. I laughed and told them, "Hey, after being married to one of them, believe me, I don't want anything anymore ever to do with any female staff. I was back in prison because of Michaelleen."

I was done with female staff or officers for good. I had come to learn that along with that pretty pussy came the rest of the woman too. With all her baggage and problems, I was tired; I was through being daddy and schoolteacher to them all. Hell, I might turn gay, I joked, because I was so burned out on women and dealing with all their issues. The gang coordinators and security laughed and said, "Well, you've come to the right prison for that. There's inmates out there now with breasts and some who look even more like women than some of the female officers who worked there." I said, "Hey, I'm just kidding around about homosexuals. I'm not ready for that, at least not yet." We all laughed. They felt better about my being released to their general population main line from the hole. I was kept in the hole since my return to the prison system in 1993.

One of the interesting things about my whole relationship and experiences with Michaelleen was that because, as I said, Michaelleen was a dedicated, loyal correctional officer, all her friends at Soledad prison were what we call "in the car" of people who ran the prison, who would go on to advance to higher positions in the whole Department of Corrections network and system. They were people she partied with and even had sex with. She was highly respected by all her peers and by all the inmates there too. I remember not even being remotely interested in her or any corrections personnel; they were all "the enemy" to me. But through her, I learned that a lot of these people who worked for the prison system were really good people. They were just human beings trying to do a job, trying to make a living to support their families. I also learned that there were a lot of dickheads working there too. Because of Michaelleen, they hated me and went out of their way to try to fuck me over.

Here's the most interesting thing I learned. It was like half the staff at different prisons I went to, once they saw I was serious about Michaelleen, they actually sympathized with me, tried to help me and protect me. I actually came to have a true respect and genuine like for correctional people, whom I once considered my enemy. They were just human beings trying to do what they believed was the right thing and just trying to live the American promise of life, liberty, and the pursuit of happiness, as they knew it. I no longer blindly prejudged or hated all correctional officers and staff. I even ran into a few on the streets later.

I actually stopped some idiots who wanted to fuck up this correctional sergeant on the streets just because they could and he was accessible and vulnerable. I told them, "No, anyone messes with this man will answer to me personally." I didn't even know this man except that I saw all the stripes he had on his sleeve, which meant he was an old-timer who had put in many years of service. I watched him, the way he carried himself. I could tell he was a good man. Funny, huh? A couple of times I intervened on the streets when people wanted to do evil against some of these people who worked for the prison system, because of all the good lieutenants and officers and associate wardens I had come to know after I was involved with Michaelleen.

Also, I want to say, some of these people I did get to know, they were not weak. They had balls as big as any of the men I had run with in the prison gang and organized crime experience. I truly respected them as men and women, too. If any of you happen to read this book, you know who you are. Thank you and God bless you still. I tip my hat in respect to each of you.

Chapter

13

I went to San Quentin. I finally made it to my people, and I was gonna get a visit from Michaelleen finally. They're not supposed to put enemies on the yard together. That's what they're not supposed to do, but they do. I was on the yard, and I got my good shoes that I've been saving for a visit, you know. I'd been there for a while, and I hadn't had a visit. I was gonna get a visit this day. She's already quit her job. They withheld her pay and a bunch of benefits she had coming. She finally was approved to come visit me, so I was finally gonna get to go see her. I went out to the yard first, and I was on the yard waiting for them to call me. I was the first one on the yard from my tier, from Fig and Casper and all of us, the original NF. I went to the yard, and I saw Ricky and Pinky. Chino was what they actually called Ricky; he's known as Chino, and he and Pinky, they're old brothers, good, old-time brothers. I love them. I saw them on our yard. They're already out there, and I went out there, and I was the first before Fig or Casper. "How you doing, bros?" We're shaking hands, and I picked up that something's wrong. "What's up? What are you guys doing here? Did you guys decide to come over here and join us or what?" They're quiet; they're waiting for Fig to come out on the yard, because they got orders to hit Fig. Now these are killers. These are not no young and inexperienced soldiers like they had been sending us. These are guys that can get it done. I picked up on it, and I told them, "Ahh, come on, guys, no, don't do it, man. Do not do this, man. Not on my yard, please. Don't do this." And they're like, "Hey, Down, we got to do what we got to do, man, you know." So I said, "No, don't do this, just stop, wait." So Fig got out in the yard, and a few of our brothers started grouping. I was going back over to Fig, and I was telling him, "Hey, just get behind me, man. This ain't going down." I saw Ricky and Pinky pull the pieces out their asses. I'd already told them, "Don't do this, don't do this." Now we're under the gun; mini fourteens were ten feet above us. But here they come; they're gonna try to hit Fig. I told Fig, "Get behind me." I took off my belt, and I was fighting with these brothers, and the paperwork will show it. I'm not just making this up. It's there in the paperwork and write-up and all that. So we're fighting, man, and one thing that happened was, what they would usually do was blow the whistle first. If you didn't get down, it's live fire. The guards, they're shooting. Then they'll shoot a warning shot sometimes. You know, and if you still don't get down, they will shoot. So what happened was, the whistle went off, and nobody stopped fighting. We're fighting, man. The warning shot went off, but we're still fighting. Next thing I know I was doing a somersault, because the guard standing ten feet above me, he's shooting down. He shot me with the M-14, and I did a somersault. Hahaha! The guard hit me in my leg and my foot; it came out my foot. Lucky shot. He could have shot me in the head. The interesting thing is, this guard, the very next week, would shoot an AB the same way and killed him on the same yard. The guard would go out on stress leave and all that other stuff, retire and shit like that, because he couldn't handle it. One thing he did do was when he made the write-up, he wrote it up that I was a hero. He said that he saw Ricky and Pinky coming with what looked like prison-made shanks in their hands, coming to attack Fig, and that Riley came across and stepped in the middle and started fighting, trying to save Fig. He then blew the whistle, fired a warning shot, and said Riley was digging up in Castro's guts, so he shot; he had to shoot me. So that was good. We came back in, and I was waiting to go to the hospital. We're all in a cage; brothers on the upper tiers were yelling, "Down, why the fuck did you get in? Why the fuck did you get involved?" I told 'em, "I told you motherfuckers not to bring this shit to me, man, and you brought it to me, so now the choice is made, man. I'm with Fig. I'm with Casper. I'm here, this is where I'm at. My choice is made." This other guy, who was not a member, was trying to clown,

"Hey, Sundown, I hear your going to the hospital to get your foot out of Pinky's ass." He thought he was being funny. I told him, "Shut the fuck up. Don't you fucking talk about my brothers like that. This is family shit, you ain't got a fucking thing to do with this. You shut your fucking mouth." I was looking at Ricky and Pinky. "Hey, you know I love you guys, but this is the way it's got to be." Pinky would go on. I think Ricky finally left, but Pinky would go on to sit on the controlling mesa with Tibbs and Hobo. They would end up getting shipped to the supermax over in Colorado, and they'd end up losing what they had inherited to what's running it now. Now I have a lot of respect for D. C. I got to say that right now. I don't know some of these other guys. I don't really know some of these younger guys that are up there now, because they're kinda new. I do know D. C., and I have respect for him, because he earned his stripes. I remember when he started with us, he almost got killed in a gunfight for us. I got nothing but respect for D. C. But I'm way ahead of myself. They say he's the new general, the only one, so D. C., I tip my hat to you, man. I got nothing against you, boy.

So it's on now; it's clear-cut what side I was on now, because it was brought to me. I had said, "Leave me out of it, don't involve me. I'm going to marry this correctional officer. I'm done. I'm riding off into the sunset. There's no more Constitution, then there's no more La Nuestra Familia. I'm free." I got tired of them trying to kill Fig, man. Fig had nine life sentences that he got just for being a loyal soldier. Hobo's on the other side. They were crime partners, and they were young kids who came into the prison for joyriding back in seventy-two or something like that. To me, you don't send recruits to try to make their bones on a loyal brother. That's just plain disrespectful to me. One thing I was glad of was they sent Ricky and Chino, because those were brothers. But don't send these guys that are new and are trying to be brothers at us; it's a family affair. You know, it's like Sly Stone sang about; it's a family affair. I was home now, I was back, and I was in NF1. So now, "What's up? Let's take over, let's do this." I brought this up because like I said, I mentioned about my mother being murdered. I kept trying to talk to Hobo and everybody else and say, "Look, this is bullshit, man. Fig didn't do nothing. Casper ain't done nothing. These are loyal brothers. They made the La Nuestra Familia. In Salinas, you wouldn't have a La Nuestra Familia if not for Casper, Cricket, and Ernie. These are the guys who helped make us. You don't treat them like this." But what it was, was some of those guys who snaked their way up into leadership positions, not all of 'em, but some of them, they were scared because, they said, "If we bring those guys back in, eventually they're gonna get us for our dirty work, so it's like, we gotta kill them." So we're fighting, brother against brother, man. For the next five or six years, we're fighting. And it was ugly, nothing to be proud of, but it got to the point where every time they sent somebody after us, we would beat them down. They would send three or four guys after one of us, and we would end up chasing them down. I mean, you grow up in this shit; you're seasoned in this shit. When you've been outnumbered by your enemies and you're on a tier, what the police would do, if they wanted to get you, they would have tier exercise, and three guys would come out at one time. The police would put you out with two Aryan Brotherhood guys who know you're there, and they will try to kill you. So when you're used to fighting like that, when you're used to being like a cat thrown into a room full of dogs, then don't send nobody who ain't been there, don't send nobody like that after me, because I'll eat them. I'll have him for breakfast. Like I said, I don't know if God was on our side or what, but we would win. So it got to be kinda embarrassing actually, you know.

Now my concentration was the streets, so I said, "Look, the only way these guys are gonna listen is if we get their families, not hurt them, just kidnap them, take them to the local cemetery at night and take photographs and say, 'Look, we have your families, lay down, cease and desist.'" I was actually always against that before. We always believed you didn't touch somebody's family, but since my mother's death, I was no longer thinking clear. We left families alone—they were innocents; they were not involved. Other gangs kill family members, like the Aryan brotherhood and Mexican Mafia; they don't have any qualms about killing someone's family. We had always stayed away from that. We wanted to be an honorable thing. We were men society said were garbage. "Let's get rid of them. We don't need them no more, forget them." We said, "Oh, hold it, we're not gonna be forgotten." Fig, Casper, and everyone said, "No, we don't do that." I said, "No, this is what we have to do. These guys are sitting there, they got life, you know. We can't touch them because they're in cells where we can't reach them. But they can give out orders, and the only way we're going to get them to stop is we're going to have to gather up their families." Casper and Fig were like, "No, you're out there, Down. That's too much, we can't do that." So I said, "Okay, well now you're tying our hands. Now we got a civil war, so let's go." So we didn't do that. That's what I'm saying though. I think that with my mother being murdered the way she had been murdered, it kinda did something to me, and so I was like, everything's fair game now, you know. But I knew better. We still left the innocents out. I came to my senses and went back to what I always believed: leave the innocents alone. I really did believe to leave them alone, that they're not involved. It's not their faults that their sons or their nephews or their whatever got involved in some shit. But we could have stopped it. Had we done what I suggested, I said, "How many soldiers do we have on the streets right now? This is what we need to have them do." Well, when you've got every day of them sending people after you trying to kill you, it's kinda hard, so I was voted down, like I said, Fig was now our general, Casper was the first captain, and I was the regimental lieutenant. I was security, then it got to where I was first captain. Both Casper and I were going home, so we had to put different people in our places. We were going to go concentrate on Salinas. Salinas was our regiment and the Bay Area, you know. We were gonna bypass San Jose. They could have San Jose. We're gonna get Salinas, we're gonna get the Bay Area, and anything else we can pick up along the way. The other thing too is we wanted to get back the brothers who had been squeezed out. I said, "Hey look, the brothers who got squeezed out, let's reach out to them and get them to come back with us, because they were good brothers, you know." So we started bringing back some of the brothers who had got squeezed out—solid, proven brothers, hits up the yin-yang, schooled and leaders. Whenever somebody would leave them, if it was somebody who'd been there for ten years plus, we would reach out to them and say, "Hey, come over here." It's all about numbers now. They got their body; we got our body. We're trying to recruit. We went out concentrating on Salinas. I would eventually be paroled to Monterey, to Salinas, Casper paroled to Salinas. We're concentrating on securing our places. I'm starting to get into some things. Let me stop for a second because I want to make sure I'm not opening anybody up to any RICO or anything like that.

There are a couple of things I need to clarify. Michaelleen, the female correctional officer I married while I was in prison, she gave up her job. Now one of the reasons why the incident in San Quentin was so good was because they had told her, "Look, this dude you're in love with, he's a piece of shit, man, cut him loose. Or we're going to have to fire you." She said, "You don't have to fire me, I quit," so she quit. Well, they owed her a bunch of back money and some benefits and stuff like that, and they weren't going to give them to her. So by me getting shot that way that day on the yard, and because the officer wrote it up that I was actually saving a life and defending a guy and that he shot me, I was a hero. So there was another way to go at it. I mean, I was going to use it, the warden. The associate warden then was Mike Cambra. He used to be a counselor and a lieutenant back when we were in Tracy, so he knew me real good. Anyway, I got hold of some lawyers, and the guards were reading all my mail, and they were reading letters between her and me and all that stuff. In my letters, I was letting them know what I was going to do, so sure enough, here comes the associate warden to see me. He asked, "What do you want to do?" I said, "Well, you see it on paperwork, man. You guys shot me when you shouldn't have shot me, you know, so I got a lawsuit, a slam dunk. But I'll tell you what I'm gonna do." I told them if they leave Michaelleen alone and release all the money that they owed her, the benefits they owed her, all the back pay, everything she had coming, stop harassing her, and let her visit me, they could put me up for transfer to Disneyland, you know. I said that jokingly, you know, Disneyland. I had requested to go somewhere else, and they said no. I knew they were going to say no when I asked on the first request. So I said, "I'm going to your pearl, send me to CMC," you know, CMC east. They said, "Okay, it's done." You know what I mean? I was there two days and wanted to get the fuck out of there. But that's a whole different story; I used getting shot in exchange for getting them to back off Michaelleen and give her her money and let us get married.

I had sworn allegiance to the Constitution, and it took me a couple of years to work my way back and to finally get back to the main body of the real La Nuestra Familia. Another thing too, the staff, they had La Nuestra Familia 1, La Nuestra Familia 2; that's how they segregated us. So that was the official designation; that's the way it went down in all the books. You got a beef with it, go beef with them. As far as I'm concerned, we were the only La Nuestra Familia. But still my brothers were over there, and this was a civil war we had to somehow bring to an end. When I got with Fig, Casper, Babo, and all them, I asked,

"What's the move?" Again, they were saying there was no Constitution anymore. We're making a new thing. And here I was again. I say, "Wait a minute. I'm done with these guys because they're not following the Constitution and now you guys are saying you're not going to follow the Constitution anymore. You're going to make changes. These are the new changes, and you know it sounded real good. Yeah, changes were necessary. I guess there's no choice, but legally, I'm free." I don't need to get involved, but then that day that incident happened, it was brought to me, so I had to get involved. From that day on, it was settled. So we had two La Nuestra Familias. We had La Nuestra Familia 1, we had La Nuestra Familia 2, and we had a civil war.

THE THIEF ON THE CROSS

Nuestra Familia Prison Gang LNF   Page 1 of 6

HISTORY OF LA NUESTRA FAMILIA PRISON GANG

A Security Threat Group - STG

Prison Gang Name: La Nuestra Familia

Other Names: LNF, NF, FNE, F, Nancy Flores

Origin and History: Originated in California in the Soledad Prison in the mid 1960's.

Ideology/Philosophy: The La Nuestra Familia prison gang was established to protect younger, rural, Mexican-American inmates from other predator gangs, most notably urban, Mexican-American inmates from the Los Angeles area who belonged to the Mexican Mafia (EME).

Membership Characteristics: Members are of Hispanic origin. There is a "Blood-in, Blood-out" requirement for membership.

Leadership/Organizational Structure: The LNF has a constitution and a paramilitary structure, with ranks ranging from soldier to general. Prison and street segments have separate organizational chains.

Geographic Location: The LNF originated on the West Coast, but has spread to other areas within the United States prison systems through transfers and other geographic relocations.

Associated Organizations: Black Guerilla Family (to some degree), Northern Structure

Some believe that the Northern Structure is a subsidiary gang of the LNF due to similar identifying tattoos.

Antagonistic Organizations: Texas Syndicate, Mexican Mafia, F-14, Mexikanemi, and Aryan Brotherhood

Typical Identifiers: LNF members may wear red rags. Tattoos may include a sombrero, a dagger, or "NF"

La Nuestra Familia Constitution - PDF

Nuestra Familia Timeline - very interesting - PDF

Blood In - Blood out

Many gangs, both street gangs and prison gangs, have established horrific guidelines for both joining the gang, or for leaving the gang. The most definitive is the philosophy of "Blood in - Blood out." This philosophy means that the only way a person can join the gang is to shed the blood of someone else. A person becomes a target and the prospective gang members is usually ordered to kill the person. The target may be another gang member, a police or corrections officer, or an innocent person on the street. Membership in some gangs, particularly prison gangs, is for life - the only way out is death.

Gangs have adopted this philosophy for one reason - to make sure that informants or undercover officers do not attempt to infiltrate the ranks. The gangs know that an officer will not kill someone just to get on the inside.

Constitution of La Nuestra Familia

(May not be up to date)

La Nuestra Familia anniversary day September 16th 1972.
The Nuestra familia philosophy:

All new members must spill the blood of the enemy to prove their nuestra familia loyalty, as the Nuestra familia will not hesitate to spill the blood of a member who turns coward, traitor, or deserter. Blood in, Blood out in, is fact, an Nuestra familia ritual, not a myth. Blood in relates to the Blood spilled during initiation, and Blood out alludes to the consequences of trying to depart from the gang.

The Nuestra Familia Original Constitution

ARTICLE I Supreme Commander

Section I. The Nuestra General (NG) is the supreme power in the organization known as la Nuestra Familia. His power shall have no limit (within ART. I, II, III). Solely he can declare war for the entire O end once in a state of war, peace shall be private until the announcement from the Nuestra General.

Section II. The Nuestra General will automatically be released from any duties and responsibilities upon receiving a date of one year or less.

Section III. The Nuestra General will be a seasoned experienced warrior. This qualification is mandatory in order to hold this high office. When the time comes for the Nuestra General to pick a successor, he will do so from the ranks of the commanders at his disposal.

Section IV. In case of an emergency and the Nuestra General is downed, the captain of the pinta will take over and automatically declare war until the first captain can automatically assume the rank of Nuestra General. In this emergency, the home captain will have no power to appoint or replace any of all position in the high command of la nuestra familia.

Section V. The Nuestra General has the power, in the state of war conditions (as regards to structures), to appoint captains. In peace time, he will retain the power to discharge any commander that is negligent in the function of his position, however he will relinquish his power to appoint captains if the familia braves where the captain has been discharged at and has no reserve captain to take command. The familia body of said disposed captain will elect a successor.

http://www.gangsorus.com/nuestra_familia.htm   10/14/2013
229

Section VI. A discharged commander will lose his rank of captain and said authority of that rank.

Section VII. Only applies in time of peace.

Section VIII. The Nuestro General, upon receiving a complaint from one of his soldados that the authority of which he is under is unjustly using their powers over him due to personal conflict, the Nuestro General will appoint a committee of no less than three soldados from that particular clan to investigate said charges, and each is to report to the Nuestro General.

Section IX. The Nuestro General will always keep in touch with all familianos leaving to the streets, until a branch in union of La Nuestra Familia is established.

Section X. The Nuestro General can have as many as ten (10) active commanders at one time. He will grade them as 1st, 2nd, 3rd, and so on according to their leadership abilities and their overall foresight.

Section XI. The Nuestro General will appoint a first captain or commander who will be his successor, and is the Nuestro General becomes incommunicado, the first captain of the Nuestra Familia will have the responsibility to see that every captain of said O works and governs within the constitution.

Section XII. The successor only applies as far as the first captain is concerned. The Nuestro General has the right to select the first captain.

ARTICLE II. Discharge from all duties of Nuestro General.

Section I. The Nuestro General may be impeached from office where it is the opinion of all commanders holding office at that time and that he isn't working in the best interests of the organization and this can be derived by a petition or document with signatures of each captains own writing.

Section II. Upon receiving the document, the Nuestro General will automatically lose all power, but he may challenge the loyalty of the signatures, in which case a soldado will be appointed by the body to write to the captains and verify their vote.

Section III. Upon confirmation of a discharge of the Nuestro General, he will lose all power, rank, and the successor will move into that position.

ARTICLE III. Objective and Bylaws of Nuestra Familia.

Section I. The primary purpose and goal of this organization is for the betterment of its members and the building up of this organization on the outside into a strong and self supporting familia.

Section II. All Members will work solely for this objective and will put all personal goals and feelings aside until said fulfillment is accomplished.

Section III. A familiano will not be released from his obligation towards the organization because he is released from prison, but will work twice as hard to see that a familia is established and will work in the hand with the organization that's already established behind the walls (pinta).

Section IV. A familiano will remain a member until death or otherwise discharged from the organization. And he will always be subject to put the best interest of the organization first and always above everything else, in or out of prison.

Section V. An automatic death sentence will be put on a familiano that turns coward, traitor or deserter. Under no other circumstances will a bother familiano be responsible for the spilling the blood of a fellow familiano. To do so will be considered as an act of treason.

Section VI. In order for [ART. II, Sec. V] to be invoked, the regiment governing body will hold a vote amongst themselves and pass sentence. Majority rules. In the case of a tie vote, the decision will lie with the captain, and his decision shall be final.

Section VII. All present familianos in said organization La Nuestra Familia acknowledge said constitution upon reading it and will be held accountable for his actions is said constitution is not followed.

ARTICLE IV. Regimental captain.

Section I. A captain is a regimental commander of La Nuestra Familia and holds the rank just below of Nuestro General. Their responsibilities are to lead and direct La Nuestra Familia regiments under his care to successfully accomplish the goals set forth in [ART. I, SEC V].

Section II. For this purpose, he (captain) shall have the choice of selecting his own lieutenant (lenientes) and shall have the power to dismiss the lieutenants if he (captain) feels that they are not accepting or handling their responsibilities of leadership. In times of peace, a dismissed lieutenant has the option of invoke [ART. I, SEC VI].

Section III. Due to circumstances beyond our control, it may be that there will be more than one captain in the regiment at the same time. If a captain is transferred from a familia regiment to another where there is already a captain, the captain with the highest rank will take command, and the other will be in reserve according to their rank.

Section IV. A captain will have a grade rating of 1st, 2nd, 3rd and so forth, as [ART. III, SEC. III] can be invoked. Also, the lower the number rating, the greater their authority. And no captain can override or contradict the orders of a higher-ranking commander without directions of the Nuestra Familias Nuestro General.

Section V. There shall never be more than ten (10) captains in the Organization at any time. This includes reserves. If there are already ten captains in the Organization and a regiment is without a captain or commander due to [ART. III, SEC. III], the 1st lieutenant will run the familia (regiment) temporarily until a commander arrives or there is an opening of rank of captain.

Section VI. The reserve captains will only take power if the governing one is downed or discharge by the Nuestro General. It will be the duty of the governing commander to take and show him the internal functions of the regiment in order for that reverse captain will be qualified to govern the regiment if the need arrives.

Section VII. All captains will hold equal rank and therefore one cannot order the other, except under [ART. III, SEC. IV] or where the reserve captain has set forth efficiently running the familia (regiment). In that case, the reserve captain will cease to interfere or he will be brought before the Nuestro General.

Section VIII. The reserve captain only has as much power as the governing commander wants bestowed on him and not more. The familia body, should at all times know the structure of the reserve captain.

Section IX. In time of war, the captain is only answerable to the Nuestro General, and no soldado shall question the order set forth by him personally or through one of his tenientes. To question said orders could be a treasonable act, as outlined in [ART. I, II, SEC. V], depending on the seriousness of the offence, which will lie with the captain to determine.

THE THIEF ON THE CROSS

Section X. In time of peace, as in a time of war, a captain is answerable to the Nuestro General; however, in time of peace, is a familiano soldado feels that the power or powers of the structure in his regiment is misusing their appointed authority against him to conflicted personalities, he has the right as an honorable member of this Organization to appeal to the Supreme Commander Nuestro General, as per (ART. I, SEC. V).

Section XI. The commander shall be responsible for the welfare and lives of the soldados under his command at all times, and there shall be no suicidal missions ordered by a commander. A suicidal mission shall be translated as an act where the soldado has no chance of survival.

Section XII. Home Captain where Nuestro General has his headquarters shall be held responsible if anything should happen to the Nuestro General. It will be the duty of the captain to personally see that two of his best warriors be with the Nuestro General whenever possible. If the Nuestro General is downed, the captain will be stripped of all rank after the state of war is over.
(ART. I, SEC. III)

ARTICLE V. Functions and qualities of a lieutenant

Section I. A lieutenant is the third in the power ladder of La Nuestra Familia, he is under the captain. He's the representative of La Nuestra Familia, as he will be in contact with all soldados at all times and, therefore, he should at all times set a good example for the soldados to follow.

Section II. While in the state of war, and the arms quota drops below the specified requirement, it shall be the first priority of the lieutenant to restore to par as outlined in (ART. V, SEC. II).

Section III. Each lieutenant shall have a certain number of soldados assigned to him. He shall be responsible for their schooling and basic needs and conducts.

Section IV. Whenever one or all of his soldados go into combat with any enemies of La Nuestra Familia, he (lieutenant) shall present the captain with a full report of what occurred.

Section V. The lieutenant shall have rating of 1st, 2nd, 3rd . This rating shall be given to them by the captain according to their experience and leadership abilities.

Section VI. It shall be the duties of the lieutenant to keep a record of all known names and numbers of La Nuestra Familia. Each day, he shall check all new arrivals who enter his territory against the record books and make a report to his captain.

Section VII. All lieutenants shall question all new familiano assigned to him for information as to unknown enemies of La Nuestra Familia. New information shall go into the record book and whenever one of his soldados is transferred to another pinta, a copy of the record book shall be sent with the soldado.

Section VIII. It shall be the responsibilities of the lieutenant to inform the captain of the departure of his soldados in order so that the familia of the other regiment can be informed.

ARTICLE VI. Familiano Soldados.

Section I. all requests for membership into this organization shall be made to the captain. Any member can make such a request for any individual providing such requesting is willing to accept full responsibilities for said individual.

Section II. Final decision for membership shall not be made until 30 days have elapsed from such a request, and the governing body of the regiment must approve the request for any new membership.

Section III. No applicant will be considered for membership if he the (applicant) misrepresents his qualifications, also once a member and soldado misrepresents his actions in battle for the benefit of making his action seem more valorous, he will be subject to be disqualified under (ART.I, SEC.V), a minor offense, or (ART. I, SEC.VI), Expelled from the Organization, depending upon the circumstances and seriousness of the lie.

Section IV. Membership of this Organization shall be restricted one those of the latin extraction. No maximum or minium shall be involved by this constitution in so far as membership into this Organization is concerned, however, such limitations may be established by the Nuestro General as to be neccessary to maintain proper control, although others of other extractions (Raza's) will will be considered with the consent of both the captain and the Nuestro General

ARTICLE VII. Discipline and conduct.

Section I. The regimental captain shall pass sentence for all minor in fractions of conduct. In time of war, there will be no appeal to the Nuestro General.

Section II. Punishment shall be administered by the lieutenant
(ART. IV, SEC.III) or by the regiment as a whole, when ordered by the familia commander.

Section III. All familianos shall be subject to disciplinary action or immediate expulsion from this Organization (ART.II, SEC.V). In the case of misconduct or behavior unbecoming of a member, said conditions shall prevail with regards to the individual towards another member, the Organization as a whole, or his superiors.

Section IV. Under no conditions will there be any fighting between familianos. To do so will bring on disciplinary action and if blood is spilled, it will result in The expulsion of one or parties involved (ART.II, SEC. V).

Section V. No member of this Organization shall put material things, whether it be drugs,money,women, or punks (related to pinta) before the best interest of La Nuestra Familia or a familiano.

Section VI. No familiano shall be about his position in La Nuestra Familia nor discussing familiano business to a superior or to a brother member. Ther shall be no lying or giving false impressions.

Section VII. It is the sacred duty of a familiano guerreo to do battle for La Nuestra Familia, and no soldado should feel that because he fought for his Organization that he is entitled to special privileges. All that matters is that you as a guerreo of La Nuestra Familia are living up to your responsibilities. remember that a true guerreo does not need to boast of his accomplishments.

Section VIII. Under no circumstance is any portion of this constitution to be altered without notification of of Nuestro General and one third of his captains staff, nor shall a familiano or familiano regiment put their own interpretation upon said constitution. It is to be read in its entirety. All Sections that relate to one concept are to be read as such.

As familianos began to be paroled, they were given advance instructions, assignments, and other orders to report to the designated location, where they were

231

reunited with other familianos already established on the streets. They were given additional orders and instructions and assigned a street regimental position. The main objective of a familiano on the street was to organize moneymaking ventures and establish a familiano bank and organizational territories. They would then be given a new set of rules, regulations and responsibilities.

The Nuestra Familia wrote a constitutional subdivision in order to avoid creating any unnecessary problems on the street's and it reads:

The Nuestra Familia constitution subdivision for the streets:

Article I

Section I. The building up of this organization on the outside will be done in these three steps.

Section II. The first step consists of establishing a self supporting familia regiment. Each shall have a bank with $ 10,000 basis, or less than $1,000, and shall have both into business in part or in whole.

The Nuestra Familia constitution subdivision for the streets:

Article I

Section I. The building up of this organization on the outside will be done in these three steps.

Section II. The first step consists of establishing a self supporting familia regiment. Each shall have a bank with $ 10,000 basis, or less than $1,000, and shall have both into business in part or in whole.

Section III. The Familia (regiment) bank will be responsible for all financial matters that occur within its own territory (Familia) town or pertains to its own business ventures, and soldados under their jurisdiction shall assist any familiano in their regiment who, due to a mission, find himself in a need of a lawyer, doctor or bail, the bank that is supporting the venture will be obligated to furnish him with these items. The familia bank, is just like the main bank, will be into legal business... but unlike the main bank, it will have no restrictions about the legality of such places. All the profit that are derived from the Nuestra Familia Bank will go into the familia bank and from it will be distributed to its banks functions.

Section IV. The Familia lieutenant shall lead and direct the regiment to fulfill the goals set forth in the subdivision of the constitution and the constitution in general. He, the lieutenant, shall be in charge of the bank and see to it that it function as described in (ART. I, SEC. II) of this subdivision.

Section V. The Familiano soldados at first will be expected to make sacrifices in so far as they commit an illegal venture. All profits will go into the familia bank. This should be until the bank is strong enough to buy its first bank. Once this is accomplished, the soldado can either be paid on a commission basis by a pay scale. The discretion will be up to the Familia until step three is put into effect.

Section VI. Mandatory rules and regulations in active service on the street

1.) Neither rank-and-file familianos shall take narcotics or any other habit-forming drugs.
2.) All active rank-and-file familianos will be expected to have a legal job.
3.) No heavy or excessive drinking while on duty.
4.) No familiano shall take upon his own personal venture without authorization from his superiors.

Section VII. Upon a familiano reaching his fiftieth (50) birthday and has given at least twenty (20) years of loyalty and dedicated service, he shall be given an alternative whether he wants to go into semi-retirement, meaning that he will be put to manage one of the main banks business and will have nothing to do with the illegal activities. However, in time of war, he may be called back into active duty by the Nuestro General. If a familiano hasn't got the mental capacity for a management job he will be given some other work with the authority within the main bank.

ARTICLE II
Section I. The second step will be to establish the main bank and the regiment captain. each regiment captain will have several familia regiments under him, depending on the ammount of active familianos under his structure.

Section II. The main bank will have dual functions of being a reserve in case of any emergency for the familia bank and will also buy into legitimate business. the first responsibility consist of supporting all wars declared by the Nuestro General and all expenses that go to the Organization in the prison system. All expenses for a familiano sent on a mission outside of his territory of his home familia, unless said mission is a monetary venture, in which case the home familia of that soldado will pay all expenses. It will be used for primary expenses of building up a new familia regiment and as a payroll source for the regimental commander and Nuestro General.

Section III. The second function of the main bank will be to buy into legitimate businesses, but will always have enough cash resources to meet any emergency that the familia bank may have. All business being under the jurisdiction of said bank will be kept strictly legal, and no illegal activities will be used to broaden the legitimate business or to establish other businesses, Except in an emergency, the main bank may confiscate money from any familia bank as needed to combat any crisis. But it will be the responsibility of said bank (main bank) to repay all cash money to the familia bank. The only exception to this rule of reimbursement is when the emergency is war.

Section IV. Regiment commanders as stated in (ART II, SEC. I) of this subdivision will see to it that all familianos function within the structure. He, the commander, should be the communication link between the familia regiment, and Nuestro General security for the familia regiment under his care shall fall under the jurisdiction of the regimental commander.

ARTICLE III.
Section I. The third step will only be activated when this organization has accomplished the two prior steps. (ART.I, SEC. I,and ART.II, SEC. I) of this subdivision and it authority in the pinto fools that the outside counterpart of this organization is strong enough to step up under their own government and in which he, the Nuestro General, will instruct the regimental commander to activate step three.

The Nuestra Familia (CAT) System:

The Nuestra Familia Category (CAT) system was designed and/or developed in order to categorize each member according to his rank, caliber and educational status. This in turn allows our leadership to keep sort of track on a member's educational standing and his progress, which will enable each member to be assigned to an individual responsibility or to a position with additional responsibilities according to his experience in a wide range of areas that coincide with the member's knowledge and know- how. All members will start out as a (CAT I). Member and the highest ranking position is that of a (CAT III). Member. A new recruit is automatically given the ranking of a (CAT). I member

CAT I. This member is basically a new member in training, and these new members are taught the very basic of the Organization and its history, functions and

THE THIEF ON THE CROSS

Chapter

14

We were regrouped and restructured. Fig was the general, and Casper was the first captain. I was the second captain. Before I transferred, I was promoted. Cricket had taken regimental lieutenant. This was our new command structure as far as the prison system was concerned. Once Casper paroled, I became first captain now, Death Row Joe's old position. Isn't that ironic? I was given authority to establish regiments and to appoint lieutenants.

I requested to CMC (California Men's Colony) in San Luis Obispo. They filmed a movie scene there about a hit on the yard for the movie *To Live and Die in LA*. Anyway, there were a lot of dropouts there, good brothers, who had got kinda squeezed out and who could be recruited and brought back in. That was one of the main reasons that I wanted to go to CMC, to talk to a few brothers whom I knew were there who were good down brothers. They were considered dropouts now because they had been squeezed out of La Nuestra Familia 1, and we were recruiting and going back and getting the old soldiers. Even La Nuestra Familia 2 was starting a reentry program, trying to get back dropouts, guys who were considered dropouts, but they were still considered brothers who could have a change of heart and still be good and still be loyal if you gave them a chance. Not all of them, because there were some that were, "Keep on going, we don't want you back." There was a handful that was out there that would come back and did come back. We already had Salinas, so Casper going to Salinas was like going home. That's the way it was; that's the way it was set up, but I want to say this. I got released. Now what it had come down to was, we were caught up in a battle for survival, because these guys were going to try and wipe us out, kill us off, so do you still believe in La Nuestra Familia? Do you still believe in what we originally were? Okay, so it's different now. Now we're actually gonna have to be like the Italian families. We're going to have families of our own, under the umbrella of La Nuestra Familia. We're going to have to go out and recruit, get our own soldiers. If we build our own families in our own towns, have our own security, take care of our brothers who were still behind the wall, that was the goal. So I was out, five years before they got me again. In those five years, I was in Salinas, in Monterey. I was all over Salinas, Monterey, Santa Cruz, San Jose, and the Bay Area. The most important thing that I learned was that I'm gonna build my own family. I'm gonna be my own *Coppo*, my own captain, my own regiment. I'm gonna have my own soldiers loyal to me. Casper, it was the same way, build your own family. So this was kinda the direction that we moved off in. As time went on and wars happened, your little nephew and nieces grew up, your cousins, what have you. They went off to Iraq, even Afghanistan and stuff. They came back, they've been trained by the United States government, and they've been seasoned and blooded by the war. This was a good pool, a very good pool, to recruit from. And again, it's family, so what we learned from the La Nuestra Familia was to be taken to the streets. Concentrate on the street. Before, the power was always behind the walls; that was what La Nuestra Familia 2 was known for. They were concentrating on the power behind the wall. They still had influence on the street, and they still ran their regiments and stuff like that.

I still had my brothers behind the wall, brothers that I love, that I will always love and I will look out for. Anyway, I'm just telling you how recruiting's done, how stuff is done. When you've been seasoned, you've learned and you've trained. This has become all you know; you've spilled too much blood to go back. It seems like you'll never be able to ever truly get away from that. You have to have your soldiers; you have to have people loyal to you, man, people that you can count on. You don't use them, you don't burn them up, and it's a whole different game, you know. It's a whole different game now.

Here we are, brothers like Fig, Larry, and all the others, they are loyal men, faithful, and they gave their lives. The Vindiolas, the Venegases, whole families, they gave their lives, dedicated themselves, and got life sentences. What do you say to them, you know? Manos, who ended up killing himself, he was Babo Sosa's little brother, but there was nothing little about him. I love Manos, and I even married him to my very own favorite of my female cousins, Roxanne. When his brother Babo was having the Nuestra Familia taken away from him, Manos agreed, because to him, Nuestra Familia was his family, even more than his own blood. Can you imagine that kind of devotion and loyalty? He chose La Nuestra Familia over the big brother he had grown up idolizing—the big brother whose leadership, no matter how fucked up D. R. had it sometimes, under Babo, his brother, it was Babo's leadership that helped create us and form us, lead us and helped to make us number 1 with a bullet on the hit parade of gangsters and law agencies. The citizens of California were beginning to become aware of this thing we called La Nuestra Familia. This thing we created to let the world know we will not be forgotten. We feared nothing and no one, not even death itself, because we were lost to this cause the moment we got in. But there will be victory, even if it's crazy, bloody, and violent, not like you see on TV, but up front and personal, and it's only gonna continue to grow and to become much more up close and personal.

This was the leadership of Babo Sosa. We gave our allegiance to this. He, Manos, too gave his all, his allegiance, following in the footsteps of the big brother he worshiped and adored and loved. You who want to be a gangster, could you make the same choice he made? I'm telling you, folks, of all the men I have ever known, there was only one I would have wished I were made more like him. It was Manos, my brother, by blood, my cousin by marriage to the beautiful Roxanne. If ever I was gonna have a kissing cousin again, it would be her, because this is what I helped raise and school her for, to be a soldier's woman. I gave her to my brother Manos in marriage. Como unfamiliar en realidad, Nuestra Familia, like a family in reality, La Nuestra Familia, Our Family—this was our shared Carnalismo. He was asked to choose. He could have sided with his brother as I had, and in doing so, he could have pulled a third of the main body of soldiers there at West Hall in Tracy in 1980. Because this was how much he was respected by everyone, especially the youngsters.

He chose what was now and forever his one family, La Nuestra Familia, and he addressed us all and explained his reasons and, in doing so, solidified all the brothers who admired, respected, or loved him. Brother against brother, just like the civil war that tore apart our country, it had torn apart his own family. In the end, Manos did not agree with some of the directions the La Nuestra Familia he chose was taking, and once he put in his twenty years and even while we're still at the winding-down stages of our civil war, Manos told his family, La Nuestra Familia, that he was done. He gave everyone his blessings on their continuance to the cause, but with all due respect, to just leave him the fuck alone. I was gone, and he could have gone then and rejoined his brother's side had he wanted to. With all the inside knowledge he had on all those who still sought to one day take his own big brother's life, we would have welcomed him with open arms, but he had made a vow to his side that he would be a faithful and loyal follower of the Constitution of La Nuestra Familia, to never betray them either, so he just stayed neutral. The big brother he loved was now dying from cancer, and Manos wanted to be free to try to be with him in whatever way he could, considering the surroundings and limitations, so he just walked away. Manos was blessed with movie-star looks and an Arnold Schwarzenegger body, the only man I was ever jealous of. I love you, Manos. May the Lord God bless you and forgive you of all your sins, and may I see you again someday in the true La Nuestra Familia to us, which we shared once upon a time in crazy Camelot, "Goodnight House." Go rest in peace, my brother, go rest in peace. You will live forever inside this thing called me. Thank you for being my brother. I didn't get to him in time, but this man was a warrior. He just said, "That's it, I'm done." He went in, and he cut all his veins. He wasn't playing around; he was serious. "I'm gone, see you, guys." Good night house—that's what he used to always say back in West Hall when we were all still united as one. "Good night house," how do you just walk away from that? How do you just turn your back on these guys? How do you say, "Hey, sorry, guys, see ya. I'm out of here"? We believed, we shed blood, we got our asses whooped together, we bled, and we did all these things together. I'd have been a fucking nut and insane if not for these guys, you know? These guys would have been crazy too, but we found something to believe in. How do you say to those guys after you are set free? How do you say, "All right, see you later, adios, good-bye," you know? Maybe some people can. Maybe they can turn their backs on that and never look back. I can't; it's not in me.

Now I got to go back to when my mother was murdered. I'm gonna go back there because something happened. I know already I touched on all this, but just bear with me. This is really important to me and to my whole life and the future influences this had upon me. I was so angry; I mean, I remember they just showed me the pictures, the field pictures of my mother's dead body looking back up at me. My mother was beautiful; she was young when she was murdered, in her early forties. The most precious thing in the world to me was my mother. You've heard me say about how I was her prize. I was her precious thing. If ever there was a mama's boy, it was me. I loved my mama; she could do no wrong. So I was angry, man. Like I said, I was in a hole. "Hey, this is your mama, yeah, okay, put him in a single cell, put him in a strip cell. We don't want him to hurt himself." I wasn't gonna hurt myself, but that's what the CDC does. While I was in there, I remember being so mad. I don't know if I said this already, or put this in here. But when I was sixteen years old, I had gone to a revival and got saved, you know. I went forth and gave my life to Jesus. It was like a Damascus road thing, man. I mean, man, there was a battle going on, voices inside me screaming for me to run. I was going to die if I didn't get out of that church. It was like a panic attack intensified a hundred times. "Get out! Run! You're gonna die!" This man was preaching, and something inside me made me go forward and fall on my face and receive Jesus. I was in love with God, man. It was beautiful; it was a beautiful couple of weeks that the guy was there with the revival. I went and got baptized. At this baptism, I thought it's gonna be great; it was a Baptist church. That's what they did; they couldn't wait to baptize you. So the lady who got me to go, she was kinda like a second-type mom, an aunt or something like that. We had grown up with Billy Mae; she was a nice lady, you know? She had talked me into going to this revival. I just wanted to have sex with her daughter Rachel, who had grown into one fine teenage girl. It was why I had come to their house to visit. I had just gotten out of the juvenile youth camp, and I had served a sentence to save Phil Harris, my friend and the Italian Mafia lawyer's nephew.

I made my brother and her sons, who looked up to me, go. "Come on, it's all your mama wants, let's go." So we were going to get baptized.

She was going in the water before me; everybody's up there and singing. And they came out of the water. Halleluiah, praise the Lord. So I was thinking, "Wow, something must be happening in that water." Billy Mae went in before me. We were wearing white robes. Billy Mae went in, they dunked her, and they brought her out. When she came out of that water, because it's a white robe, it's see-through. Billy Mae had some of the biggest breasts and big dark-chocolate nipples. I remember seeing them and lusting. I remember I was getting ready to go in there and get baptized, and I was looking at those nipples and those tits, and I saw her body naked. I was standing there with an erection. Oh my god, I was turned on, right, but then I was also ashamed. "Man, you're getting ready to be baptized. What the hell is wrong with you?" I put it out of my mind the best I could. I was next to go in. All right, I was ready for this, so they dunked me. It seemed like time stood still. I went in the water, I looked up, and I could see everybody. My girl-friend at the time was there. She would become my first wife, Netty Lou. Everybody was singing and clapping. I came out of that water, and I was waiting for something to happen, but nothing happened. I came out, and I was just wet. I didn't understand the significance of the baptism at the time. Nothing against God, nothing against baptisms, I just didn't understand. But I didn't want to disappoint everybody, so I yelled, "Halleluiah, praise the Lord!"

If you ever read the Bible, it says Jesus, after He gets baptized, immediately He was driven into the wilderness by the spirit to be tempted by Satan for forty days and forty nights. Well, I swear to you, I mean, when I came up out of that water, I couldn't wait to leave. I was in a hurry. I was changing my clothes, getting dried off, and the baptism service was still going on. For whatever reason, I had to leave. Something was telling me to leave and pushing me. Something greater than me was telling me to leave. I went out there, and I grabbed my girlfriend. I said, "Come on, let's go!" She said, "Why are we leaving? The services ain't over." I said, "Let's go, let's go, we got to go!" We got to the church door, and I did not understand why I was being driven away. I stopped at the door, and I looked back. They were all up there still singing and baptizing people. I was confused, and all of a sudden, I heard something inside me say, "One day you'll be back, don't worry. Go!" So I left. Jesus had forty days in the wilderness, forty days and forty nights. I went for forty years into the wilderness of the world and sin. I became an animal, a beast, an ugly creature with all the things and sins I did. It took me forty years.

Anyway, the night my mother had been murdered, and I found out, I was in the hole. That was what? Ten years later, yeah, roughly ten, eleven, years later from that time. All these things have happened in that time, a dozen or so years, and I remember being so angry! I was mad at God. "How could You let this happen? How could You? I prayed to You. I asked You when I first came to prison. Please don't let my mother die while I was here."

Well, He hadn't. I got out, but then I came back again, but still, I was so angry. Like I already said before, I said, "I wish You would come down here so that You could taste my knife, so I could kill You! So You could feel my pain!"

All of a sudden, I heard His voice inside me, loud and clear, "I did, and you did."

In other words, "I did come down, and you did kill Me." I swear to God, there on that cell wall, I saw Jesus Christ. I don't know if it was a vision or what, but I saw Him hanging on the cross. I almost stumbled. I was, "Oh, I'm sorry, forgive me, God, forgive me, Lord. I don't want no problem with You. I'm sorry, I apologize. It's not Your fault. This is my own fault. I don't want war with You, God." I was trying to make peace with God. "But, God, You got to know that I'm gonna get out and kill cats, dogs, chickens, man. I'm going to get out of here, and I'm gonna do what I have to do. This cannot go unanswered!" I just kept on going, and like I said, I did all the things and everything that I continued to do and the lifestyle I continued to live. I mean, it was a good life when I was married to Michaelleen. I went out there; I was recruiting. I was doing all the things I was doing. I was living with her. Oh, by the way, guys, yes, you know that fantasy of having sex with Mikey , the correctional officer, in the skintight jumpsuit, it was all that. But that's all it was. I mean, we would fuck each other's brains out to the point of exhaustion, but that was all it was, although this once straight square female correctional officer had become one of my main crime partners, and we did more than a few armed robberies together. She wanted to know what it was like to do an armed robbery, and when we did our first robbery together, we threw the money on the bed, ripped each other's clothes off, and fucked like two animals in heat, all night long, from the adrenaline and excitement of having committed our first robbery together. Every time we did an armed robbery together, we would have wild, crazy, uninhibited sex after; it was crazy. I mean, all the freak would come out of that rodeo cowgirl. She had never had anal sex before. Now she would get so excited she would be begging me to have anal sex. After a robbery, she would ask me after hours of regular sex, "Fuck me in the ass, daddy big dick." When you have a woman calling you daddy big dick and begging you to fuck her in her ass, what can you do but oblige. She said she had orgasms from it, but that they were a different kind of orgasm that felt just as good as regular ones.

But there was nothing substantial there, so it didn't last. We stayed together a total of ten years—from the first day I met her on my birthday in the hole in Soledad until the divorce became final on my birthday ten years later to the day. She divorced me while I was back in prison over some stupid shit man, some stupid shit. I was going to kill her that night and then commit suicide, but instead, something else happened, and I ended up getting arrested and going back to jail. I did eighteen years straight. In those eighteen years, when I came back, I saw that shit was not the same. It had changed, but I still had my schooling, and my schooling had always kept me alive. I did those eighteen years, and I walked every main line, I think, in the state of California. I used my schooling, I went undercover, I did everything I could, and they put me on enemy lines. I guess God's favor was with me. I would end up taking over the lines instead of getting killed. It was crazy; all the while, I was recruiting from different races and groups and people. Except that I was keeping them loyal directly to me, and it's all about Omerta, the code of secrecy and silence. I was sending some to our regiments on the streets. I learned that if you control the drugs and the law, you control the yard. So everywhere I went, I control all the drug traffic, and because I was so good with law, I won almost every case I took. Everybody knew that when it comes to the law, I was better than a fifty-thousand-dollar lawyer. When gang members and leaders see you changing their prison sentences from two hundred years to twenty years, they love you and they protect you as long as you are working on their cases.

I had gone to the Indians, the Native Americans; some called it hiding behind the feather, but I never hid. I had some battles with the Indian circles sometimes because of who I was and what I was. But as long as no one else on the yard seemed to have any problem with me being there, neither would the Native Americans, the Asians, the Samoans, or the others. Like I said, whenever I did get challenged by some wannabe prison chief, I would deal with them too.

I got at everybody on the mesa, the ruling table, of La Nuestra Familia 2 at the time and told them I was done; I was retiring. I let all my own people know that I was done too. They picked their own successor to me, and they even decided to abandon the old La Nuestra Familia 1 title and now go by what they call themselves, which I will not discuss.

Tibbs, I loved Tibbs; we were good friends before he got in, and I had raised my hand in favor of his membership years before. He had inherited the Familia by then. Storms were coming, and it was the right time for me to strike out on my own. I would keep my own family, my own soldiers, and we would only be concerned with ourselves. "Congratulations, Tibbs, Pinky. You guys are now the only remaining La Nuestra Familia. Leave me the fuck alone. I'm done. I did mine, I gave my all. I owe no one. By the Constitution, I am free to retire. Still, I will have my own family, I will raise them, and I will teach them to be a family." It had been my plan all along. Hobo was right in the end; all you need is a handful of dedicated and loyal brothers and, even now, sisters to share your cause and your beliefs. I will protect my family with all that I have learned, and I will do whatever dirty deeds needed to be done. But no more will anyone be killed for stupid shit. It's all about money; he who has it rules.

Now a lot of people will say I went to the Indians because of all the casino money they were getting, millions of dollars. But I didn't go back to the Indians for their casino money. I went back because when I was a child, my mother told me that I was of Blackfoot heritage. Her Uncle Manuel used to be the one who was proud of his Indian heritage and who would teach me of my Indian blood and heritage. He would take me to powwows and sweat ceremonies. I was looking for a way to live. I was a warrior and would always be a warrior; it was in my blood.

The Indian way, the true Indian way, what we call the Red Road, was a good and honorable way to live. It needed warriors to guide and lead them too; I came to love all my Indian brothers. When I was first accepted back into the circle, the elder gave me the name "Two Hats." He was a blind Apache elder who had killed a man in a knife fight on the streets because this big-ass bully didn't like him and thought a blind Indian had no need for a bike. He tried to take this old blind Indian's bike from him and sell it for drugs. But this blind Indian defended himself; they fought, and the blind elder stabbed him to death. He was much loved and respected throughout the prison system. Although he was blind, he lived free and did things normal blind men didn't do, like run the track every day, work out, and stuff. So he was much respected, and he accepted me. He knew all about me. He told me that "Grandfather" had called me home to my true people and that "it was the beat of the drum that led me home." He gave me the name Two Hats; he said, "Because you walk in two worlds, you will be called Two Hats."

Okay, let's backpedal again. I know I keep doing this, but I found that this is the best way to get this story out, to just tell it. Like I said in the beginning of this book, this is my story, let me tell it. When you tell it, you can be the hero.

I came back to the penitentiary. I drove up, and they escorted me in a convoy because I was still active. I was still dangerous, as far as the officials and the powers that be were concerned. Because I had never been debriefed, I guess you could call this my debriefing. Except I'm not debriefing to any police; I'm debriefing to the world. There's a reason why I'm doing this, because I feel I need to speak for all my brothers that are back there who are never going to get out and for all my brothers who are dead, who are never gonna be remembered, for all the brothers who are on death row, and for myself.

I was not liking what I was seeing. Like I said, we were schooled that you try to infiltrate your enemy's lines. You deny being anything. One time, I even remember pretending to be a Christian just long enough to get to an enemy line to go hit an enemy. I went back, and I was an Indian. I went back with the Indians. Like I said, this was my schooling. There're a lot of people that are probably going to be upset. I don't really care; you know what I mean? Because that's the name of the game, shame on you if I fooled you. I didn't care who you were, but I did care, and I still do care. You didn't care who I was. I did get to know some people, and I did get to love them too, good brothers, good people, as Two Hats. There were people who knew me as Sundown too; I had to deal with those things when those things came up. For the most part, I was pretty much moving on my own. The other thing too, the Indians started getting a lot of casino money. Right away the Mexican Mafia and everybody were thinking, "We got to get them Indians, because that's steady bucks." A lot of people will say that's why I infiltrated the Indians, so I could recruit from them and have that money there too. I did what I had to do to survive, because that's the name of the game, that's what I was taught, that's what I learned. I didn't care because they were putting me on all these active enemy lines; everybody there was my enemy. What was I supposed to do? I was gonna deceive them up the ass. I was gonna get what I get. I was gonna take what I take, and I'm gonna hit whom I hit. Shame on you if your feelings are hurt now. You know, "Oh, Sundown, oh Two Hats, why didn't you tell us?" Hey, that's not the way the game is played. But if you don't know anything about it, then you don't know what the game's really about. So just think about that. You know, I think that like the Twenty-Third Psalm. It says, "The Lord is my shepherd; I shall not want. He maketh me to lie down in green pastures: he leadeth me beside still waters. He restoreth my soul: he leadeth me in the paths of righteousness for his names sake." But this part, "He prepares a table before me in the presence of mine enemies," you know? "He anoints my head with oil, my cup's overflowing. Surely, goodness and mercy will follow me all the days of my life." The Lord literally blessed me with favor among my enemies. I was like David when he was among the Philistines; you need to read the Bible. You know a lot of guys sit in there thinking the Bible's weak, Christians are weak. Well, you haven't read the Bible. I'm telling you; there ain't no weakness here, brother. You want to try me, come on; my Bible did not come with no miniskirt.

I pray for you, God bless you. You challenge me, let's do this. Flip the coin, man, call it heads or tails. I've been here before, you know? Sundown, the hour of the gunfighter. I'm not saying that I'm invincible. A child can kill. If there's one thing I learned, it's that anybody can kill. The difference is, who's the smart one, you know? Who can get you anywhere any time? Who's been schooled, who knows all that you know? Here I go, anyway, like I say, the schooling that we had, the schooling that I taught, it's what kept me; it's what helped me, but honestly, I believe that it was the grace of God that kept me. Because you know, I had to stand, I had to fight, I had to get busy, I had to put in work, and for eighteen years, I walked active main lines, you know what I mean? I paroled as an active from an active main line. The thing is, in our Constitution, like people say, there's no such thing. Yes, there is. I followed the Constitution. I killed for that Constitution. I spilled blood, my own blood, for that Constitution. One of the things we were guaranteed was that any brother who had served twenty years of active service and loyal service and had reached the age of fifty, he could retire. So me, hell, what did I put in? I put in thirty years of active service. That's more than the twenty that was required. So I had every right to just say, "Okay, I'm done, I'm through." As my last act as our last Nuestro General, we disbanded. Captains were allowed to form their own families under whatever they call themselves today, tomorrow, or forever. There would now be just the two factions of La Nuestra Familia remaining—the State and the Federal. Let them work it out; we're gone.

I have mainly addressed La Nuestra Familia and myself in this story, but for example, an FBI agent came to see me once. He told me that I was a very interesting person because, he said, we can put in all the different organizations that are active in California and in America, right now, in the computer, like La Nuestra Familia, the Black Guerilla Family, the Crips, the Bloods, the ABs, the Hells Angels, the Tribal Thumb, the SLA, even the Weathermen and the Black Liberation Army, for just a few. And when they check the computer for people they have in common, my name appears as having dealings or associations with them all, even the Italian Mafia, the Bonanno Family.

Throughout my life and my service in La Nuestra Familia, I have had to have dealings with all these different groups, if for no other reason than as the spokesman for La Nuestra Familia in dealings with all these different criminal organizations and groups. I mean, like when you're establishing regiments, you have to have talks with different groups in the course of business or war. Most of these meetings and associations I'd had were beyond my control, simply the result of authorities placing me in the same jail tanks or prison tiers, as well as on the streets where you have to discuss territories with other criminal elements, all trying to work the same jungle to make money. I was just a likable guy, and when it came to business, I was always professional and respectful. Even when delivering potential threats or promises of violence if something was not worked out and agreed to by all involved. I used an example of how sometimes, even though in prison, we had a death-on-sight policy with any and all enemies of La Nuestra Familia. But sometimes on the streets, in order to prosper, establish, and make money, we needed to work out agreements with our enemies.

There was this very well-known Mexican Mafia lieutenant working out of Decoto, California, a small city outside of Hayward. We could have continued to send soldiers after each other to kill each other, but no money would be made. I told this Mafioso, "Look, you can have Decoto and a small part of Hayward that spilled over into Decoto where the heroin trade was very lucrative." In exchange, they would stay out of the rest of Hayward and Oakland and the rest of the Bay Area that belonged to us. D. R. could have had me killed for this had he found out about it or pushed it, saying it was cowardice during wartime. But it allowed us to establish stronger, more effective, and prosperous regiments everywhere else in the Bay Area instead of losing my soldiers to murder charges and have them sit in the county jails, not making any money for the organization. Same with the Hells Angels. They had their massage parlors and speed, methamphetamine business, which was big for the Bay Area. Even with them, there had to be agreements and understandings. Like when I was sent to speak with the Italian Mafia members representing the Bonanno Family in Northern California, I told them, "Look, you guys may have the money and the connections right now, but all your soldiers making your hits are in their fifties and sixties. We have an unlimited supply of shooters and hit men, and we want to do business."

You know, it's funny; in the movie *American Me*, a few of the scenes they attributed to the Mexican Mafia were actually about us, not them, like our first meeting with the Bonanno Family representatives and the killing of their leader Cheyenne Cadena. The Mexican Mafia was pissed off because of that scene in particular; it made it seem as if they betrayed their own leader, played by Edward Olmos. Some people associated with that movie ended up getting killed by the Mexican Mafia for it.

La Nuestra Familia killed Cheyenne Cadena, their leader, there in Chino Palm Hall, stabbed him and threw him off the third tier. Cheyenne was ahead of his time and was actually trying to broach a peace treaty to organize all prisoners and prison gangs under a common cause. His own people did cause him to be killed by us by violating the peace treaty in DVI Tracy. The idiots leading us at the time fucked up and ordered him to be hit as depicted in the movie *American Me*. Cheyenne had heart; he could have stayed in his cell until the shit could be dealt with, but he believed he could still talk sense into us. It cost him his life. I never agreed with that hit, but then again, there were a lot of hits I didn't agree with.

But I want to pay homage to my enemies too. I'm not glorifying them, their causes, or their tactics. But I do want the record to reflect that even these enemies were soldiers at heart. Men like Cheyenne, Joe "Pegleg" Morgan, "Ahce" or Axe, Barry "The Baron" Mills of the Aryan Brotherhood along with Tyler "The Hulk" Bingham—all these guys were and some still are as dedicated and loyal and vicious as even the best of the La Nuestra Familia legends. I in no way intend any disrespect to any of my former enemies or brothers.

I lived this life; they lived as I did, and some still live. It would be stupid for me not to recognize and respect even all my enemies. Because their loyalties, dedications, and viciousness was part of what also trained, educated, and made me. Without my enemies, I never would have known if I was really Familiano material. In the old days, we had a lot more direct access and interaction and violence against each other than the prison gangs do today. Today, for the most part, everyone is segregated away from each other, and most of a soldier's experiences and violence is among themselves.

It's easy to talk shit about enemies you have never even really done battle against, but once you have experienced battles like we experienced in the past, you will respect your enemies; and if you are a true warrior, your enemies will even respect you too.

To all my enemies, I tip my hat to you.

Underworld mob figures flocking to California

SACRAMENTO, Calif. (UPI) — Mob figures from all over the country are coming to California in increasing numbers because of the absence of organized crime controls, the good weather and the state's vast wealth, a confidential report disclosed Thursday.

The report by Attorney General Evelle Younger said known underworld gangsters from New York, Arizona, Michigan, Pennsylvania, Ohio and Louisiana have in the last year either moved into California or visited other mobsters there.

"Persons with organized crime connections are indeed coming west to reside, visit, or exert criminal influence within California," the report, obtained by UPI, said.

It said organized crime in California involved the garment industry in Los Angeles and San Diego, pornographic films, loan sharking, and to a small extent automobile dealerships.

The annual report on the status of organized crime in California also disclosed that prison-spawned gangs are carrying out major sophisticated narcotics selling operations and "contract" murders in California.

The gangs, once confined to California prisons, have established new operations throughout the state, developed better communications and have placed emphasis on "financially rewarding crimes."

The prison gangs named in the report were the 1,000-member Mexican Mafia, its smaller rival Nuestra Familia, the Aryan Brotherhood and the Black Guerrilla Family.

"Through a combination of collective support," the report said, "detailed organization and criminal skills, prison gangs have become strong enough to conduct major street

Brown joins ranks of crime fighters

operations in narcotics, robbery, forgery and contract killings."

The confidential report made to the legislature said drug trafficking was "one of the most enduring problems plaguing California."

At the present time, the report said, the Southern California Mafia has about 21 known or suspected members. It said the California Mafia was not as well structured as many of the East Coast Mafia families.

"Although this group is small, its influence over over hundreds of non-Mafia figures and its association with other Mafia families allows it to accumulate power and profits for illegal purposes," the report said.

It said the average age of Mafia members in Southern California is 67 with the youngest known member being 50.

(Mount Clipping In Space Below)

Meximafia, Vast Swindle Suspected

Washington Post Service

SAN JOSE MERCURY,
SAN JOSE, CALIF.

PAGE 1

SACRAMENTO — Officials voice growing concern that millions of dollars in state, federal and local funds for social programs are being diverted throughout California into the hands of Chicano-run, Mafia-style organizations.

Their concern was sparked by the Feb. 17 murder near the Sacramento Metropolitan Airport of a South Pasadena woman. Ellen Anne Delia had been shot, gangland-style, three times in the back of the head.

Later, it became known that Mrs. Delia, the estranged wife of the operator of a halfway house in Los Angeles, was on her way here to tell officials what she knew about the misapplication of federal and state funds and fraud in social programs in the barrios. A briefcase of documents, which she said supported what she knew, was missing when her body was found.

No one knows just what she had to tell. Her husband, himself a suspect in her murder, later reportedly told health department officials and legislators that she had possessed canceled checks from the operators of drug-rehabilitation programs to gang figures.

amounting to as much as $1,000 a month per counselor, that go into the pockets of Chicano mobsters.

In addition, methadone reportedly is being siphoned from drug treatment programs and sold on the street.

"It's bound to be going on wherever there are programs like this, in all the cities," said a law enforcement official who asked not to be identified. "That's where the money is."

The gangs themselves were formed in California's prisons as self-protection units. They began to spill out of the prisons in 1972.

The two main gangs are "Nuestra Familia" (Our Family), which is composed mainly of rural Chicanos from California's Central Valley, and "EME," pronounced "emmeh," as is the Spanish pronunciation of the letter "M." Composed of urban Chicanos from East Los Angeles, EME is also called the Mexican Mafia, or sometimes "Emilys Brothers."

As long as three years ago officials were warning that the organizations were moving to the streets, but there was no real concern until recently, when they apparently began a gangland turf war over the control of hard-drug traffic and funds for social programs.

As blacks have in major Eastern cities, Chicanos have begun to attempt to wrest control of organized crime from the older Italian Mafia in California. One informant, only recently out of prison, said the Italian Mafia had passed the word in the state institution that Nuestra Familia and EME could fight it out for control, and "to the victor belong the spoils."

The war has been bloody. In 1975, according to Charles E. Casey, head of the Organized Crime and Intelligence Branch of the California Department of Justice, 33 murders were traceable to intergang rivalry, 16 of these occurred in prisons. But in 1976 there were 75 such murders, and all but 14 occurred on the streets.

The Bakersfield Californian Sunday, Feb. 16, 1986

Deadly prison gangs carry warfare from cells to streets

...four most deadly gangs are moving ... power struggle ... prison cells to city ... law enforcement ...

... illegal drugs, ... prison rackets ... loansharking, ... prosti-...

... inmates of the ... Correction Insti-... Tehachapi and the ... a man in Bakers-... been linked to the ...

... San Diego Evening ... reported that ... now became the ... one of the ... powerful Mexican-... prison gangs, La ... Familia.

... Familia, "our ... English, moved ... to San Diego to be ... its jailed leader, ... by investigators as ...

... described by state ... officers as the ... leader of Nuestra ... gang officials say ... of becoming ... Mafia and a "hit ... long.

... man is the ... is the general ... is unlimited," ... report quoted by ... Sosa is report-... gang circles as "El Nuestro General."

He is currently being held in San Diego County Jail, awaiting sentencing on two counts of robbery with a gun. Police think he wants to return to prison to put down a rebellion within his own gang.

Nuestra Familia has been at war for the past few years with the other big Mexican-American prison gang, the Mexican Mafia. The two have been responsible for many of the stabbings in California prisons in the last three years, corrections officers say.

Both are vying for control of the state's narcotics traffic and both are making alliances with other lethal prison gangs.

Nuestra Familia reportedly uses members of the white supremacist Aryan Brotherhood as contract killers, while the Los Angeles-based Mexican Mafia has aligned itself with the Black Guerrilla Family, described by some observers as the parent of the Symbionese Liberation Army.

All four gangs are on the streets of San Diego in numbers unknown to police, the Tribune said.

Nuestra Familia is said to have extensive plans for evolving from a gang into a full-fledged crime syndicate.

These plans include establishment of "gang regiments," with "strategic advisers" to run the gang's street activities and a "think tank" of lawyers and legitimate business ventures.

There's even a retirement plan. The Tribune quoted a captured gang document saying that gang members who reach age 50 can retire from crime if they have given "at least 20 years of loyal and dedicated service."

However, even retired gang members can be recalled by the general "in time of war," it said.

Investigators say Nuestra Familia has already established three "regiments," one for robbery, one for burglary and one for assassination.

But their main efforts, investigators said, are still channeled into narcotics. The gang was shipping a pound of heroin a month from San Diego to Northern California until San Jose police arrested 17 Nuestra Familia members there, the Tribune said.

Police are not the only ones disrupting the gang's drug operation. Officials say the rival Mexican Mafia has been disrupting Nuestra Familia traffic and terrorizing its drug pushers throughout Southern California, which the Mexican Mafia sees as its private territory.

One disruptive tactic is for a Mexican Mafia member to approach a local pusher and order him to deal with the Mexican Mafia, also known as the EME.

"If he doesn't agree to this, the EME will send enforcers to rob him and work him over," said the state report. "If he still resists, they will kill him and set up their own neighborhood operation."

The two warring gangs also have been forging links with big-time organized crime, the Mafia, the Tribune said. Law enforcement officials found names and phone numbers of high-ranking Mafia members on the body of a Nuestra Familia man killed with his brother in Bakersfield, the report said.

Some corrections officers view the gang members as violent, but not bright enough to operate a statewide syndicate, the Union reported.

"On a scale of one to 10 these guys are about two," said one corrections official.

But local law enforcement agents say they plan to take a hard line with any gang members arrested in their area.

"We take a very hard-nosed stand," said ... Huffman, chief deputy district attorney for San Diego County.

"Anytime we catch these guys doing anything wrong, we're going to come down on them with both feet and send them back to their prison gangs for as long as possible."

RICK RILEY

NUESTRA FAMILIA

The bones of La Nuestra Familia (NF) originated in September 1967 with the initial name "La Familia" at the Deuel Vocational Institution in Tracy, California. The gang's initiators then changed the organization's name to "La Nuestra Familia" on September 1968 at the Northern California's Soledad Correction Training Facility. The violent prison gangs founding fathers, Haero Morgan, Robert Joseph Gonzales, Bobby Joe Barkley and Freddy Gonzales believed that the gang would unite all northern Hispanic inmates. Their main objective was to divide prisoners from northern California and compete with the southern California based Mexican Mafia.

GANG PROFILE
Symbols: Huelga eagle "XIV" Possible NF number, Norteno, Norte, 14, catorce, ENE, sombrero over a bloody machete.
Ranking structure: Paramilitary
Territory: Northern California
Alliances: Northern Structure, Nuestra Raza, most street gangs in northern California.
Members: 8,000.
Racial make up: Hispanic
Threat: High

MEXICAN MAFIA VS NUESTRA FAMILIA

As soon as Nuestra Familia members began arriving at the San Quentin maximum security prison in 1968, high ranking Mexican Mafia members attempted to kill the NF seed before it grew. NF member Sonny Pena was the first victim to be murdered by the Mexican Mafia. Pena's brutal murder was the Mexican Mafia's way of informing California's prison population that new gangs would not be accepted. The Mexican Mafia wasn't the only prison gang to reject the idea of a new barracuda in the pond. The Aryan Brotherhood also joined in the attack by murdering Nuestra Familia member Fred Charles Castillo on February 3, 1972. All Mexican-American prisoners from northern California became immediate targets, leaving the California Department of Corrections with no other choice but to segregate all Nuestra Familia members and northern California inmates. This gave Nuestra Familia the perfect opportunity to unite all northern California inmates and opened the doors to thousands of new members.

Bakersfield, California soon became the dividing line between the Nuestra Familia and Mexican Mafia territory.

This is new to N.F. Two

NUESTRA FAMILIA RANKING STRUCTURE

The NF operates in a paramilitary fashion. The gang has a Supreme Commander, several Generals, regimental captains, lieutenants and soldiers.

Valley News (Van Nuys, California), Edition - Page
Printed on May 7,

Page 6 Section 1 Part 3

VALLEY

6 Fresno deaths may be linked to prison gangs

FRESNO (UPI) — Six recent assassination-type murders related to Fresno's lucrative heroin traffic have authorities concerned it may reflect a power struggle between prison-spawned Mexican-American gangs.

None of the local officials publicly want to call it a "War" or "Conflict" for fear of stirring passions even higher or impeding investigations. But privately they admit it appears to be a territorial battle.

The two rivals are the Eme, also known as the Mexican Mafia or Emily's Brothers, and the Nuestra Familia, which means "Our Family."

The gangs are bitter rivals inside California's prison system where gang violence and murders are common; and are coming into increasing conflict in outside society over control of drug traffic and other criminal activity.

Eme is basically urban and Southern California-based, while the Familia is mainly from rural and Central Valley and Northern California. Eme influence begins waning north of Visalia but Fresno is still an area where dominance is unclear, authorities say.

Consider the murders:

On the night of last Oct. 17, Antonio Garcia Ocon, a major heroin pusher just out of prison and believed to have Eme connections, was shot to death in an alley behind his home. The assassin, wearing a red bandana, fired two shots from a handgun at two witnesses who saw him walking to his car. He missed.

On Nov. 10, Daniel R. Duran, 28, of Sanger, a known local heroin user and pusher, was gunned down by a youthful assassin along F Street in West Fresno's Chinatown, a popular connection point for heroin transactions.

While Duran had no known connections to either gang, authorities say a possible murder motive is the fact he owed people money and was known to be selling bad

drugs and passing off floured chalk as heroin. He died with a balloon of the fake stuff in his mouth.

A young heroin addict with Duran, Mary Shannon, 18, was wounded in that shooting.

On the evening of the same day Duran was shot, Milton Europe, alias Richard Hamilton, 48, a known heroin user and small time peddler, was stabbed to death in a pool hall a short distance from the Duran slaying. Duran and Europe were at least acquaintances.

The murders halted temporarily in December following . the arrests of three suspects: Frank "Sleepy" Villagrana, 32, and Carloe "Casper" Silva, 16, both known members of the Familia charged with the Duran slaying, and Bobby Reyes, charged with the Europe stabbing.

Dep. Dist. Atty. Steven Noxon, who is prosecuting Villagrana and Silva for the Duran murder, introduced evidence at a preliminary hearing for Villagrana which showed the Duran murder may be gang related.

No one has yet been charged in the Ocon murder. Villagrana, Silva and Reyes are all awaiting trial.

The murders resumed again in January, on Jan. 6 Guadalupe Rocha Venegan, 25, a drug dealer believed to be a member of the Familia and known to have relatives in the Familia, was executed in the parking lot of a West Fresno service station when two shots from a small caliber handgun were fired into the back of his head.

Five days later, David Nava, 27, of Modesto, known to be a member of the Mexican Mafia, was found dead in a field near Fresno. He had been shot twice in the chest with a shotgun.

Noxon says it is hard to "tie the thread" connecting all the slayings but some are definitely gang related.

One motivating factor may simply be greed and the desire to reap

the overwhelming profits made in heroin.

Fresno County has an estimated 6,000 heroin addicts, who commit burglaries and robberies at an incredible rate to support their habit.

Another possible motive in the slayings is the natural animosity between the two gangs.

The Familia is known to have at least a dozen members operating in the Fresno area. The strength of the Eme is unknown.

The rivalry between the Nuestra Familia and the Eme stems back to the late 1960s.

According to a Department of Corrections Intelligence report, the Eme was first formed in 1957 at the Duell Vocational Institution near Tracy, and was comprised of a small group of Mexican-Americans from the barrios of East Los Angeles who specialized in illegal activities within the prisons such as narcotics, gambling and collection of debts.

The organization grew in numbers and spread throughout the California Prison System and even into the California Youth Authority System.

In the latter part of 1967, members of the Eme fatally stabbed a Mexican-American inmate at San Quentin. This was the first known assault on a Mexican-American inmate as a direct result of orders from the Eme leadership.

The makeup of this second group, comprised mainly of valley and Northern California residents, came from San Jose, Santa Clara, Gilroy, Salinas, Santa Barbara, Oxnard, Stockton, Fresno and rural areas and took the name "Nuestra Familia."

Estimates of the membership of each gang, "A very loose number," between 30 and 400 out of a total California prison

The Fresno authorities refuse to speculate on where the orders for the Fresno murders might be coming from, inside or outside of prison.

253

Chapter

15

We had disbanded; this had been a hard decision to make, but it was the only decision to make. I had sworn an allegiance to a Constitution, which had long been discarded. I was holding on to a dream, trying to justify it and to justify along with it all the blood that had been spilled, both the good and the bad. We had butchered brothers behind violating this Constitution, and for me to just let it die was to admit that all those murders and life sentences brothers received for those murders were all for nothing.

We had moved to a variation of our original Constitution. We stuck with the military structure of chain of command. But in reality, all our main captains were already on the streets and running their own regimental families under their own guidelines. They would still kick down assistance to brothers behind the walls, and we would still send recruits to some of these established regiments if they were good soldiers or if there was a need or request. For the most part, we were done as Nuestra Familia already. We could not keep up with the other side; they had retained control of the Northern Structure and had ten times as many soldiers and recruits to keep sending after us, all day long, because of it.

It was time to sue for an honorable peace. We gave up claim to the name of La Nuestra Familia, and it now belonged only to them. But being a Familiano, a gangster, was in my blood, and like I said, I would continue to have my own family, my own people, dedicated and loyal to me. I only had to walk enemy yards and try to find the occasional recruit to my own Familia from everyone around me and in all the different prisons I would go to.

I was scheduled to parole in 2004, and everyone was in place, waiting upon my release, before we went full speed, guns blazing, quietly and secretly as we had planned. I knew I would probably have to do all of whatever killings came up in the course of my dreams and plans for this family in the beginning, until I could teach each soldier how to do a hit without leaving evidence that might lead to the knowledge of our family or the turning of any of my future soldiers.

I had learned that from all the mistakes and experiences of the past thirty years, I became a forensics expert in murder evidence. I figured that if I got out, I would secure my own organization well enough to run on their own. I was going to find some major drug dealers sitting on millions. Go in kill four or five people, however many were there, as long as I was only killing criminals and then take all their money. Then I would go buy some village and have that village prosper; the end would justify the means. But I became involved with this little square court clerk named Luci.

I had turned this square little court clerk out, but she loved me, and because she really did love me, I came to love her, to care for her. Then they tried to prosecute her for bringing drugs in to me. I had always lived by the code that you always protect your woman; I had taken a twenty-seven-year sentence to protect Michaelleen. Now I could have beaten the case against me, but it would have cost Luci in the process, so I made a deal for five more years added on to my sentence. In exchange, they would let Luci go and leave her alone; it was my good-bye gift to her. She had come along when my wife Ruthie had abandoned me, and Luci helped me more than she could ever know. Mostly, it was her innocence, her sincere love for me that affected me and made me begin to think of possibly one day settling down and pursuing legal businesses and opportunities. She helped to plant the seed in me, but she would not be the woman for me if I did; we both knew this, I think, so I sacrificed five more years to protect her and to free her from me. God bless you, Luci, mi nalgona Mexicana, my big-butt Mexican girl.

So I was alone, as far as any women in my life. I had women friends who were still visiting me, like Taffy and Monica. Taffy, I could write a whole book about my relationship with her. She was always my friend who always loved me unconditionally as a brother and a friend. Though we had messed up and had sex once together, we recovered from that mistake and remain best friends still today. These women were Christian women; they tried to help me, to be there for me in their own way. But none of them was the right one, that right woman whom the Creator had made just for me. Besides, I was still thinking of, if I ever got out, just getting my guns and taking anything and everything that I ever wanted or needed. I was a very dangerous man, with nothing left to lose; the sun had gone down on me. Like the Elton John song from which I had first taken my name, Sundown.

I felt sorry for anybody who opposed me or got in my way once I was released. I feared no man or beast or no demon from hell, and inside of this thing called me, I was the living dead, looking for a reason to believe or a cause to die for. I lived like a king inside prison. I was even bored with being rich in prison. Doing law still seemed to excite or challenge me, and women, even the forbidden fruit all around me, I was no longer interested in pursuing or getting involved with. More than a few still expressed interest in me though.

Then one night, after a week of straight partying with prison-made whiskey and every drug available, I had gotten addicted to pornography and loved nothing more than staring at women's naked photographs of their most intimate body parts. I was sick with it. I especially loved big women. To me, the bigger the woman's butt, the better. I could lay there in my bed and just stare at a certain area of a woman's anatomy and not turn the page for hours on end; I lived in my mind's fantasies of all I wanted to do with that woman's body. So while I was no longer interested in being involved with any women, I still loved to see them naked, especially bigger, thicker women.

Anyway, one night I can feel something's not right with my body. At first, I think it's just the drugs and the alcohol residue wearing in my body. But I had been shot point-blank in my chest and bled internally for three hours while I evaded every cop in Humboldt County, including the K-9 unit back in 1981. While I escaped from the manhunt, I even used a stray cat I had grabbed. While running from the manhunt for me, I turned the cat loose just as the police dog was closing in on the spot in the field where I was hiding. The police dog chased the cat instead of finding me, but I couldn't escape the internal bleeding in my lung, and when I started choking on my own blood, I knew I was gonna die. I made a death prayer telling God, "Well, God, I guess I'm gonna be seeing You here in a few minutes. I'm sorry for wasting my life like I have, and I'm sorry that this was how my life that promised so much potential was gonna end like this." In a field of tall grass with the soft rain falling all around me, I remember, once the fear of dying was faced, I was filled only with regret for the waste I had made of God's gift of my life. I may have been born poor, but I was blessed with intelligence, good looks, and charisma, and this was how it was gonna end, with nothing to show that a great man like I had always strived to be was ever even here on earth, except for a headstone with my name on it.

Back then, at that time in that moment and that experience, with my certain death from three hours of internal bleeding, I asked God to let me make it to a bar where I could tell my friend Taffy to call my crime partner Jimmy Boy and to meet me, pick me up, take me to the beach we had spent the night before at, hold me until I died, and then have Jimmy Boy take my body home to my father.

There was this very devout Christian detective who worked for the Humboldt County Sheriff's Department. He had been off duty that day when the manhunt for me had begun. After over three hours of evading all the police, they had called off the dragnet for me, believing I had gotten away. But this Christian detective told me that God spoke to him and told him exactly where to find me and even showed him what I would look like. God told him to go to me, to help me, to save me. We met on a backstreet. He walked up to me, and I asked him if he had a cigarette before I collapsed into his arms. He caught me before I could hit the ground. I remember going in and out of consciousness. He was asking me what my name was as they were rushing me to the hospital. I remember telling him it didn't matter what my name was, but that if I lived, I would tell him my name.

Anyway, years later, in that prison cell, I began feeling and sensing that something was seriously wrong with me. My cellmate was passed out drunk, and I began to feel the pain in my chest and all I could do was say to God, "Really? Really, God? Not like this, I know You don't owe me nothing, and I've got a nerve to ask You for anything after all the wrong I've done in my life, but really? Lord, come on, this is me, Your boy. Can I get a break? Not like this, don't let me die in prison."

I remember the pain in my chest kept intensifying with every breath. I thought it was a heart attack, and I warned my cellmate and friend, Victor, that I was gonna have to go man down. That means you have to go to emergency, to the hospital, and for Victor to make sure everything in the cell was secure, in case they searched us once I told the officer on his next round when he walked by taking count. It took about twenty minutes more before he came by.

When they took me out of the cell, the pain was so intense that it felt as if every breath was going to be my last. It felt like my chest was going to explode, and I'd be dead each time I inhaled. The cops asked me if I could walk to the hospital. I took three steps, and I collapsed. It took almost four hours for them to get me out of the prison and on the road to an outside hospital. The nearest hospital was ninety miles away in another state, Nevada.

With each breath, I expected to die, and I began to get right with God. I knew this time, He would not save me as He had before when I had been shot in the chest. As I prayed, I remember that all that mattered to me as I was dying was my real family—my father, my brothers, my sisters, all my children. I kept praying over and over for them, giving them to God to watch over and to take care of for me, my real family that I had abandoned in my heart of hearts years ago when I chose to make La Nuestra Familia my family instead of them, my own blood. I did not pray for my La Nuestra Familia family, but for my real family, whom, in that time between life and dying, I realized was the family I had always loved and had been looking for all along.

I remember praying, "God, send an angel to help them find the paperwork to get me out of this prison before I died in this ambulance still inside those prison walls." Once they found my paperwork and we exited the prison and pulled out onto the highway heading for the hospital, I remember feeling such relief, and I told God, "Okay, God, now I can die, I'm free; I'm outside that prison hell. If I die now, I'll die outside of prison." At first they took me to the local hospital in Susanville. There was a black guy there faking a heart attack so he could get out of prison for a few days, have a kinda vacation from the prison. There were two other guys there, a white dude too. The doctors were always on the lookout for this kind of bullshit game some of these weak-ass inmates would play just to get out of prison for a few days.

I remember thinking these assholes are messing it up for me. I was gonna get sent back to the prison along with them fakers. By then, I was in so much pain with every breath I believed my heart couldn't possibly take any more and I was gonna just explode and die. I began praying in tongues aloud, and with every breath, I was raising up against the restraints. I was tied to the hospital bed, in twisted knots from the pain. As the cops are waiting around for the on-call doctor to come and decide who stayed and whom he thought was faking, the nurse came and told me, "We don't know yet what's going on with you, but I'm gonna give you a shot of morphine for the pain." It was obvious I was in extreme pain. She whispered to me, "Don't worry, you're not gonna be returned to the prison," like the other two fakers might be returned to the prison. Sure enough, the doctor said to the guards that the other two can be returned to the prison hospital. They couldn't find anything wrong with them. But me, even though they couldn't tell what the hell was wrong with me, the pain, and my straining against the hospital bed restraints, my whole body was twisting up from each breath. They were going to have to rush me to the bigger hospital in Reno, Nevada.

They went to take me by helicopter, but the helicopter was taken by an off-duty guard suffering a heart attack. He got the helicopter, and I will have to be transported by ambulance to Nevada, ninety miles away, for help, where there're more doctors and better equipment to find out what's wrong with me.

I heard the ambulance drivers and guards complaining that Reno was too far away and I should be in the helicopter too. But they said it couldn't handle the weight, so I was stuck like chuck with the long drive. They even were told to prepare for the reality that I may not live long enough during the drive in which they will have to go into a whole different protocol. As they were securing me in the ambulance for the long drive to Reno, I could actually hear the guards and the drivers making bets whether I'll make it all that way or not. I remembered the closing scene from the movie with Paul Newman, *Cool Hand Luke*, when the evil warden orders them to take Cool Hand Luke to the farthest-away hospital so Cool Hand Luke will die on the way, and everyone's saying he'll never make it. Just like they said, he would never be able to eat fifty boiled eggs within an hour. Of course, Luke did eat all the eggs just within the allotted hour, and in that closing scene, just when you think they're right, Luke will never live long enough to reach that far away hospital. The movie ends with Paul Newman smiling that Cool Hand Luke smile that says he'll make it against all odds. Well, I smiled that same smile through the insane excruciating pain I was feeling with each breath.

I made it to the hospital in Reno. The nurse, on her own, had given me another shot of morphine just before they loaded me up to go, and after a hundred tests and a dozen doctors and thirty-six hours of this pain, they were just about to release me back to the prison because they couldn't figure out what was wrong with me. I remember praying aloud, "God, don't let them do this to me," when this young doctor said, "Let's try one more test." They had me drink a dye, and they gave me an x-ray of my chest, and they saw it. It's a big old blood clot in my lung; this is called a pulmonary embolism, and most people die from this, and the doctor said, by all the evidence, I should have died already. So they knew what it is, and they admitted and kept me and immediately began treatment to try to keep me alive.

I woke up later in my hospital room, needles sticking all in me and oxygen hoses strapped to my nose, and I knew I was gonna live. The pain was subsiding, but for over thirty-six hours, it felt like with every inhale, my chest and my heart were just gonna explode and I would enter into eternity. I had made my peace with God and had come to realize that all along I had had a family that loved me and cared for me in spite of how distant I had become to them inside of me. Because I could only see one family, my prison family, for all these years, so much so that I never even noticed my mother's descent into drugs and darkness, or my own wife Ruthie's cries and pleas for sensitivity from me.

She used to refer to me as a rock. When I asked her why she referred to me as a rock, she said it was because I had the sensitivity of a rock. Thirty-six hours of being between life and death in that kind of pain will make you realize a lot of things. I knew I wanted to change. I wanted to be right with God, but I was still on an active enemy line. My wife had returned to the streets and abandoned my babies. Even though I was not the biological father of her children, they were still my babies to me.

I tried to make a compromise with God, for his having saved my life yet again, when I didn't deserve being saved because of how evil a man I truly was when it hit me. So I went back to rereading the Bible, especially the Old Testament, about Samson, Gideon, Joshua, Caleb, and King David. These men were blooded warriors, and I could relate to these men, especially King David. People who saw me reading the Bible so much would ask me what was up with that. I would tell them, "Hey, there ain't nothing weak about reading the Bible or trying to get to know and understand God, and make no mistake about it, my Bible didn't come with no miniskirt." I was still the same gunfighter I always was. It was like I was trying to dictate to God the terms of my relationship with Him. Maybe I won't destroy as many people when I get out, maybe I'll only kill half as many people as I have to in the course of this goal I had set for myself. Maybe I'll only kill really bad guys, take the money they killed and wasted lives to acquire, then I'll really give it to the poor. I figured it was the cold equations, if I have to kill four or five guys who are sitting on millions of dollars in illegal money and I take that money and I save a village of poor people, raise them, and teach them how to make it and how to provide for and protect their own village and family. It's fair to me, and if I handpick a handful of young innocent virgins to plant my own seed into, to give me sons and daughters to raise and teach them to be soldiers myself, wouldn't this be fair? Wouldn't this make up for all the people I've killed and all the lives I've helped to destroy?

Then something happened that blew my whole life wide open in two ways. The first was for the good and the other was devastating. It would involve the two great loves of my life, two completely different women, my wife Ruthie, and Lori, my future.

With the weight of the world on my shoulders,
I know how Atlas felt.

Thank you, Luci. God bless you!

Nuestra Familia

From Wikipedia, the free encyclopedia

Nuestra Familia (Spanish for *"Our Family"*) is a criminal organization of Mexican American (Chicano) prison gangs with origins in Northern California.[4] While members of the Norteños gang are considered to be affiliated with Nuestra Familia, being a member of Nuestra Familia itself does not signify association as a Norteño. Some law enforcement agents speculate that the Nuestra Familia gang, which operates in and out of prisons, influences much of the criminal activity of thousands of Norteño gang members in California.[5] The gang's main sources of income are distributing cocaine, heroin, marijuana, and methamphetamine within prison systems as well as in the community and extorting drug distributors on the streets.[6]

Contents

- 1 Origins
- 2 Operation Black Widow
- 3 Renewed organization
- 4 Operation Knockout
- 5 Membership
- 6 Symbols
- 7 Allies and rivals
- 8 See also
- 9 References
- 10 External links

Nuestra Familia	
Founding location	Soledad, California Correctional Training Facility
Years active	1968 – present
Territory	Northern California
Ethnicity	primarily Mexican/Mexican Americans
Criminal activities	Drug Trafficking,[1] Extortion,[1] Racketeering,[1] Murder
Allies	Black Guerrilla Family,[1][2] Norteños,[3]
Rivals	Mexican Mafia,[3], Mexikanemi, Sureños, MS-13, Texas Syndicate,[1] Fresno Bulldogs, Aryan Brotherhood

Origins

Nuestra Familia was organized in either the Folsom, California, or Soledad, California, Correctional Training Facilities in 1968.[7][8]

In the late 1960s, Mexican-American (Chicano) inmates of the California state prison system began to separate into two rival groups, Nuestra Familia[4] and the 1957-formed Mexican Mafia, according to the locations of their hometowns (the north-south dividing line is near Delano, California.)

Nuestra Familia were prison enemies of the Southern Latinos who comprised La Eme, better known as the Mexican Mafia. While the Mexican Mafia had initially been created to protect Mexicans in prison, there was a perceived level of abuse by members of La Eme towards the imprisoned Latinos from rural

THE THIEF ON THE CROSS

farming areas of Northern California.[9] The spark that led to the ongoing war between Nuestra Familia and members of the Mexican Mafia involved a situation in 1968 in which a member of La Eme allegedly stole a pair of shoes from a Northerner. This event put into motion the longest-running gang war in the state of California.

In addition, it is common knowledge for many California gang members that a member of the Crips gave a pair of replacement shoes to the Nuestra Familia member as a way to protect his manhood and dignity. Since then the Crips and Nuestra Familia members have been "cliqued up" in the California Correctional system. In normal penitentiary rules, there are certain politics among the various races which regulate how inmates of different races can interact with each other. These "politics" take supreme precedence over all issues; Blacks deal with Blacks, Whites with Whites, Mexicans with Mexicans, etc. Ultimately, this moment of friendship between the Crips and Nuestra Familia is a classic element of California gang history for those who are familiar, because "politics" (i.e. race) were put aside in the interest of bringing justice to another man's life.[9]

Operation Black Widow

Federal law enforcement agencies, long unable to infiltrate Nuestra Familia, began to step up their investigations in the late 1990s. In 2000 and 2001, 22 members were indicted on Racketeer Influenced and Corrupt Organizations Act (RICO) charges, including several who were allegedly serving as high-ranking gang leaders while confined in Pelican Bay.[4] Thirteen of the defendants plead guilty; the other cases are still ongoing. Two of the defendants face the death penalty for ordering murders related to the drug trade. The largest of the federal investigations was Operation Black Widow.[6] At the time of Operation Black Widow, law enforcement officials had estimated that Nuestra Familia was responsible for at least 600 murders in the previous 30 years.[10]

In the aftermath of Operation Black Widow, the five highest-ranking leaders of Nuestra Familia, James "Tibbs" Morado, Joseph "Pinky" Hernandez, Gerald "Cuete" Rubalcaba, Cornelio Tristan, and Tex Marin Hernandez, were transferred to the United States Penitentiary, Florence ADX, the federal supermax prison in Colorado.[11]

Renewed organization

Since the written constitution of the Norteños stated that the gang's leaders resided in Pelican Bay State Prison in California; the relocation of the five leaders led to confusion among its members. The leadership vacuum resulted in a power struggle between prospective generals.[11]

Eventually, three new generals came to power at Pelican Bay, yet two were demoted, leaving only David "DC" Cervantes as the highest-ranking member of the gang in California.[11] Cervantes' rise marked the first time in decades that the Norteños had a single leader at the helm of their criminal organization.[11] The remaining leadership of the organization in Pelican Bay consists of Daniel "Stork" Perez, Anthony "Chuco" Guillen and George "Puppet" Franco. While all Nuestra Familia soldiers and captains in California are expected to follow the orders of Cervantes, a small percentage of the gang remains loyal to the former generals and captains imprisoned in Colorado.[11] California Governor Arnold Schwarzenegger has complained that keeping the five remaining gang leaders located in the same prison

RICK RILEY

continues to add to California gang violence, and that they should be scattered throughout different prisons. While the recognized leaders of Nuestra Familia in Pelican Bay ask that members respect the former leaders, they have been effectively stripped of their authority.[11]

Operation Knockout

In April 2010, federal and local law enforcement agencies concluded what was considered the most significant effort to dismantle the Central Coast leadership structure of Nuestra Familia.[12] After months of investigation, at least 37 alleged gang members were arrested during the raids conducted. Law enforcement authorities seized 40 pounds of cocaine, 14 pounds of marijuana, and dozens of firearms.[12]

Membership

While Nuestra Familia is primarily a Chicano gang, membership sometimes extends to other Latinos as well as non-Latinos. Members of the organization are considered to have taken a "blood oath" to join the gang, and are considered lifelong participants.[7] Nuestra Familia's written constitution allegedly states that no member should prioritize women, money or drugs over their membership in the gang.[13] Membership in the gang extends beyond prison.[7] Women are not allowed to become full-fledged members of Nuestra Familia, but are sometimes used for communication and drug-running purposes as they are considered less likely to be noticed by law enforcement agents.[15] The NF has a formal written constitution and claims about 2000 inmate members.

Symbols

Members of Nuestra Familia are known to wear red bandanas to identify themselves.[7] Other symbols include use of the number 14 or XIV, as the letter "N" is the 14th letter of the English alphabet.[7] Nuestra Familia members often use the image of a sombrero with a machete as their gang symbol.[7]

Allies and rivals

only made veterans can wear this tattoo

The primary rivals of Nuestra Familia is the Mexican Mafia. Other rivals include the Texas Syndicate, Mexikanemi, and the Aryan Brotherhood.[7] Nuestra Familia has a loose alliance with the Black Guerrilla Family prison gang, primarily as the response of sharing similar enemies.[7]

See also

- List of California street gangs

References

1. ^ a b c d e Prison Gangs - Gang and Security Threat Awareness (http://dc.state.fl.us/pub/gangs/prison2.html#inf), Florida Department of Corrections
2. ^ "Nuestra Familia" (http://www.gangpreventionservices.org/nf.asp), Gang Prevention Services

Chapter

16

Ruthie, what can I say about Ruthie? She was my best friend, and she was my wife, and she wounded inside this thing called me, because she was the only friend and woman I had let that close inside of me. She betrayed me by being human, not only stepping down from the pedestal I had always placed her on, but by pissing all over it and then kicking it over, smashing it along with my heart into a thousand pieces. I first met her when she was just eighteen years old and attending Humboldt State University. I met her while I was in the Humboldt County jail. She was the girlfriend of my best friend there, Michael English. She was drop-dead gorgeous, so fresh and so innocent, a poet with a wide-open heart who met Michael because she was babysitting his daughter, whose mother was somehow related or involved with the family of Clint Eastwood, the movie star in Carmel, California.

Michael was in jail facing the death penalty. Ruthie wanted to help Michael's young daughter, who was at that age where she wanted to know about her real father. So Ruthie, on her own, went to visit Michael. Ruthie was the champion hero of lost causes, not that Michael was ever a lost cause. She became fascinated and infatuated with Michael; she wanted to help him in any way she could. Michael was mad at the world, and his only concern was finding a way to escape and a way to fight his death penalty case. He would tell me how bad he felt for turning Ruthie out and using her to help take care of his needs.

How beautiful, wonderful, and innocent this poor girl was, and he had taken advantage of her big heart and infatuation with him.

At first, he had her bringing him drugs to escape the madness of being locked up in a maximum-security cell for twenty-three hours a day. Then he hooked her up with some older dope-fiend drug addicts, a husband and wife Michael had met there while he was in jail. These two older experienced dope fiends immediately saw potential for making money to support their own drug habit. If only they could turn Ruthie all the way out and have her become a prostitute. I've enclosed a beautiful picture of Ruthie as she was then, so young, so innocent, and so beautiful.

This broad Anita gave Ruthie her first shot of heroin and started filling Ruthie's head with fear for Michael receiving the death penalty as long as he had a public defender. She convinced Ruthie that Michael needed a real lawyer, and he would be expensive.

Naive Ruthie was like, "What can I do to save him?" and Anita, the snake, pounced. Anita kept sticking needles in Ruthie's arms and telling her, "You're young and beautiful and new to this city where prostitution is big business." Ruthie told Anita that she was still a virgin, so Anita told her that she knew a man who would easily pay her a thousand dollars to have sex with Ruthie because Ruthie was so young, beautiful, and a virgin. With that thousand dollars, she would be able to a take better care of Michael; she promised Ruthie she would get her only top-paying, good, clean customers who would be mostly old men.

Ruthie ran it all by Michael, and Michael confessed to me that at first he felt like, "Hell, no!" His conscience and his genuine like of Ruthie made him say no at first, and he even got all over Anita's husband, Bob, who was in jail with us, about this. Michael said one day Ruthie showed up to visit him all dressed and made up with makeup and everything, loaded on heroin. She told Michael that she really wanted to sell her virginity to help Michael. Michael got pissed off and told her that she could do whatever she wanted; he was through trying to talk her out of it.

So Ruthie's virginity was sold to Anita's highest bidder. Anita even burned Ruthie. Instead of giving her the thousand dollars she promised her for her virginity, she only gave her five hundred. Anita actually did get the thousand dollars, but she lied to Ruthie and then kept five hundred for herself. The old man whom Ruthie lost her virginity to told her he gave Anita one thousand dollars and that Anita had lied to her. God bless this old man; he told Ruthie that she could leave Anita's house where Ruthie had been dependent upon for shelter and come live with him. He would take care of her; he would give her five hundred dollars a week to live with him and have sex with him. This became Ruthie's way; from then on, she was a prostitute. She would always find an older man, what's known as a sugar daddy, to take care of her in exchange for sex. With the money she would receive, she made sure Michael lacked for nothing while he was in jail. But after only a year of this lifestyle, it began to take its toll on Ruthie's once innocent and kind, compassionate, poetic soul. She became dependent on drugs and wrote some of her darkest yet beautiful poetry during this period.

Now enters me, yours truly, on to the scene. At first, while Michael would share pictures of Ruthie and her poetry with me, I would tell Michael, "God blessed you, man, you need to hang on to this one." They were having problems, and Ruthie had overdosed a few times. She had gotten pregnant, and although she was half Jewish on her father's side, she had been raised Catholic. When she had a miscarriage and lost the baby, twice, she believed it was punishment from God for all her sins she was committing. That because of the drugs and prostitution, her womb was now cursed and she would never have the big family of children she dreamed of having someday. So she tried to kill herself by overdosing.

Michael asked me, "Rick, would you talk to her for me? You know everything I've told you, and you've read her letters and her poems. I just think maybe she will listen to you, because she's not listening to me! I feel bad for her. Can you talk to her like you talk to me?" I said I would, so that's how it started. I spoke with her long distance over the phone the first time, and we talked for a whole hour about her poetry and about her. She told me about her belief that her womb was cursed and how she could never have a child now. I remember I told her, "Ruthie, listen to me. You know, I used to be a Christian at one time, and I'm promising you right now. You will have so many kids someday, and they are gonna drive you crazy at times and you will remember that I told you today that this was gonna be your destiny, and you will laugh again. I promise you this." She said she was coming back to California from Washington, where her sister and father had been living. She was coming back for Michael, but first she had to have a visit with me, face-to-face and eye-to-eye. I asked Michael, and he said, "Sure, anything, just get her to come back, because I'm afraid she'll kill herself if she stays in Washington."

In the meantime, Ruthie and I exchanged poetry. I sent her some of my poetry, and she sent me some of hers. We talked a few more times over the phone. Now, I like to sing, I always have, and the Eagles had a song called "Desperado"; it had been my mother's dedication to me.

So Ruthie's coming to visit me in Humboldt County Jail. It's behind the glass visiting with telephones. You can see everything and everyone else through the glass. I don't know why, but as soon as Ruthie came in and picked up that phone, I smiled at her and I started singing the first verse of the song "Desperado" to her. I only intended to sing the first verse, but the way she looked at me with tears pouring out of her eyes, I didn't know what to do. So I kept singing the whole song to her. By then, she had stopped crying, and she told me, "We have a problem. I care for Michael, and I even love him and I'm his old lady, but I'm in love with you too now. I will still marry Michael and take care of him because I gave him my word, but I will always be in love with you too."

I went back from the visit, and I told Michael, "You promised to marry this girl if she came back. She's expecting a marriage." Michael had been changing his mind about going through with the marriage, so I told him, "Ruthie is special, and she deserves more than either you or I could ever give her, and all she wants right now is to get married. Brother, I love you, but come this Friday, one of us two is going to marry her. She's yours, so I'm giving you first shot, but if you say no, then I will marry her instead." Because now, after our first visit and seeing her and looking in to her soul, seeing her full beauty in person, I too was now in love with Ruthie. Man to man, friend to friend, I was telling Michael this and giving him respect of being the first to marry her.

So Michael married Ruthie, and I was the best man. Thirteen years later, I would marry Ruthie, and her ex-husband, my best friend Michael, would be there as my best man, in a visiting room in Folsom State Prison. Michael told us that day that he felt like everything was set right, that all along he knew it should have been me who married Ruthie the first time in Humboldt County Jail and not him. He was happy that we had found each other again and that he could see for the first time that Ruthie was finally happy. Ruthie had five wonderful, beautiful children now, there with us—her son, Christopher; her twin daughters, Alycia and Elena; her wild child, Shaina; and her baby, Chelsea—just as I had promised her when I spoke to her that first day over the phone in Humboldt County Jail.

I loved those children. Everybody did. They were such good and awesome kids, and the main reason that I said yes to Ruthie's request that I marry her was these children. I wanted to be their father. For a couple of years, we were happy. We had visiting a few days a week, and my job allowed me to be free to have all four visits every week. Ruthie had moved to Folsom to be close to me. She was only a few miles away, as Netty Lou had once done when I was in Tracy prison. Ruthie brought the kids on the weekends to visit, and we had Thursday and Friday to ourselves for a while. Then we made Friday a rotation day for the kids so each child could come alone with her to visit me. We had conjugal visits between every forty-five days to every sixty days depending on the availability and waiting list.

On our first conjugal visit, it was like our honeymoon, finally forty-eight hours alone. Ruthie's favorite song was "The Rose" by Bette Midler. That night on that conjugal visiting apartment patio, that song came over the radio. I asked her if she wanted to dance. I was shocked when she shyly admitted she did not know how to dance. No man had ever asked her to dance before. Men had asked her for sex, but no one had ever danced with her. Therefore, I took her in my arms and told her to just rest in my arms and follow me. We danced our very first dance ever there on that prison patio.

I forgot to mention that we had gotten married in front of a packed visiting room. All the children were there, and I told my beautiful step-daughters, "Don't ever marry a man who doesn't love you enough to sing to you on your wedding day." I turned and took Ruthie's hands in mine in front of that whole packed busy visiting room, and I sang to her "Forever My Darling," an old song by Johnny Ace. My friend Michael told me later that he was surprised I was able to sing in key throughout the whole song. Michael knew I could sing, when we were cellmates in Humboldt County. He heard all my greatest hits, as I would sing the entire jail floor to sleep. Some nights everyone would ask me to sing for them. One night, one of the sheriffs working there brought in his guitar. He pulled up a chair outside of our cell and played as I sang every request from the prisoners that he knew how to play.

It seems I've always sang the prisoners to sleep at one time or another over the thirty-three years of my life I've spent behind bars.

Ruthie told me the first time on our conjugal visit that she had never experienced an orgasm before with a man, in spite of her sexual exploits. Then she said, "I've never even been made love to or made love to a man." She had only had sex; more specifically, she had been the receiver of men's selfish thrusting and emptying in her womb. She was mine now. I had fantasized about her and about being with her for almost eighteen years, when we were alone and I was singing my song for her. She had five children; she was concerned about how her body would look naked before me. But she had already sent me naked pictures of herself that I had asked her to take just for me. Now at last I was not only gonna see it all for real, but I was gonna be free to totally enjoy her naked body. She did not have her big breasts anymore; they had been drained from breastfeeding five kids in a row. But to me, her breasts were still so beautiful, as well as the tattoo she had put across her chest of the sun going down between her breasts, fifteen years before to honor her love for me then. "Sundown" looked so beautiful that after I had covered it with kisses, I laid my head and face against her tattoo of love for me, before we even made love. She was Jewish and, like most Jewish women, very hairy with a nice big butt. But it was her eyes, her smile, and her face; she would smile and look just like Angelina Jolie. To this day, I can no longer watch Angelina Jolie movies because they remind me too much of Ruthie.

I made love to Ruthie as if we were Adam and Eve making love to each other for the first time, and that night Ruthie had her first orgasm ever with a man. It was like the genie in the bottle had been let out after that. She lived for our conjugal visits. We became like *Leave It to Beaver*, with our happy little family, and for a while, Folsom State Prison and our time there together was like Camelot to us.

But the storms were building up within the prison system, and I could sense it was coming. Fig was stepping down completely from La Nuestra Familia, as was his right to do according to the terms of our Constitution. He was done; he was tired of being in a civil war for something he had given his whole life to, and him and Larry and everyone else. But Fig especially wanted me to take the mantle as the leader and Nuestra general of what was left of the original La Nuestra Familia. He told me they had already voted, and everyone agreed with Fig's pick of me to take his place. I did not want this; to me, Fig was the last Familiano. He had been a loyal soldier; he had given his all to the point of nine murder convictions. For this, his once own Familia was still trying to kill him. Fig was always curious about how I had got a female correctional officer to quit her lucrative career, to risk it all and marry a man like I was. But mostly, he was curious about how I had actually changed from hating the whole prison administration and anything in green, no matter how good she looked in that skintight green jumpsuit uniform, to actually being in love with the enemy, so to speak.

Well, Fig eventually found out for himself when he met and fell in love with a female correctional officer too. To her credit, she knew everything they had on file about Fig, that he would most possibly never get out of prison and that conjugal visits for them might be many years in the waiting, so they could be together the way their love for each other longed for them to be. But she saw, possibly, what I always saw in Fig too. He was just a kid when he first came to prison on a joyriding crime, with a maximum sentence of five years. But he was loyal to his friends, and when his crime partner and best friend, Hobo, told him they had to step up and take out this Aryan Brotherhood shot caller, Fig could not let his partner do it alone. Ever since, he was just a loyal soldier following orders, and for it he received a total of nine murder convictions and then was turned on and against by the very cause he had served faithfully and loyally. If ever they should make a movie about his life, they should name it *The Last Familiano.* Her love for Fig and her knowing willingness to give up that very prosperous lifestyle and income as a correctional officer in California, where correctional officers are among the highest paid in the country—she was willing to give it up for him and to stand by him forever, as long as Fig could walk away from the whole gang lifestyle. So this, I believe, is the main reason Fig walked away and stepped down when he did.

The love of a good woman can bring any man to his knees; I believe that. So Fig rode off into the sunset in search of their own piece of Camelot, wherever they could find it together. God bless you both. You are a living proof that love conquers all. One of the things Fig had done was to make a truce with our biggest and oldest enemy, the Mexican Mafia. He had secured our loyalties with our biggest and strongest allies, the Black Guerrilla Family as well as with the Crips and the Bloods. These people all respected him and us still, even though they also had allegiance to Black Bob's faction of Nuestra Familia too.

I did not want to become the last Nuestro General ever of this dying shell of what we had once been when some hero made his bones and paid his price of admission into what was then a blood-in blood-out organization on the verge of criminal history. But if I was gonna be, then I would change it and try to salvage what I could for its remaining members.

It would cost me my happy little *Leave It to Beaver* family, and Camelot would be over. Everything would be undercover; no more spotlights, no more chatter. Times had changed, and by all rights, I had the right to walk away. I had put my twenty years in. I didn't need to prove anything to anybody who was not with me or about how we were gonna fight and manipulate and do the things that we needed to do for us.

I told them to hurry up and find a new leader out there or in here. I was more than willing to step aside. Ruthie could sense a change had come over me. I was becoming harder and more quiet as I tried to balance her and the kids with all the mouths I now had the responsibility of feeding all over the prison system and even in the streets. Most men would have wanted to be the Nuestro General, but not me.

The storm hit, an all-out race riot, and people were being killed. They were shipping out all the undesirables to other prisons, and though I tried to prepare Ruthie for this, she couldn't handle her happy little *Leave It to Beaver* family being over. It didn't have to be over; we could have made the adjustments, but she couldn't see that. She had been going to church regularly and learning her Jewish ancestry and heritage. She loved God and Jesus, but she couldn't understand how all of this could be happening. I would be shipping out to the farthest end of the state to a prison in the desert called Calipatria.

Ruthie had a nervous breakdown and ended up in a mental hospital. The children, she had believed in her broken mind that she was doing what was best for them by giving them over to Child Protective Services to be returned to their biological father and his family. Even though she hated him, she thought her children would be better off with his family than with hers. That's the reason I fought in the courts and against the Child Protective Services, against this, for the next few years, because Ruthie had told me how much she hated the children's father, and his older children, she was now hoping would take care of her abandoned children. She told me how the children's father would abuse her, both physically and verbally. How he always reminded her that she was just a *gringa puta*, or "white whore," and even though she had children with him, he never once made love to her. She never even kissed him during sex. She also told me the children's father had older children who also hated Ruthie and Ruthie's children. They would tell Ruthie all the time, even in front of the children, that Ruthie was just a whore who caused their father to leave their mother.

This is what Ruthie told me. That is why I fought so hard and teamed up with Ruthie's father and sister from Washington to try to get custody of the children granted to them. But I was only Ruthie's legal husband and only a stepfather, and I was in prison. I stood no chance, but I tried, and it is there in all the Child Protective Services files and court records. I wanted the record to be there so that someday, if my stepchildren ever went looking, they would see that I never gave up on them or how much I loved them all and wanted them to remain in my life. Whether Ruthie told me the truth or lied about all of this, I don't know. The children's biological father's older children came to love and embrace them as their own family. In the death of their father, they all became one and loved each other.

It gets painful here to continue on about all that I watched my wife disintegrate into, and all I could do was try to get custody of the children. I'd come to love them all very deeply, especially my daughters who called me daddy and Christopher, who was such a good kid. The records will show how hard I tried for the next few years. It's there in black and white in all the court records.

Fuck this shit. I'm done with this part of my story. Let's move on. She is dead, she was murdered, and I can't bring her back from the dead. I can only make sure everyone involved and responsible are brought to justice and that they pay. Like they say, every dog has its day. Since I've been out, I've been able to find out that out of the three men who I believe were responsible, two of them have already died. God will deal with the third one too. She deserves justice too.

Ruthie

Me and James

RICK RILEY

Authorities say Nuestra Familia's revisions mean more violence in streets

By JULIA REYNOLDS, Herald Staff Writer-Monterey County Herald
Posted

MontereyHerald.com

Monterey County's deadliest gang has new leadership and a new constitution, forcing changes that law enforcement officers say is translating to increased violence in the streets.

After several years of upheaval — stemming largely from the massive federal prosecution called Operation Black Widow — the top leadership of the Nuestra Familia is once again firmly established.

For the first time in decades, one man sits alone at the helm of the criminal organization that for more than 30 years has called the shots for thousands of Norteño gang members in the Salinas Valley.

In 2004, when the prison gang's top five leaders were transferred from California to a federal supermaximum prison in Florence, Colo., a struggle for the gang's top positions brewed in Pelican Bay State Prison in Crescent City, the Nuestra Familia's traditional headquarters.

In the aftermath, some of the gang's thousands of Norteño associates — street-level addicts who answer to Nuestra Familia — stayed loyal to the exiled generals and captains, while others looked to Pelican Bay because the gang's written constitution said its leaders must reside there.

Three leaders soon emerged at Pelican Bay, filling the ranks of the gang's mesa, or board of directors: David "DC" Cervantes of Chino, Jose "Huesito" Gonzalez and James "Conejo" Perez.

But in a coup d'etat of sorts, Gonzalez and Perez have been "demoted" to "Category 1," the lowest level of the Nuestra Familia, investigators say.

That leaves Cervantes, who has always kept a keen eye on Salinas affairs, firmly in control as the organization's only general.

The next rung of leaders in Pelican Bay includes Daniel "Stork" Perez of Salinas, Anthony "Chuco" Guillen of San Jose, who was involved in the murder of a Nuestra Familia member there and is serving a 25-year sentence; and George "Puppet" Franco, 39, from San Jose, responsible for the gang's activities in Stockton, Tracy and Fresno.

Nuestra Familia is organized in a military-like hierarchy, with generals running the gang from inside prison and paroled regiment captains running the streets outside.

Last year, a newly revised constitution for the gang was distributed through underground channels, allowing for change in the mesa's structure, said Santa Cruz County sheriff's Sgt. Roy Morales. But copies were intercepted in Pelican Bay, giving investigators a heads-up about the leadership changes.

Like other major prison gangs, including the Aryan Brotherhood and the Mexican Mafia, Nuestra Familia issues orders from its power base in the Security Housing Unit of Pelican Bay. And though prison officials recently reorganized the housing in a way that slows down gang communications, orders themselves are still smuggled out that translate to violence in California cities and farm towns.

One such order last year told Norteños across Northern California to close the streets of Salinas.

Police surmise that the order was responsible for many of the shootings in Salinas in 2007, which increased by 50 percent over 2006 levels.

Now, nearly all Norteño soldiers and Nuestra Familia regiment captains across California answer to Cervantes, gang experts say, but re-establishing the gang's control over the streets has not been easy.

"DC Cervantes is calling the shots," said J.R. Amon, a former gang investigator for state prisons and now a consultant for federal and state law enforcement. "He's trying to regroup these guys. The Norteños are trying to establish (in Salinas) but every time they try to, there's shootouts."

A small minority within the gang has not transferred loyalty to Cervantes, Santa Cruz County's Morales said.

"There's literally members still loyal to the guys in the field," he said, referring to the exiled former generals and captains in Colorado.

When the five were transferred out of California, Gov. Arnold Schwarzenegger promised the feds that the five were not scattered across the federal prison system, as former U.S. Attorney Robert Mueller's staff had promised.

And the transfer led to internal power struggles played out in the streets, police say.

The five former leaders are James "Tibbs" Morado, 59, whose common-law wife, 20-year-old Salinas resident Crystal Neequez, was found slain on Hecker Pass Road near Watsonville in 2003; Joseph "Pinky" Hernandez, 58; Gerald "Cuete" Rubalcaba, 52; Cornelio Tristan, 46; and former Monterey resident Tex Marin Hernandez, 53.

Despite the governor's complaints, all five are still housed in the same supermax unit.

The gang's new constitution says the five should still be respected as former leaders, but has stripped them of their power in California.

What they will do within the federal prisons remains to be seen, but investigators and snitches have maintained and communication with the outside has been established through cell phones smuggled into prison.

http://www.montereyherald.com/ci_8350955

5/9/2013

Chapter

17

So I was still on an active enemy line. I had to survive, and I had to continue to prosper; it was all knew. But there was a big emptiness inside of me that no alcohol or drugs could fill. I don't know what it was, except that I had always lived as a gangster who always had a woman who loved me and believed in me. As long as there was a woman in my life who truly loved and had faith in me, I was invincible, and I couldn't be killed.

One of the things I remember telling God was that no matter what, I was a man who would always have to have a woman, not just for my strong sexual needs and appetites, but more importantly, a woman whose love for me I could believe in. I made it clear to God that the only way I could ever follow Him would be with a woman as described in the Bible, called the virtuous woman of Proverbs 31:10 and on.

When I was sixteen years old, I was the leader of my own little group of followers and friends. We used to all hang out at this big elementary school called Stanton School, on Stanton Avenue. The police and everyone else even called us the Stanton mob or gang. We hung out at this school because after school hours or weekends, it was the perfect spot for us to party. It had a good football field and basketball courts. We may have been young delinquents, but we were sports jocks too, who loved playing both football and basketball. All the neighborhood girls would hang out there and party with us too. Of course, I was the great Rick Riley, one of the best fighters in the whole town; at sixteen, I could whip almost every senior in town, even older guys too. So naturally, I was the leader and, naturally, every girl's dream, at least I thought I was.

Anyway, there was this girl named Lori Rau; she's my wife now. I was sitting across where we hung out with my friends; I could have any girl I wanted. This girl, she was fourteen, and she wasn't little. She was tall, she was pretty with blond hair, and she was coming home from school across the street. You hear about this, but this really happened to me, man. I looked across the street, and I saw her walking home from school, holding her schoolbooks, all shy. I looked up and I saw her, and I have never felt what I felt in that moment. It was like, like what they say, the thunderbolt hits you, you know. It just hit me. I was like, "Who is that? Who is that?" I was asking everybody, "Who is that?" "Oh, I think her name is Lori. I think she lives up the street there." I was like, "Oh my god, I have to know her." So the next day, I borrowed my partners' car, and I was waiting for her. I was trying to get her. "Hey, let me give you a ride home." She's carrying her schoolbooks, and she's smiling and blushing. "No, that's all right. I just live up the street." So I tried to get with her. I found out one of my sisters was in her classroom. She knew who she was, so I had my little sister write a letter saying, "My brother, he's just crazy about you. He doesn't know that I'm writing this letter. He doesn't know that I'm telling you about this." I was actually telling my sister what to say. I gave a picture of me, all sexy, my sexiest picture. "I'm enclosing a picture of him. He will give you this letter for me. He doesn't know what it's all about." So I went to her house. She's in the window, washing dishes. I could see her there, so I went up to the door and knocked, and her mother answered. I asked, "Does Lori live here, Lori Rau?" She said, "Yeah," then she said, "Lori, there's a young gentleman here to see you." Lori came to the door; I was playing it cool, like I didn't know what's in the envelope. I said, "Hi, I'm Rick Riley, my sister Penny, you know her, well, she wanted me to drop this off with you. I told her I would because I was on my way down to where we hang out there on Stanton." I was playing it cool when I gave it to her. Well, this girl just didn't even care about me. She shines me on, ignored me, you know? Like, okay, whatever. Another girl at the time that I was also interested in had started hitting on me, Judy. This girl looked like a young Jane Fonda. She was fifteen and a virgin; she wanted me to be her first lover. Point-blank, she approached me and offered me her virginity. So I thought, "This girl Lori don't want me, I'll go for this other girl and her offer." Lori ended up marrying my little brother five years later. I never messed with that. I always honored that, and I was jealous my little brother ended up with her, but it didn't work out. They stayed married for a year. The funny thing is, well, I'm not going to go there. They had a child, Melissa, my niece. She divorced him and she went off and she ended up marrying another guy. She's married to him for twenty years. She divorced him, and thirty-seven years later, my little sister's renting a house from her. So my little sister told me, "I'm living over here, and I'm renting a house from Lori." I was like, "Lori?" Because all those years, when I found out she had divorced my brother, I was always asking about where she was. I could never hook up with her. Anyway, thirty-seven years later, now here's my little sister, the same sister I tried to use at sixteen years old to get with Lori. She told me, "Yeah, I'm living here with Lori, at Lori's place." Right away, I was shooting her a letter. *Wham,* you know? We started corresponding. As soon as I saw she opened that door, I said I may never get another chance. I'm just gonna tell her the real, "Hey, look, all these years I've thought about you. I never felt anything like that before," you know, the whole nine yards. I was pouring my heart out, so I was thinking, "All right, I should get some kind of response from that." Her response when she wrote me back was, she told me, "Cut the crap, cut the con. I'll be your friend. You don't have to try to con me, cut the crap'.' I was like, "What? I just poured my heart out to this girl and she tells me to stop conning her." Anyway, so she's in my life now; we're corresponding as friends and what have you. Ruthie ended up getting murdered. The police said it was suicide, but it was no suicide—it was murder. They notified me while I was in prison. I was really pissed off because Penny had known for months and didn't tell me. I was pissed off because it turned out my so-called friend Monica had known too. One of her best friends' husband was the officer who responded to the call of Ruthie's murder. She and Penny decided to keep it from me, to shield me from the pain. Not to mention I was devastated knowing that my Ruthie had been murdered, here we go again, just like my mother's murder, all over again. My sister Penny knew about it but felt I shouldn't be told, because Penny didn't want me to suffer from finding out. Penny told Lori about it, and Lori told

Penny that she should tell me, that I had the right to know, so Penny notified me.

You know, before I caught the case that put me back in the hole, I was just taking shit and burning people, wanting to push it to a violent end. Then because of Lori, I started to have a change of heart. I began paying everyone all the monies I felt they were owed. There was this one black guy who had never heard of me, nor cared about my past. In his eyes I was just this old guy, and he decided he was gonna add a tax of interest to what I had owed him. One day he got all in my face, loud, on the yard, talking shit. What he didn't know was I had a knife in my crotch, and as he was in my face, telling me all his tough guy shit. I was reaching through the cut hole in my pants pocket, untying the knife, and I realized that I was gonna hit him right there in the yard, in front of God and everybody. This feeling of euphoria came over me. I could see it all in my mind. I was not gonna just kill him, but I imagined how I was gonna stab him in the face and neck, but I was especially gonna cut his whole face up, mutilate him, make an example of him. I didn't know what it was he saw in my face. Did he see the joy I was feeling in my face and eyes? Unknown to him, I was loosening the string that held the knife to my penis. He stopped in midsentence as he saw this big, joyous smile on my face, instead of fear or anger or anything. I'll never forget how happy I felt. Finally somebody bit; this was gonna be for Ruthie and for my mom, for my children, for all the pain and madness I had been living with. This man was already a dead man in my eyes; he saw it, because all of a sudden, he froze in midsentence of his threats. He began apologizing to me, telling me he was sorry. He didn't want no trouble; I didn't owe him nothing. The knife was in my hand now, in my pocket. He started backing away from me, still apologizing, in front of everyone there. I bring this up because of how I felt in that moment when I knew I was gonna kill him. How good and excited I was feeling. This was what I was; this was who I was—I was a murderer. This was what I knew; this was all I would ever be, and now the loudest-mouthed idiot on the yard was gonna be my parting gift to everyone there. They were gonna have to shoot me off him.

When he backed off me, apologized in front of everyone, and got as far away from me as he could, I felt cheated. I felt robbed, I wanted blood, and I wanted to carve him up. Later, back in my cell, there was a letter there waiting for me from Lori. She finally wrote that she would give me a chance to show her that I had changed and that I wasn't just trying to con her. This was all I had been asking her for, and I had almost completely blown it. Had I killed this black guy, I could not have used my self-defense argument that I had been keeping as my ace in the hole these past eighteen years I had walked on all the active enemy lines, because that guy was unarmed. Like I said, I was gonna butcher him. They would have had to literally shoot me with the mini 14s from the gun tower to stop me, to get me off him.

I was out of control with pain and anger, and a need for vengeance for Ruthie being murdered and for having lost my children too. Everyone called me the Lawyer, because I was better than any fifty-thousand-dollar lawyer. I studied that Bible like I did the law, looking for any loopholes I could find that would allow me to challenge God to deliver me and allow me to continue to be like King David, the warrior king I had admired in the Bible and through his Psalms. I studied that Bible like it was a law book. I had become an expert at law; most lawyers are lucky if they manage to win 50 percent of their cases. They usually never give any guarantees. After thirty-three years of studying and practicing law behind bars, I won 85 to 90 percent of my cases I worked on. I could usually give a guarantee of a win of some kind. So when I tell you that I studied the Bible like I studied law, you can take that to the bank.

Like I said, I knew I owed God big-time. I knew He had prepared tables before me in the presence of my enemies. But here I was again, like when my mother had been murdered, only now it was my wife Ruthie. Even though she had abandoned me and, worse in my eyes, our children, she could have come back to me at any time and asked my forgiveness. I would have accepted her back because of the children. I had even told her once when she asked me what it would take for me to take her back. I told her not until I see Chelsea walking in the visiting room with her could she come back. That would mean she had gotten my babies back, and all would be happy in Camelot again. But Ruthie was right. I still had the sensitivity of a rock. I should have allowed her to come back as she was and then worked with her to get the kids. But she knew the price of being my woman; it was all or nothing.

You see, back when Ruthie had started losing it, right after the storm had hit at Folsom, which tore apart our happy little *Leave It to Beaver* family and our Camelot, she did come to see me for one last conjugal visit there in that prison in the desert of Calipatria. I remember she was a wreck, crying over and over again. "Forgive me, forgive me, forgive me." She hadn't nutted up yet and given up the children and went back to the streets to prostitution. So why the forgive me, forgive me?

I had never seen Ruthie look so completely broken. She was right about me being a rock because I was as sensitive emotionally to whatever was going on with her as a rock. I just told her to soldier up, and I thought having sex with me, my wonderful penis, was all she needed and then she would be all right. But all she kept telling me over and over again, as we had sex and made love, was "forgive me, forgive me." Finally I'd had enough and I got off her and I looked her in the eyes and I told her, "Ruthie, I promise you right now that I forgive you whatever it is you imagine you need my forgiveness for. Now listen to me, Ruthie. I promise you on my mother's grave that no matter what you should ever do, there is no sin or wrong you could ever commit or do that is greater than my love and my commitment for you and to you. No matter what, I forgive you now, and I forgive you forever."

She left that conjugal visit feeling better than when she first came in, but it was not enough, and she ended up making the choices she made and doing the things she did, except she got pregnant by me on that last conjugal visit. My son Ricky was conceived on a conjugal visit many years before with my first wife. Ruthie did not realize she was pregnant until after she had done all the things she did, giving up the kids and going to the nut house for observation. It was while she was in there that she discovered she was pregnant. She began to write me letters filled with new hope and wonder because she had her tubes tied, and it was a tubal pregnancy, which meant if she tried to carry the baby to full term, it would kill her. I told her no. I wanted her more than I wanted her to give me a son. Ruthie was determined to give me a son. She ended up losing the baby, and it almost cost her her life. She went nuts and began to live a life that would inflict punishment upon her. It was the Jewishness in her. She had it bad, and she was filled with guilt and shame for abandoning me and her children. She thought God was punishing her by her losing the son she had wanted so bad to have with me.

It led to the lifestyle and the people who would kill her in the end. But in the end, she had determined to take her life back, to go straight.

She got a job, she got clean, she wanted to get herself right and to go back and get her children, but the devil made his move, and she was murdered viciously.

Here's Lori, the girl, the only woman whom I had ever had the thunderbolt with. My beautiful elusive Lori, Lori whom I had secretly adored and wanted when she was my brother's wife. Lori whom I always thought of and had tried to find or get a hold of once I knew she was no longer with my brother. My beautiful Lori, my Lizzy and the Rainman Lori, offering me at least a fair chance to win her heart.

But what about Ruthie? I owed her vengeance; I owed her children and my children justice. I would kill cats, dogs, and chickens, wipe out whole family trees as soon as I could to avenge her and to give our children justice. The people she had gotten involved with would not let her just leave and go back to her children. These three men, they deserved to die and to suffer first before they welcomed their deaths. They would beg me before I was done not to wipe out their own innocent families. This was my promise to Ruthie and to her children, who, for a time, were mine.

I was mad with pain, and drugs and alcohol could only numb it for a while. But it was there to greet me when I lay down to sleep in my dreams and when I awoke every morning. I was a killing machine, I was a murderer and a thief, and I will be released again back into society. I was afraid for the first time of just how vicious an animal I had become. Maybe it's better if I die or catch a new murder beef and never get out. But there's Lori, what about Lori? Lori was so beautiful, not just in her physical beauty to me, but now I was learning through our correspondence just how much more truly beautiful a woman she had become. From that vision of loveliness, I had first seen that first day thirty-seven years before when God had imprinted her upon my very soul, and I didn't even know it then or understand why until now, when I could finally appreciate what a real virtuous woman was, just as God described in the Bible.

I had studied that Bible, and I discovered something, a covenant promise that, according to God's own words, now belonged to me just because I had chosen to believe in Jesus Christ and had faith in God's Word and in God. It was the covenant promise of Abraham, and according to these scriptures, I was now Abraham's seed, and these promises belonged to me. So I tore out the very pages from the Bible that guaranteed these promises to me, and I put them in my shirt pocket. I said, "All right, God, I'm going out to do battle this day with this whole prison yard, and if they are gonna kill me today, their knives will have to go through these pages to hit my heart and kill me. It will be self-defense on my part, and if I live and if I hurt or kill anyone today, at least I will be able to win the case against me in a courtroom."

Anyway, I caught the case, I was in the hole, I was going to court, and I was looking at another life sentence. Lori used to send me pictures of this waterfall that she went camping at, Burney Falls. I always liked waterfalls, and I loved these pictures of this waterfall. I said, "Someday we'll go there." I was starting to write her, and I was starting to fantasize about being with her. You know, dream about it. We're starting to get a little closer, but hey, I was facing another life sentence. One day I was sitting there in that cell. I was sitting on the floor; I had just finished working out. I was sitting on the floor, looking up at the wall where I used to have the pictures she sent me. I had her picture, I had the picture of Burney Falls, and I had some spiritual stuff, like those pages I had torn out of my Bible and wore in my shirt pocket. I was looking up at them and heard a voice, you know, challenging me, telling me, "Step up. It's time." I said, "Huh?" It's been a long time since I heard that inner voice like that, so I said, "All right, I'll step up, all right, God. If this is really You, and I know nothing's impossible for You, You know my parole dates coming up here in three days. I'm not going to be able to parole because I'm facing another life sentence. But if You're really serious, then in three days, I want to get out. I want to have this woman, and I want to be at Burney Falls, all three." Well, about a month before, when I'd went to court, the judge, the DA, everybody knew I was going to beat this case. But they were still trying to prosecute. Like I said, I was a lawyer by now; I've had thirty-something years of everyday studying law. Winning, that's what I did, so I knew I could beat the case. But what I told the Judge, I said, "Your Honor, look, I'm gonna beat this case and you guys know that, the district attorney knows that. Because you guys put me on an active yard, with all my enemies, knowing who I was, so I'm going to beat this case. But I haven't seen my father in eighteen years because they wouldn't let him in to visit me. I know he is getting old, and I am worried that he is going to die before I could say good-bye to him. I promise you I'll come back. I'll plead guilty, and I'll spend the rest of my life in prison." The judge said, "No, that's not going to happen." He said that he wanted me to see my father, then he made a special court order. He said, "On June 16th, when Mr. Riley's parole date comes up, I order that he be taken to the county jail and he be allowed to post bail." Okay, well, he had never done that before for anybody, and nobody else who was facing a case like me had ever gotten out. So part 1, on June 15, I was not even rolling up my stuff, because other guys who are going to court and have parole dates, they come and go and they are not released or moved because they have active court cases like me. I didn't pack my shit, nothing, you know. I was not going nowhere. About three o'clock in the morning, the spirit told me, "Hey, pack your stuff, man, get ready, you're leaving." I got up, and I started packing my stuff. Sure enough, at six o'clock in the morning, here they came. They got me and took me to county jail. Part 2, I got a phone call, and I called Lori. I did not know if Lori had any money or anything. Her grandson Chance answered the phone. Thank God he took the call; he was only ten years old, but he accepted the call. I told Lori, and Lori's on her way. Before the day was up, she drove, I think, four hundred miles or something, five hundred miles; it is up to Susanville and then to Red Bluff. She bailed me out, picked me up, I was out after eighteen years, and the next day we're at Burney Falls together, just as I had challenged God to do to prove to me it was really Him talking to me that day when I accepted His challenge for me to step up. When God brought Lori into my life, I was ready for her. I realized that she had been imprinted upon my whole being that first time I saw her, like the song says, "Ever I saw her face." I had enough sense by now to realize just how beautiful and awesome a woman Lori had become. She had always been beautiful and strong and independent; time had seasoned her into the virtuous woman I had asked God for. I had put all my women and wives upon pedestals they couldn't help but kick over. But none of them were Lori. She opened her soul and her heart to me and all the pain she had been through in her life. But like that pearl of great worth Jesus spoke of in the Bible, the pain only made her more beautiful in my eyes. In my eyes, the only pedestal I placed her upon is the pedestal that she came with that very first day when I looked up, saw her, and was hit by the thunderbolt. God, who knows the end from the beginning, knew I was not ready for Lori. So He imprinted her forever in this thing called me. She's my Elly May Clampett and my eternal fourteen-year-old maiden who forever lives in all of me. I realize more each day how useless, lost, and empty life would continue to be, no matter the glories of hardened men like me, without her. She was the other part of me that had always been missing, and she was more than worth whatever God would ask of me in exchange for my freedom with her and our anointing at Burney Falls. So I made God a vow when He challenged me to step up that day. I vowed to God that if He gave me this woman, Lori Rau, I would want no other woman and that just as the Bible says that a man should be, that I would always be satisfied with her breasts alone. I vowed to be faithful to Lori and that I would always be grateful for her and that I would always love her, cherish, adore, and honor her. So God has done what I asked, you know. He got me out. He gave me this woman that I had asked Him for, and I was at Burney Falls. I returned to court twice while out on bail. They had even had the attorney general's office there against me, because if I won, my case would cause great problems for the prison system. Every prisoner would be able to use the same self-defense I was using. The judge who let me post bail married Lori and me. He dismissed the case against me as a wedding present, I guess. God bless that judge. I did not know where that was going to go, but today I am married to this woman. She is the greatest. Everybody wants a virtuous woman, you know. In Proverbs 31, the last chapter of Proverbs, it describes a virtuous woman. I got a virtuous woman, Lori. My father, whom I only wanted to say good-bye to before he died, lives in my house now with me. He's lived here for the last four years now. He is doing well. So did God answer? Yes, He did. You know, miraculously, every day that I'm out here, I'm like, okay, I can't deny, the very same things I had on that wall on that prison wall, they're on my bedroom wall now. So every day when I get up, I look in the mirror and see them over my shoulder behind me. They remind me from where I've come. It was a big question as to what I was going to do when I got out. Was I going to stay active? Was I gonna still go to war? Was I still gonna be in organized crime? So I just let everybody know, "Look, I'm done, you know. I have the right to retire. I'm retired, leave me alone. You guys do what you do, just leave me alone. As long as you leave me alone, we ain't got no problem." But now, like I said, how do you just walk away from all these guys that you've eaten with, that you've slept with, you've fought with, you bled with? How do you just walk away? Some people can, again, maybe just another case of misguided loyalty. But I'm not that guy. I can't walk away, so I'm starting a prison ministry, and Lori is helping me. We are helping prisoners already as it is; that's what we're doing. I want this prison ministry to be the kind of ministry that I always thought one should be. Not just, "Hi, Jesus loves you, God bless you, good-bye." You know, that's nice; we appreciate that, but that's not what a real prison ministry should be. Prison ministries should be someone that goes in and says, "Hey, God loves you. God has hope for you, and I'm here for you, man. As much as anything I can do, I'm gonna do what the scripture says." A lot of Christians forget that. They don't read the whole Bible. What they need to remember if they look, look in your concordance, see how many times *prisoner* is in there. One of His commands is *to remember the prisoner as if you were chained to him.* That's what I'm doing now, you know. There're lots of things I may never be able to do, and I've read the Bible from *A* to *Z.* Let me explain something. What I found out is this: the only requirement that God had of me, you know, or of any of us, was not that we shouldn't do this, don't do that, stop doing this, stop doing that; it wasn't a whole bunch of rules. It was one simple thing, you know, because if He'd have asked me to stop picking my nose or stop, you know what I mean, guys, stop lusting, stop all this other stuff, I couldn't promise I could do that. Don't ever hurt anybody again, don't fight. I can't promise any of that stuff. The only thing He asked was that I be merciful. You know, that I be merciful, that I could do. I could be merciful, so that's what I'm gonna do. I'm gonna remember the prisoners as if I were still chained to them, and I'm gonna be merciful. To the best of my ability, I'm gonna try to leave all that other stuff behind me, hopefully never have to kill another man or woman, never have to kill anybody ever again, never have to hurt anybody ever again. I'm a work in progress; that's the only thing I can say, and I want to say this: you know, I think the reason why God has so much love for prisoners is because of what a lot of people forget. When Jesus Christ himself was on the cross, there were two murderers and thieves on each side of him. There's a murderer and a thief on this side; there's a murderer and a thief on the other side. Now even as these guys are being crucified, they're killing Jesus, you know. But one guy catches on; the other thief, he says, "Wait a minute. You know, this is that guy that only did good. I heard about Him." You know, and he changes right there on the cross. He's dying, and the other guy's going to hell cursing God. You know, but that one thief changes right there on the cross, and he says something as Jesus has His darkest moment. "Eli, Eli, lama sabachthani" (my God, my God, why have you forsaken me?). In His darkest moment, His darkest time, that prisoner, that murderer and thief on a cross, looks over to Him, and he reminds Jesus of what He's there for, why He came. When he calls Him Lord, he says "Lord, remember me," and in that moment, I believe that thief on a cross gave Jesus strength, blessed Jesus, reminded Jesus what it was all about, why He was doing that. And maybe that's all I am. I used to tell people, and I still do, there were two thieves on the cross. I just know which one I am. There was one that cursed Him; there was one who blessed Him. I know which one I am. Which one are you? And so maybe that's what I'll call this book, *The Thief on the Cross*. I thought of calling it *The Trial of Sundown*, but I think I'll call it *The Thief on the Cross*, because that's all I am, all I was—a murderer and a thief hanging on a cross, whom Jesus remembered.

Burney Falls, Rick, Lori & Chance

Isn't God Great!

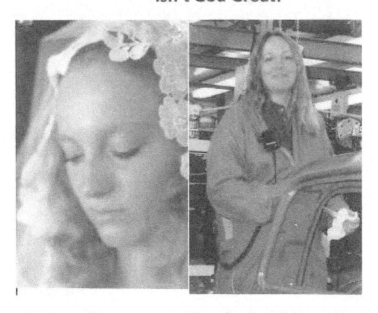

Pictures of Lori on my cell wall, my Virtuous Woman

God gave me more than I even dreamed, Lori

Bringing my father home, R.J.

Trip to Texas with Dad and brother Patrick

My brother's daughter my niece, Melissa, and her son, Chance. My grand nephew, "My heir apparent."

My son Ricky, born in my Heart, conceived on a Conjugal visit, my miracle.

My heart, Olympia, my step Daughter, and her heart, her son, Ean.

Reunited, God answers prayers

Mine and Ruthie's kids

My first Christmas after 18 years in Prison

My best friend, forever, Taffy

Me & Cousin Roxie, Manos's wife

Family Reunion

Epilogue

I have been out of prison five years now. These have been the most amazing years of my life with my wife, my virtuous woman. It has not been always easy, but it has always been good. Before, when I would get out, I could have walked away from all the violence and the gangster lifestyle. But there was always a strong pull to go back toward this gangster life, toward vengeance, and violence. Always before, even after God had done some miraculous things in my life for me, there was always a strong pull, the call of the wild.

In the past five years, there has still been that pull calling to me. Sometimes I want to jump in my car and go plant some bodies in a field somewhere, when money is tight and I know I could easily go back to my old ways real quick just to get enough money to live comfortably.

I find that this time, there is a difference that was never there before, and that's that the pull on me to be with Lori, to live my life together with her, and to experience all that God has for me with Lori and Chance, my brother's grandson, whom we are raising together. Chance is Melissa's son, whom Lori had raised since he was five months old. He is such a smart, handsome, gifted, and good boy. I wish he were my own son. Melissa too, my brother's beautiful daughter, my wife's fondest love, my niece, my blood, and my heart too. This family God has given me, this pull is much stronger than any pull of the streets or my old life.

I am learning how to trust in God, and so far, God has never failed me. I am an ordained minister now—from gangster to pastor—and my flock are all the prisoners we are helping through our ministry now. Maybe this is why God saved me, because I know exactly what prisoners and gangsters are all about. I'm one of them, or at least I was, and maybe I was the worst of them. Maybe just by being there for them in whatever way my ministry can allow, maybe this is why I went through everything that I went through, so that I could reach men other people cannot reach or whom other people don't even care to reach.

I want to say that next to God, if not for this one woman, Lori Riley, my wife and my love for her and her love for me, I could do nothing, and I would have gotten out and went back to being a gangster with a vengeance, leaving bodies all up and down the state of California. So there is something to say for the love of a good woman. I had been loved by a lot of women; some of them were good women too, but none of them was Lori, my virtuous woman, the only woman strong enough to be the one woman God had made just for me, my Elly May.

Not a day goes by when I don't thank God for all He has done and given to me, above and beyond all that I ever could have imagined or even asked for. He has blessed me, and if He could and has done all this for a man like me, He can and will do it for anyone who is willing to just "step up," as I did that day in that maximum-security prison cell, facing a whole new life sentence in prison. I was appointed to die in prison, but God said no, I didn't have to die; I could still live and be free.

Sometimes I am asked if I am still that tiger, and I say, "I am still a tiger, a tame tiger, by the grace and for the grace of God and for Jesus Christ too. But I am still a tiger, and if you stick your hand in my cage and start poking me, I can't guarantee that you won't pull back a nub, because I am a tiger."

Joshua, King David, and Caleb too—these men were mighty warriors and warrior kings, very bloody men, just like me. Like Joshua, King David, and Jesus, I am a warrior king too. God is my Father; my Heavenly Father really loves me. So I wouldn't go sticking your hand inside my cage. My Bible didn't come with no miniskirt. It's all about the spiritual battle, and I've got angels for soldiers now. I'm just looking for a few more other believers like me to help me with my prison ministry. Because there are still a lot of good men inside our prisons, and even the worst of men in prison, God gave His own Son's life for them too. Whether you believe or not, there will be a dividing between His sheep and the goats. Just remember, the sheep blessed the prisoners.

You've read my story; you've seen what kind of man I used to be. The message of this book is simple: "What God has done for a man like me, He is willing to do for you too." It's not rocket science, and it isn't weak. It's not about my good and my bad; it's not even about me. It's all about His free gift that One Man paid for and bought with His life's blood. It's only about that cross at Calvary and Jesus Christ, who gave Himself for you and for me.

God bless you all.

Love and rage,

Sundown
Pastor Rick Riley
The Thief on the Cross
Prison Ministries

Pastor Rick

The Thief on The Cross

Prison Ministry

About The Author

Rick "Sundown" Riley, a.k.a., Two Hats, was born in Santa Maria, California, and now lives in Northern California with his wife, Lori; his father, RJ; and grandson, Chance. He has spent thirty-three years of his life in and out of the prison system and has now become an ordained minister. He has created the Thief on the Cross Prison Ministry, which he hopes to be able to help many prisoners with. Rick's mission in life is to speak in public forums on gang-related topics and how God helped him through all situations in his life in spite of himself. Rick believes that because of his own life of misguided loyalties and the violence he was involved with as a member of prison gangs and organized crime, he is uniquely qualified to work with and help other such men as he once was and prevent others from following in his blood-stained footsteps. Rick says he is still a work in progress.

CPSIA information can be obtained
at www.ICGtesting.com
Printed in the USA
BVHW07s0844130618
518947BV00019B/446/P